THE
WAY OF THE
FLAMEKEEPER

David Kala Ka Lā

Published in Great Britain 2004 by

MASTERWORKS INTERNATIONAL
27 Old Gloucester Street
London
WC1N 3XX

Tel: +353 (0)86 325 2645
Email: books@masterworksinternational.com
Web: http://www.masterworksinternational.com

ISBN: 978-09544450-3-4
ISBN: 0-9544450-3-1 (10 digit ISBN)

Artwork by David Kala Ka Lā
Cover Photograph - Sunrise at Kapa'a - by Phil Young

The Way of the Flamekeeper

by **David Kala Ka Lā**

The Diary

The Handbook - On Being Human

ACKNOWLEDGEMENTS

No human can find the truth without assistance.

I have had many teachers, even some whose names I do not know. No matter how small the lesson, I thank every one of them.

Words cannot express the gratitude I feel, and the debt I owe, to Kuoha, Kihonua, Kiri, and the secret one, without whom I would never have known. It was my magnificent good fortune to meet you, and there is no greater thanks I can give you than to embody that teaching in my life.

Halehale ke aloha

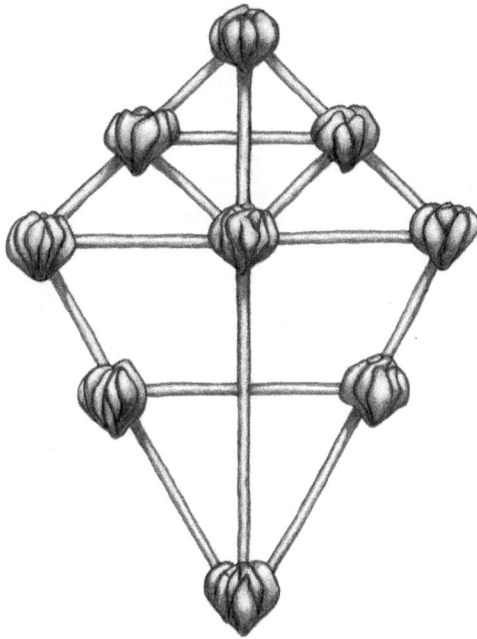

The Diary of a Flamekeeper

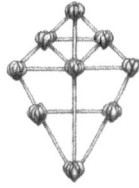

THE GLIMMERING

I awake. My limbs and body feel leaden after a deep and heavy sleep. I am so warm and comfortable that I don't want to move. Bright light filters through my consciousness as I turn over and glimpse the day.

The first thing I hear is the sea; as ever the crashing sea greets my morning yawns and stretches. Today I groan as I sit up and place my feet onto the floor; I really do feel tired. At the first sign of significant movement the cats enter my room and various bodies rub their soft gentle fur against my legs. There is gentle but insistent mewing because they want to be fed, but first there is the morning ritual of strokes along backs and soothing scratches behind ears.

My tiredness is yesterday's: it was an intense and important day and I expended much during the ritual for my apprentice's acceptance onto the path. I smile to myself: it is good that he has decided to walk this narrow path. It is a brave and mighty decision. And I feel deep love, concern and respect for him, as my teacher felt for me. I know that now, but I didn't at the time. A wry smile passes across my lips because the old man knew all along that it would turn out this way. That is why he was concerned for me, as indeed I am for my apprentice. That is why he loved me like a son and a brother; that is why he protected me and put up with my ways, my incessant questions and my irritating nature. As I sit and wipe the sleep from my eyes I think of him deeply now. I send my heartfelt greetings to him, for I know he is close. Of course he is.

I pass the other bedroom and look in at Kawowo. He sleeps, looking just as beautiful as all humans do as they sleep.

I walk out of the cabin. The bright sun stuns me fully awake. There is light. Bright sparkling shards shoot from the sea. There is the warm wind on my skin, the smell of the salt, the green foliage of the mountains to my left and right, and there is the cool sand beneath my feet. This is my life. Everything that I need to feel fully alive is here. I feel at peace; I feel an utter and complete peace knowing that now there is another who knows the secret ways and is treading the earth. The line will continue, as it wends its gold light through history and beyond, further than I can know. I laugh now at the many things I thought would make me happy and fulfilled. How wrong we can be.

I eat some fruit and feed my little companions. Then something more urgent calls. I walk into the forest behind me.

That done, I walk along the beach, my staff in hand. There is no one else around. The cats walk off to various sunny and perfect spots in order to groom themselves. The sea is crashing the shore, the foamy white surf greeting my feet. I walk onwards from the end of the beach, up the hill, along the path through the woods, over the brow of the hill and down onto the sand of the next bay. Unlike the other bay, this one has many scattered rocks, pools and unusual stone formations. They must be very old, and have been used in the past as I use them now. There is one in particular that I've always used. About a third of the way along the beach there is a large piece of rock. It's as if someone had gouged a seat out of the centre, so I am able to sit in it—all my body supported and surprisingly comfortable—and look out at the horizon. The sea only reaches this far up the beach with the Spring and Autumn tides.

I put my feet onto the cold rock, swivel around and sit down, and rest back onto the smooth dark surface. My staff is leaning up against the side. I shiver as the rock touches my back and legs, but it soon warms up; it always does. I look up at the sky. Above me it is blue, with a few clouds here and there. Then there is the sea in front of me. I settle down and take in a few deep breaths.

In this place I meditate and think. The stone has special qualities, as has rock in many parts of the world. It is so good at retaining thought forms that it can act almost as a battery, a repository, and a transmitter; a place for me not only to contact my thoughts and beliefs but also to be renewed and revived with energy from my beloved Earth. Together they often produce new thoughts, new ideas;

I can refresh and revitalise my mind and its beliefs with regular contact. It is almost as if the mixing of the two—my thoughts and the consciousness of the Earth—is facilitated within the medium of the rock. Today I am here simply to install some new thought forms, some little changes, that have taken place since the initiation last night. My evolution goes on and on, there is never an end point.

I close my eyes and breathe deeply; gradually taking less and less interest in the sounds and smells of my surroundings. I become aware of my many bodies, centred and calm, and sink my attention into the rock. It is an act I have performed many times, but this time, unexpectedly, instead of me controlling and observing the process of exchange with my bodies, I am at once caught, like a fish in a net, and manipulated skilfully in a totally unexpected way; in a new direction.

I see a picture coming towards me. At first I observe myself, and then I am seeing through my own eyes; yet I am young again, probably about seven or eight. They are eyes I haven't looked through for a very long time: I live in the present moment as much as possible and try to move from a timeless space. It is a real shock to look through this child's eyes; to feel as I once did and at the same time be conscious of observing everything from my present state and age. It is fascinating to me.

As a child I certainly played as a child. Yet always there was that difference, that feeling: that of being an outsider. Not only an observer but a thinker. I reflected in my own childish way on everything. But at least I did reflect. It is only now that I realise how very few people actually do, whatever age they are. Perhaps it was because of my skin disorder that my self reflection was always active. I was born with, and have always had, eczema. At times it was severe and at all times it was present. It drew attention to me and from me, especially with other children. Yes, perhaps now that I see myself and see through my own eyes, I can see from this age that it has orchestrated much of my seeking during this life. Perhaps it came from that initial feeling of alienation, of drawing attention when others did not, and on to the desire to find a cure so that I might be normal, average, not noticed, invisible; to disappear amongst the crowd. Perhaps I didn't want to be singled out, different from the everyday. In retrospect I wanted to fit in with my peers as if I was just another member of the gang, and not taken account of, not noticed.

11

Yet, of course, it is the only reason why we are noticed: a difference in some aspect or other.

I feel great tenderness for this young man with his bandages, fair skin and freckles, and an innocent depth. I wonder what it would have been like if I'd encountered myself as I am now when I was this young, or indeed at any age. How would it have been if, as an eight or nine year old child, I had seen this old man walking towards me? How would I feel if this man, with a twisted staff in one hand and dressed in scruffy clothes, stooped down to me, looked into my eyes, so very seriously, deeply, sincerely and said softly "do not worry young man, do not fret, do not become desperate. Your life will not end up how you want it to, but you will be happy with the result of it. You will survive all the traumas and disappointments and your often broken heart; you will endure. You will know more than practically any other man alive. I am already seeded inside of you. You will survive…" And how would it be as his eyes watered at the thought of all that his own self would have to endure, to suffer, to crawl and grab the earth in desperation; to cry to the heavens in bitterness, in anger, in hate, for help, just someone to help him. Then he would hug me; this total stranger would hug me so tight and say "I love you, never forget that I love you…" And he would hold me as if there was never going to be another hug in my life like this; with his strong yet gentle hands, his tears falling down onto my face and neck, and I would be scared of him and his intensity yet feel absolutely and completely valued and loved and protected at that moment; a moment I would keep alive in my memory through all the days and weeks and years to come. How would that have felt? What difference would it have made to me as I grew? I think it would have been huge and lovely. A drop of rain in a parched desert. A ray of sun. Love. I would never have forgotten it. I wish it had happened.

But it didn't. In the long run it's probably better that it didn't. Such a vision, such an incident could have left me complacent, or arrogant, or very, very sad. For, at that age, the man that I saw would have appeared unkempt, poor and perhaps lonely; and I wouldn't have wanted to turn out like him. His strength would have been invisible to me and I would only see that which was before my eyes. His power was secret; unexpected, and I wouldn't have appreciated it. But his eyes would be mine, and I couldn't have denied that. And his words?

I didn't even understand what 'endure' meant, or its ramifications. There would have been this conflict to do with an undeniable truth about my destiny: because at the time, the only real feeling I had about my future was a distant foreboding. Some indescribable fear that it was impossible to put my finger on. I never did discover its identity. It was something to do with dying young, a sense of urgency and a poor sense of self-esteem; all contributed to this dark cloud inside me. However, it did disappear. I can't think exactly when, but I do remember that it disappeared without a trace of where it went. And it was a relief. And it disappeared for one reason and one reason only: because I continued to walk the path.

But that was much, much later. Many years were to pass with this hidden bleakness inside me; so long in its company. And here I am now, I am that unkempt man. Yet I am happy.

How did this come to be?

I can't remember what I thought about as a child. I suppose they were childlike concerns. They were the usual traumatic and terrifying encounters with life. But I don't think I was happy. There was something in me that wasn't happy; and I'm sure the reason I ended up as I did was because I was looking for that supporting happiness, that enthusiasm, the pulsing of life through my body which I somehow realised should exist. That is why I began to search, but I knew not what for. Nobody walks up to a parent or guardian and says "I need to search for my happiness." Yet somehow it's the unspoken sentence of many children. Only a few seekers will continue what seems like the never ending quest for its resolution. At first, when you begin to walk the narrow path, you are sad, dragging your feet; enthused at the next discovery but soon disenchanted that it didn't lead to that expanded state of happiness. And only much much later do you walk the path with happiness and simply seek to maintain its presence as powerfully and for as long as possible. But it's not a giggling, lightweight, companion. It is a deep and fulfilling contentment that radiates both inward and outward at the same time.

Of my childhood companions I remember little. I was verbally bullied for most of my teenage school years. It was intensely painful to me.

Just as pack animals will sometimes chase an albino out of the group lest it draw unwanted attention to them—but the animal itself having no idea about why such an action is necessary—some of my peers picked up on something that I had no inkling of at the time, which only left me feeling confused, hurt, lonely and isolated. It was as if they had identified me as not being one of them. That is one way in which the seeding takes place: a need to find out why we are treated differently from others. There were names and some faces and faces without names. But they are the past now. I wish them well and I hope that they are happy and loved, yet I suspect that they are not. Only a few are lucky enough to end their lives in such a state. Most are numbed into an existence that forces them to ask "what the hell is this all about." Although I have envied their comfortable existence I wouldn't wish to be them. For, with their numbness, comes the closing off of the light. Perhaps there is the occasional flicker; a distant sound that draws their attention away from the shopping and the car, away from the holiday and their day to day existence. Sometimes a piece of music, a film, a feeling in the air during a holiday. But they haven't enough enthusiasm or desire, or energy, to pursue and own the light, that tear in the comfortable cloth that clothes their existence. They should make the effort. Then the desire for self-knowledge and thence the knowledge of their existence would rekindle life for them, and in them. Like waking from a dream—one that really wasn't that much fun in the first place—and really feeling glad to be alive: that feeling is incomparable.

Of course I remember my family and they are good people. Their lives walk on as lives do. And I love them. They never abused me, there was always food on the table, and I was allowed a freedom of reflection and thought that instilled a lack of dogmatic beliefs, which I now believe enabled me to absorb the truth wherever I found it, rather than it having to pass through an imbibed orthodoxy that only serves the shadow-light of human discovery, of speculation rather than real knowledge. It was a priceless gift. I have seen many since who found it nearly impossible to eradicate this wretched dogma from their selves. It never enhanced their life but only gave them a false sense of purpose; it never allowed them to glow and radiate as individuals but only to shine weakly as part of the subservient majority. And it certainly never served humanity, as it only caused their lives to become sad replicas of what life and aliveness is really about. Yes, for this reason alone, I have myself refused one or two students who sought me out for instruction. Perhaps they will come back in the future if their desire is strong enough: if it can overcome their fear of retribution. My own master was notorious for refusing the requests of others, mainly for this reason. Their minds were not open to the degree that is required and—as is the case with every one of us—he only had a limited time on Earth. This quest is hard enough for even the most suitable student, let alone those who are strung by wires that hold them tightly to the ground; wires which have to be cut by our own hand—nobody else can do it for us. Yet the potential which is available once we take that action is greater by far than that of a hot air balloon which, once untethered, soars upwards into the sky. But the real prospect of that free flight into the unknown is not for many.

I remember one such occasion which demonstrated this very clearly, though I'm not sure of the student's name. I think it may have been Peter. I had been apprenticed to my master for a while and, as long as I remained in the background, was allowed to watch his interview.

We had been walking along the beach after visiting another site for a few days. There he sat, at the door of the cabin. He stood up as we approached.

He looked my teacher in the eyes "Hello" he said, "I am here to place myself under your tutelage, I wish to learn everything you can teach me. My name is Peter."

My teacher looked to the sky above, took in a deep breath and after a minute or two said, "You had better come in then."

Peter pushed in front of me and behind my master as he walked into the cabin. Did I hear my master give a little chuckle? It wouldn't have surprised me!

Over the next few days I was left much to my own devices, as they spent time together. As you can imagine, I was a little irritated—not that I am proud to admit it, but that is how I honestly felt. Now, of course, I realise it was simply my master acting with purpose: it is an unfortunate fact that—after all the trials and tribulations—every apprentice is forcibly ejected from that protected place he or she has become used to; it is essential that we become self-sustaining. Perhaps he was giving me a foretaste of the future, and enjoying every minute of my discomfort. But probably the main reason is that the decision to take on an apprentice cannot be made lightly. Our lives on Earth are finite, better to cast your fertile seeds on ground that at least contains the possibility of growth. How unfortunate to spend so much time; to give to another the proceeds of your refined knowledge; the bare truth; the love and light of your own learning, and to realise that this vessel was, in the end, unsuitable. How painful to see that it wasn't free from the restraining influence of the pre-determined plans, life and beliefs of a rigid mind in order to liberate the essence: the light seed of life. He had to decide, very carefully, if this man—who had obviously made a decision to give up everything to become an apprentice—was the right type of person to

17

hold the truth. He couldn't afford to waste so many years of his life trying to loosen and free the rigid structures of an unreceptive mind; to free them enough for the seed to grow strong. Of course the desired stress of dispute and challenge would be needed: only in this way would the plant grow vigorous and the flower be beautiful—but there must be few enough clouds to let the sunlight through; the weather must not be too cold to kill off the growth; the sun just warm enough to encourage the plant to grow upwards. Without a lack of dogma no one could take in the knowledge. And because no man knows when he will die—not even my master—he had to make a decision about whether this human being was likely to be a good and positive vehicle; a carrier; a holder of light; a flamekeeper, or not.

As I mentioned previously, I did not see them for the next few days: I think he was talking, simply being with him in the forest; I don't actually know, he never told me. Only years later did I ask him why he didn't accept this offer from an apprentice. "He wasn't suitable." That's what he said, "I was very sorry to let him go, but he just wasn't suitable...." His voice trailed off. I thought he seemed regretful and sad about the matter. Now I understand why. It is very disappointing to work so hard, to sacrifice so much for the clear light, and to have so very few people understand it, to know it as intimately as their breath. A great sadness. We can only rely on life to support the very few who do know, in order that they live long enough to carry the lineage on. In a world of so many people, why are there so few flamekeepers? That's a question I have never been able to answer.

If, as I thought, my life was pretty average, how was it then that I became a flamekeeper? It is only now that I realise the internal dialogues I had with myself, about all aspects of my life, were not ordinary and were clearing a path which would enable me to walk in a certain direction. The goal I didn't know; and certainly whatever ideas I had in mind for myself and my life fell by the wayside a long time ago. In the end it is whatever life has in mind for you that will decide your path; not that it is pre-determined but there are certain fields of activity; styles of life, occupations, that you will be suited to, and usually these are not what you expected.

I suppose, if there was a starting point to my journey, it would be my relationship to my childhood friend Mr Johaness. He ran the village sweet shop. Like all children, I spent more time in there than

I should have done. He was very good to me. Some might think it an unusual situation for a young boy to be in but I would disagree. Everyone needs somebody to believe in them; and all children need someone who will listen, who talks to them with respect and fun in their voice, someone who recognises an awakening spirit and wishes to nurture it. Somebody who knows.

When I was a little older he would often ask me behind the shop counter to help him; a kind of shop assistant at entry level! Of course, weighing the bags of sweets was great fun—it always is when you're young—but the real enjoyment was when the shop shut and he would sit me down, make me a cup of tea, and offer me a few biscuits or cakes. He'd ask me about my day at school, about home, things like that. It wasn't only that I enjoyed this attention from somebody very interested in me and my thoughts, but also that his home was fascinating to me. He had books on shelves all around the room, and musical instruments here and there from overseas. They were more primitive than the instruments I was used to and even though I played an instrument at the time I had never seen anything like them before. He said that that their sound was closer to nature, and therefore closer to the beginning. I think he was right. There were also figurines of gods and goddesses utterly new to me, and on the walls were black and white pictures of distant times, when he was much younger and surrounded by what seemed like very different people.

Our conversations were usually initiated by one or more of the objects. I would point something out, or perhaps he would take an object from a shelf and let me handle it, look at it, and then I'd ask my spontaneous questions. He was like a marvellous book which had a plain cover: you actually needed to open the book to find the golden words inside. For me he was inspirational. It always strikes me as an infinite sadness that there are so many people with so many wonderful and amazing stories who die alone. Their experiences evaporate with the ceasing of their breath; their unique and magical tales of strange and remarkable meetings, trials and traumas surmounted, and the distilled wisdom of so many years on this Earth—with its people and the natural forces that shape our lives—are gone forever. Even the most ordinary life has experiences to share of the most human and touching intimacies, exchanged with others whose life's tales will fall into the same great void. As a race there must be few who can match us. An infinite variety of individual lives.

It was Mr Johanness who helped me to see the flame within. He directed me towards its faint light; a light which I'd always somehow known was there but which I hadn't identified. It was a subtle process and yet, later, it was a sudden realisation. It was his highly perceptive nature which led me to identify something within: the essence of myself that is permanent and crystal clear; a most subtle and profound distillation of the true nature of me as an individual. Of course it would be years before I could work with this, before I even came to know it. What Mr Johanness did was to awaken within me the fact that I was interested in finding out more about it. He gave me snippets of information from the cultures he'd visited that were parts of a massive jigsaw, the overall picture of which was not even remotely visible, but which I somehow knew was behind it all.

The time I spent with Mr Johanness was very special, and it is only with the passage of all the time in-between that I can see his secret light, the one he passed to me all those years ago. He had that gentle quality of those who have a natural and matured perception of life. He saw me for what I was, a flamekeeper; as a small, young and immature boy who nevertheless had been given a gift. For many years I didn't see it. But I have since paid my respects to his great gift of friendship and the love with which he gently led my enthusiasm in the right direction, the one that was right for me.

He died when I was fourteen. I arrived after school as usual, but the shop was closed. The blinds were down. I'd never seen it like this other than late at night. I knocked on the door and it was quiet. No one in the street, no back door on the latch. I was simply confused and unable to comprehend why it was so. On arriving home I innocently asked my mother why Mr Johanness' shop was closed.

"Oh" she said, "The thing is you won't be able to work there anymore."

"Why?"

"Well, you see, Mr Johanness has died."

He was the first person I knew well who had died. I was shocked. I ran upstairs and fell onto my bed crying. Immediately I could see nothing but the sheer bleakness of life without Mr Johanness. I felt utterly lonely and desperate; one more cup of tea, one more smile, one more word from his croaky voice. I wanted to say goodbye because I knew he had something special to give me. At the time I didn't realise that his gift was invisible, an invisible seed that grew and grew over my life. His gift was an act of pure love.

Although my parents knew I was upset, they never, even until they died, realised his significance in my life. I kept this precious and secret memory alive all of my life until I met my teacher. Yet when I look at it in the clear light of day, all he did was talk to me. But his talking came from a different centre than that of other people I knew. It was as if he inhabited a different world. His thoughts, deeds, and words had the definite rhythm of spirit; of that special drumbeat that only actions from the void can issue forth with. Perhaps he was one of the few masters, living in secret, in the world. Waiting and biding his time until someone came along in whom he could see the precious commodity of light. His secret work—that of holding consciousness for the whole world to imbibe—was the invisible gift that shone every day of his life. And it still shines today.

A few years after Mr Johanness' death I fell into a depression or, more accurately perhaps, a kind of melancholy. I was, at times, subject to a deep melancholy which might last for weeks. My normal everyday life would carry on, but inside I was sombre and unhappy. Something was wrong but I could never put my finger on it. I spent a great deal of my time in introspection, reading and seeking any information I could from as many sources as possible. This nearly always took the form of books and pamphlets. I sought out all manner of obscure information in an attempt to grab and hold onto that very special consciousness that I had experienced with Mr Johanness. I didn't find it. And so, at eighteen or nineteen, I sought work, with mediocre exam results and a heart that yearned for knowledge and truth; feeling more distant from my friends and family and yet not transferring my friendship to anyone else. I became more isolated. However, it wasn't the kind of isolation that is bought upon oneself, or the result of a concerted effort on other peoples' behalf: it was, as I now know, the natural consequence of seeking that which other people do not. It's a difference that cannot be isolated or distinguished by others but still they sense it's powerful and invisible aura. And so did I.

It is difficult to define my restlessness. During this time I already had an eager interest in many teachings, especially those from the east. My knowledge was quite in depth and as usual I threw myself into investigating all aspects of whatever I was interested in. However, one of the problems I continually encountered was that I could never find a term or description for a certain feeling or awareness that I always encountered when meditating. I can only describe it as an absolute certainty that at my centre there was an identifiable radiance that was certainly the source of my being an individual: it was something that definitely wasn't anything other than the very essence of me. So often, teachings said that their highest understanding resulted in one realisation: that there was nothing that was identifiable as an individual self. My experience was other than this: I could directly contact my centre and it was absolutely, definitely, real.

I lived with this realisation for years without finding its name. It often reappeared to nag my consciousness: it said "I am here, I am here." But, somehow, it was simply submerged under the trials of everyday life. I certainly remained interested in these teachings but felt a negative space at the centre of them that it took many years to identify. Now I know that it is simply evidence of their incompleteness. At the time though, their certainty bought me into conflict with my own definite experience.

My life continued on its wavering path.

I had a dream one night. I visited somewhere not of the Earth; beyond the place where no time passes; beyond the dark clouds with an edge; above my numbness, which dissolved and became invisible. Was it accident or chance that I visited, or a deliberate act at someone else's behest? I crossed over the border and landed into a separate reality. A life like nothing I had known before: of pleasure, of music, of such peaceful and original pure experience that when I awoke my heart was full of sadness after such a transient visit. I realised how isolated I had always felt; how far away from home I really was.

Such memories and visions. That peace. A peaceful security so sure that I could bear all that I was, all that I had been. I unfolded, at first tentatively, then in a bloom of movement I shone: I had no fear. There was no pain, no trembling, none of that awful and dreadful anticipation I presumed everyone carried around with them at that time. And there was no examination. I was allowed to be one, with all my faults around me—for they did not disappear—I could approach and not be looked upon with disdain or criticism. All the defences that a life on earth can muster dropped away like a useless dead skin; yet I only felt relief, not exposure. A pure unburdening. A wonderful radiant existence.

And music: sounds so all pervasive and penetrating; curved; drawing nearer and moving away; surrounding; vibrating; enrapturing; changing at each perfect moment for that note. Wave upon wave of living sound; so unlike anything heard on this earth that I cannot hear them at all, now I am back here. This music was like bells and birdsong; of running water and growing. And within there was the soothed sounds of a comforted child; of the embrace of a warm human body on a cold and unhappy night. Outside there were stars and the black void, around which were the infinite eyes of compassion. Watching; always watching. And the infinite ears, listening to the cries of pain and anguish; the pleas for help and support; the joy; the laughter. Inside was the heart bearing the love and the pain. The love and the love and the love. Inside and outside were the valleys of the moon; the teeth of the rat; the eye of the sun and the folds of our skin. Everything; everything in that sound. These vibrations sang through my body as I sat on the edge of a precipitous cliff and looked out at mountain tops jutting through a blanket of cloud. The blue sky above combined with pure sunlight to give an overwhelming sense of light; living light. More than anything, I was at peace: I felt I had returned home. I was safe there. Beyond my bruised exterior, there was my bruised interior; my secret and damaged heart was enfolded. I felt as if I stood in the middle of a huge protective hand: enveloped, loved and safe. It was like the moment before my birth.

I awoke and burst into tears at my loss. The separation from that place affected me deeply for many years. Whenever I was sad or lonely, when I felt alone and fearful of the future, I could occasionally glimpse my memory of that visit and didn't know whether to curse, cry or rejoice in my experience. From that point on I was a different human being.

My work was everyday and of no particular consequence. My search went on and on. I became interested in alternative therapies and then trained in a variety of them. This began to stimulate an interest in the much more subtle and secret knowledge that is often hidden in the origin of such therapies. Very often I found that the originators of these alternative viewpoints were inspired and inspiring individuals whose frustration at the methods of the day—or whose radical insights into our bodies, our healing and our development— were the result of an ability to isolate and separate their thoughts from those of the time. They rose above or below to the place of inspiration, of truly evolutionary thought. Criticism only drove them onward, and I considered and consider them to be great examples of manifested human potential. So very often, truly marvellous humans are those that were pilloried in their time. Attempts were always made to discredit their inspired insights and to deny them their viewpoint. There is and always shall be such individuals in short supply, and the status quo will always try to deny the movement to greater variety, greater individuality, and to change. So much is invested in the maintenance of the present, as if it could be frozen in time and live as it is, forever. It is such a stupid idea. As if there could there be too much diversity, too much variety, too much individuality. Yet it is simply a macrocosm of the individual human being. As I have found out to be the case time and time again, the main obstacle to a person's growth is an inability to change, the fear of newness and challenge, and the temporary instability that may ensue. But it is absolutely essential. It is indispensable. There are so very few who are brave enough to walk this path of instability and to search for a unique and hard-won point of balance.

During this time there was the slow ripening. It was and is an invisible process. Rather as if you lived underground and tunnelled everyday, only occasionally surfacing to get your bearings and then being surprised at where you actually are. There is nothing more untrue than the fact that there is a peak—a zenith—of experience; of achievement; after which there is simply continuation; no more advancement or maturing because you have the insight which is all that every seeker searches for. It is totally untrue, yet there are innumerable people who teach that it is so. They, content in their own fluffy woollen blanket of illusion, guide others into the same soft space. If they are challenged they retreat into it, saying condescendingly "one day you will understand." So patronising, and such a disservice to true seekers. Then again, perhaps it is a necessary evil in order for one to feel revulsion at their condescending actions: for time and time again, true seekers will find themselves, as I did, pushed away from that warm place. As if a traveller on a cold and windy night came upon a cottage with glowing firelight in the windows and a spiral of smoke rising from the chimney. A knock on the door, in the middle of nowhere; a hope that here is a place to stay with some comfort and kindness. Indeed, at first, you are taken in with open arms. But, within a few short hours, you are forcibly ejected, or realise that to stay in such a place will prove stifling to your growing spirit. Because no actual growth took place there, you have to leave. Again and again you find yourself walking that cold road alone, more worried and aware than ever that the next house you encounter will probably offer a similar experience. Gradually, as you mature, you will resist the urge to knock on those inviting doors and realise that the sky above your head and the earth beneath your feet are your only true home; they provide the environment which facilitates your flowering as a human being.

As I have said, my maturing—invisible and undetected—moved on. There were relationships that failed; there was unsatisfying employment. Occasionally there were glimpses of a light so bright, of happiness, of love, that they burned themselves into powerful and distressing experiences. Rather like my visit to a different place, they inevitably left me wondering "what was all that about?" I still do not know; but they are part of life and we must accept them and move on if there is ever to be a hope that one day some sense, some purpose, can be attributed to them.

At a certain point in my life everything changed. I was in my early thirties. My eyes opened. I took a great conscious leap into the unknown; it was a radical decision that affected the rest of my life. How can I describe it other than to say that I simply decided, seemingly suddenly and quite out of the blue, to leave my employment when the offer of redundancy arose. I can only suggest that the apple had fallen down from the bough, a certain set of circumstances had coalesced and produced a doorway for me to step through, into a wider world; into a world that would answer many of my deeper questions and produce answers before I had even consciously formulated those questions. I took the chance and leapt through with all my might. This coincided with me entering into a period of instruction in a little known therapy which worked with distinct patterns of energy and their manipulation in the human body. Let me tell you how it came to be.

A few years before, I had trained in yet another therapy. It was interesting and certainly worked for a general variety of body conditions. Unfortunately, after obtaining my qualification, I had two insights which infected my desire to move into premises and begin my business. It became apparent to me that deep inside was the feeling that by healing and helping other people I was actually justifying, to myself and the world, that I had the right to live. I literally felt that I had to help other people in order not to draw upon myself the title of 'ungrateful and idle occupant of the earth.' Does that sound peculiar? I soon realised that this unspoken impulse was behind the seemingly benevolent acts of many healers and helpers in this world of ours. It does not in any way invalidate the great good gifts that their benevolent gestures towards others bestow on the world, but for me—once I had realised one of the deep impulses feeding my desire to heal—I could not, in all honesty, continue. My words here are important. Honesty was, and is, an important quality to me. My honesty and integrity were in question, not from a source greater than myself, but from the centre of my very own self: some part of me could not accept my duplicity and necessarily required me to find out why I should feel such a lack of self-esteem, such an unsureness about myself; as if I was alive by accident, or maybe the result of an experiment after which I had to justify the food and water wasted on me in order for me simply to live. Although the notion may seem rather crazy now, it is a presence that can haunt many a seeker for the whole of their life, and this makes its resolution absolutely essential. I did resolve it, but that was to come later on. From the moment of that realisation I went back to working as I had before. There I was, the holder of this unusual knowledge, and I kept it hidden and in the dark until I felt I could unlock the box and show the jewel without a hint of pride at my accomplishment; without a glittering medal pinned to my chest as a material gesture towards the creative force of the universe—the justification for my very breath shining there for all to see.

The second reason for my lack of enthusiasm for the business of healing in this way was the overwhelming sense that I had only touched, very superficially, on the true art of healing. In some part of me I was sure that there was a depth, an unplumbed secret depth of knowledge. I was only skimming the surface, which was at first tempting and beautiful to look at but whose shiny reflections I soon tired of. I knew there was much more to explore underneath, but that this particular therapy wouldn't show me how to reach the secrets.

It was as if my life went onto hold. My maturing process was somehow unable to move more quickly: it is much safer to remove blockages slowly. Of course there is one major reason for this holding—I simply wouldn't have understood. Quite what the details of the process are if we are continually growing I do not know, but I can only describe it in this way: it is as if the layers that are shed, as we move forward, reveal more of the potentials and possibilities available to us—not only of the light within but also of our ability to absorb and understand true knowledge. As I grew, I definitely understood more; could take in more; and yet even this is a simplification of what seemed at the time to be a complicated and somewhat chaotic apprehending of reality. But then it is also true to say that if we become simpler in our lifestyle—its issues and knowledge—somehow we understand much more of life itself? I would not understand this seeming conflict for many years.

At the same time I was looking at and investigating the more esoteric and stranger forms of therapy. Nothing I read really seemed too outlandish; certainly there were therapies about which I was startled to read, but the explanations for such approaches seemed, at least in part, to have some validity. It also occurred to me that certain practitioners were much better than others. Even in my early training this became evident. One person intuitively knew how to touch another's body and those that did not, even if taught well, never had that same quality of touch. It was nothing to do with their upbringing or experiences, it was a talent; a gift. That is why it was so important that I had absolute confidence, interest, and passion about any therapy I wanted to use. It had to involve and somehow draw on me, my life, my experiences, my knowledge, my beingness, in order for it to be real and important to me. In healing and growth the quality that we own and manifest will influence proceedings in a certain direction. It should not be otherwise. We have to be further along the path than anyone who asks for our help, simply so that we can shine a light for them to follow. If we are not, then we can only point out to them possible routes which they may like to try. This is not the work of a master. Certainly we cannot know what is best for another, but we must be able to say "this is where I am, my words, my actions are of and from this region, I can tell you the good and bad of this place and you might like to come and visit here if you cannot find better." Is that arrogant and presumptive? You see, the further along that path you walk the less and less real choices about belief you can have. Rather like the flowchart of evolution, there is only one source, and it divides and divides. We can be caught by any number of enticements, but only a very few have enough uncorrupted wisdom and teaching to lead us forward to the fundamental knowledge that is the inherent birthright of all humans; and even fewer are clear and precise. That clear precision comes from the refinement of your life's experience; from the wisdom and knowledge gained; and those beliefs that you still have yet to find a good argument against! I knew that I must be an intrinsic part of anything I practised; I must bring myself to the process because I am human, and I am dealing almost always with other human beings. My full participation is absolutely essential. True sincerity born of hard work and experience is very hard to ignore. It can have incredibly powerful effects. I began to surround my life with these thoughts.

It was in this atmosphere that I found myself embarking on a journey, to a place far away, for instruction in a little know teaching. I travelled with that forgotten thrill of adventure. Somehow, I had the perception that here I was catching sight of the thread of my existence; as if long ago it had moved too quickly out of my view and I'd lost the path it had taken and wished me to follow. I had a general idea, but specifically was lost as to where to tread. Now I had sight of that ever enticing trail of light moving in front of me; too far away to touch but close enough for me to see. I can only tell you how I felt, and I felt exhilarated, thrilled, expectant. My previous life was forgotten easily as I quickly moved into the present moment. For once in my life I didn't want to be anywhere else but here, on this train, travelling towards the future, literally and metaphorically. It was one of the great journeys of my life. It still is.

The building in which this teaching was to be initiated was humble, and I had some trouble locating it. I was lost; the thread had moved too fast once again. But, with the help of a man and a dog, I found the right place. On entering the calm room, with the few other participants, I was greeted by a human giant. She was everything I knew a true teacher should be; perhaps exemplified by a simple word: real. A real human being; eyes wide; grown; loving and yet light and secure; calm and ageless. She had the gravity of one who knows. She is great. From this distance I can see her greatness. I know her courage to follow the narrow path was great and good. Her name was Kanaka Nui.

So what do you do when you meet a great human? Why you greet and enjoy the radiating light that is given freely. You share the gift of your own life with others. Then there is connection. With connection comes transmission, even if it is secret and unsaid. If it finds a place to hide, to sit, to wait, to secure itself in the dark until the light of attention activates its innate capacity to grow, then it will reside in you. Like a clock with an alarm, its constant ticktock reminds you that life is moving on, and so must you. If you wish to hear when the alarm is sprung, then to live with the rhythm of the clock is all important.

Having witnessed, met and conversed with someone who was absolutely giving of herself in her healing it was beholden upon me to take that leap and say "Yes, teach me." It is such a simple phrase, yet if I had but known then what I know now I may have taken much longer to think before saying it. I would have made the same decision though, no matter how long it had taken to decide. How could it have been otherwise: I needed to know, and she so obviously knew. The truth is that I had no real choice if I wanted to move forward.

Over the next few weeks and months I learned so much that I looked upon my previous knowledge in exactly the way I suspected I should: it was superficial and but a reflection of a deeper knowledge of how our beautiful bodies work. More important to me though was that I began to grow and mature in unexpected ways. By methods that I wasn't fully aware of a transformation had begun through simple instruction and experience. Obviously this process was to continue all my life, but I can say that this was one of the great leaps in my development. Perhaps not since Mr Johaness had my evolution made such a jump; and little did I know that in some way it would influence me on a totally different level; point me towards a totally different path, not even suspected yet. That would be my great leap, the one great leap that is made during a life, when I was entrusted with the sacred flame of light and love. How quickly it all seems to have happened, yet there were many years in-between. The reason I mention it now is because, without this one particular stage, I would never have progressed towards the truth. Without this key, the door would have had to be knocked down with violence—which is never a good way to approach the light—and still I may not have been admitted. Much better to approach humbly and ask to be allowed in: always give the gods the opportunity to refuse your request; then, if they do, you will not be devastated. In the end, the uncomfortable truth is that they know more than we do about our real selves and the possibilities that are potentially available to us.

So how did I change? There was a dawning. After the unconsciousness of the night, with all its confusion and misinterpretation, there was a promise that the land would soon be seen and I could find my feet. As if, at last, I had begun to learn of the real, not the illusory; and since I was taught by those who had followed the process themselves, it had much more impact on me. Behind it all was the real feeling that although it may not turn out to be exactly what I sought, it was a very real step forward and I was much closer than I'd been before.

I travelled too and fro for quite a time, and this in itself was interesting for me as I generally preferred to stay at home. So there I was, seemingly all of a sudden, enjoying this travel for knowledge and actually finding what I sought. My respect for my teachers grew over time and my initial assessment of them was confirmed: they knew. As I travelled physically I also travelled mentally. It was as if the many different influences from my past had suddenly began to coalesce and, by their sheer force and number, create enough power and speed to force me through the invisible barrier. Now I found myself on the other side of this separation; one that is totally unsuspected by most of the population. Yet, as seekers begin to approach this secret impasse, the suspicion arises that there is an invisible difference between what is already known and what it is possible to know. But it seems impossible to break through. In fact there is only way to achieve this, and it is a secret way. By this I mean that it happens without the seeker being able to do anything about it, other than to persist. Then suddenly—but in retrospect—you realise that you have passed through a barrier that has changed you forever. The veil is lifted; not in some mythical, fantastical, rainbow lit spectacular, but in this peculiar perception of the world around us and within us. It is very subtle. There is still your body, the trees, flowers, cars and buildings, but they are changed. I can't in any way tell you what it is like, but it comes down to the fact that your consciousness has altered forever, as has its place of residence; and then, of course, everything else must change as a consequence.

Still, my life carried on in its way. However, there was much more of an awakenedness about me now: not only was I internally reflecting more, but I was aware of the external world in a more comprehensive manner. Issues which I had known about only as rules suddenly became part of me. Prejudices of all kinds; the separateness of things; matters such as these I now knew were wrong: not because of what I had been taught or because they were rules that I had to hold to, but simply because they were intrinsically right. I felt they were right. At that time I also had a great sense of my own righteousness. As I now know it is a constant pitfall for the seeker and one which was, and is, obvious to all but oneself. However, at this stage I could be forgiven this fault: for above all I was excited. I had a youthful enthusiasm for my new knowledge of a subject that I was in love with. I had an appetite that couldn't be sated—consuming knowledge like a teenager although I was in my mid-thirties. Finally I felt I was learning something that wasn't known by many people—not even suspected—indeed I felt at the time that it was a secret teaching. Even though this was an openly taught therapy, only a few people had knowledge of it. I was a step closer and I knew it.

After qualifying, I tried once again to set myself up in business. To a certain extent the problems I had with my self-esteem had been addressed. Although I realised that I was a minuscule cog in a massive and infinite machine, I felt very positive about healing. Now I was not justifying my life: I realised that my life was given to me as a gift with no need for recompense, and my work in the world would only be one aspect of my thanks for that gift. Far more important to me at this time was the fact that I felt I had an unusual and valid knowledge which could help to heal others. It was not practised by orthodox medicine and was little known in the unorthodox world: it was a truly alternative approach to healing. Of course, if there was a dramatic and life threatening accident or illness that had befallen someone, hospital was the only place to be; but even here my skills would be a useful adjunct. And certainly, after their crisis had passed, I knew I could benefit so many people.

I had one problem though: the people themselves were not interested in any benefit this therapy could bring to them. They didn't know of it, nor did they wish to. Even at this level my knowledge was far beyond that of those who lived in my catchment area. This was at a time when certain alternative therapies were well known and quite often used, but their success only confirmed to me that they had often played into the hands of orthodoxy. Did I really, as a sick or unhappy individual, want to walk into a place that greeted me with curtained bays, each with a "patient" in, each visited by a man or woman in a white coat; as if the coat itself bestowed an aura of one who was to be hallowed and revered. Someone who took no risks and was always covered with over ample insurance: the security blanket that keeps them from breaking through into real healing. The answer was no, I did not; but that was my answer and wasn't the answer of the majority. Their conception of "alternative" medicine was structured and pre-formed. It was not open ended. It was not expansive and it certainly didn't contain individuals like me. I therefore found myself with these unique tools waiting to be used for, and on, human beings; but they lay on their own, shiny and unused; like tools in a workshop where the key to the door had been lost. What was I to do? My few clients definitely benefited, but somehow the word didn't spread and my earnings were too small to support me. I was facing real hardship and had to return to paid work. It wasn't difficult work, but it did require me to learn some new skills, and it was work that I didn't want to do. I wanted to earn my living healing, not sitting in an office. I couldn't understand my lack of success. I was very disappointed. I remember one important turning point.

Out of the blue I had been offered a stall at a local exhibition. It would be well attended and there wasn't too much cost involved. As the day approached I worked hard on producing leaflets and handouts, on preparing photographs and charts for people to read and enjoy. I even asked the gods for help and in return received, only a few moments later, a sign that I had become used to: a rainbow adorning the sky outside my front door. Everything augured well for me and I hoped for a positive result to this final push at financial independence and success.

The day was a disaster. Because of a local sporting fixture the attendance was very poor. I stood calm and relaxed; my little stall with its bright candle and calm atmosphere attracted a few interested visitors, and from these people I hoped for a response in the future. But the truth turned out to be that they never would visit me. When I arrived home I already knew it had failed. My last gasp attempt at running my life as I wanted and wished was not to be. I broke down in tears as I shut the door. My hopes had been dashed against the rocks of fate and lay shattered and useless on the ground. I hated the gods; I hated the creator; I hated anything that couldn't allow this seemingly innocuous request to manifest. It was a devastating end to my dream. And yet, in retrospect, it was another beginning.

When I began to rid myself of my anger and disappointment I realised that I simply had to face reality. I had to face the world as it is and not how I wished it to be. At the same time I came to a realisation and a decision that would shape my life and my attitude for ever; for eternity.

What became apparent to me over the next few weeks and months was this: as seekers we have one simple choice to make, yet as simple as it is, it has the most profound consequences on one's life and even more on that which we are able to attain. At some point or other—but it is well after the beginning—there arises certain knowledge of one simple fact: we choose whether to attach our evolution to those of our group, our fellow human beings, or we detach from that consensus-evolving and fly freely, fuelled by our own potentiality. It was clear to me that this is why I hated to be attached to groups and societies: they constrained me. In many collections of so called "like minded" individuals there was a group dynamic which restrained and contained those who moved faster than the majority and, since the majority moved little if at all, it led to the wholesale abandonment of the impulse to forge ahead with adventure, and instead to sleep with the afeared and manipulating individuals who strove for power over others. It may appear to be otherwise, but that is a fact. It is such a rare being who can teach you and, at the same time, allow you to advance freely and joyfully towards the attainment of the self perpetuating flame that is the long sought goal of the true seeker. With this realisation I made a choice: I decided on freedom. Not the freedom of those with no rules or moral code—not the freedom of hedonism and its consequent degeneration and degradation of the human spirit—but the freedom not to attach my evolution to anything or anyone but the guiding light of my soul. What exactly my soul is I was to learn of later, but I could no longer ignore its subterranean callings; its deep dark hum that I had always known as far back as I could remember. How was it possible for me to tether its mysterious and magical light to the ground, for it to be attached to others who knew not what they did? I had to free this burning brightness so that its rise into the air gave me nothing other than the breathtaking joy of advancement at my own pace; that which was, above all, suitable for me. I was filled with excitement when I realised what I had uncovered: for I instinctively knew that it was the right choice. No matter how many teachings and teachers you partook of, there was only the single "I" that could evolve; it was, and is, so very clear, and yet it took so long to realise this truth. However I would never regret the length of time it did take for this realisation to break the surface of my mind, because ultimately I was incredibly lucky that it finally become a conscious realisation: many people, even on the path, never understand this simple truth and are unsuspectingly bound by others who have nothing but their own selfish interests at heart. Most groups are run by those who haven't the faintest desire to facilitate another's growth. How could they, they haven't even facilitated their own.

So what did I do with this new freedom? After the euphoria of the moment it became apparent to me that, as is usual with such realisations, there was as deep a darkness as there was bright light contained in, what now seemed, a glaringly obvious insight. One who searches alone will have to endure degrees of loneliness; one who walks the single path can become enchanted and even entranced by a new teaching, a new insight, even a new group of 'like minded' people, but will leave much sooner than was suspected. Because it only offered a tiny fragment of the vessel of knowledge—not the whole—there yet again arises the thirst; it is as if one had craved a certain nutrient and, because some visually appetising food was offered, ate greedily thinking that this food must contain whatever it is your body sought. However it doesn't take very long before the meal lies heavily in the stomach and yet again the feelings of hunger arise. To put it another way, your ship had become anchored in a harbour that wasn't the place you'd set out for. Even if you hadn't any idea where that was—and you can't know that until much later on in your journey—you simply knew that this place couldn't possibly deliver you any further along the path. I discovered that all I had to do was look at the main protagonists in the show before my eyes. Did I want to be like them, or were they shadows of what I thought such a being should be like? It is a difficult decision, because the vision—the ability to discern—is only revealed as you yourself approach that which you seek. That is the only time you can even remotely identify its telltale radiation; the freely far-flung evidence of a burning flamekeeper: alive, beautiful, clear toned, integrated, loving and unpretentious. It is real, so real, so very real. It is rare. It will hit you between the eyes. But first your eyes must be able to see.

One of the greatest pitfalls—after the recognition that the road is travelled alone—is that of arrogance and self-satisfaction. It is easy to become entranced with one's own self-discovered truths; as if truth could be anything other than self-discovered. This entrancement is the downfall that continually awaits flamekeepers: hiding just around the corner for all, or else it can be continually shadowing your every move, your every word—behind your thoughts. Over the next few years it was my twin. Not only was I proud of the knowledge I had—and rightly so—but wished for it, in subtle ways, to be recognised for its depth and clarity. If only I had known then that the clarity I possessed could be likened to following the pavement edge in a dense fog, compared to the free flight of a bird on a clear sunlit day, I would have been much more reluctant to open my mouth. But that is a pitfall that it's easy to fall into; for the excitement of new knowledge fizzes over the top of the vessel which contains its exuberance, and in the process losses its long held power. How careful we have to be with its accumulation and exhibition.

I began to explore the more distant and remote of therapies. Perhaps that's the wrong way to put it. I began to explore those teachings where healing was but a smaller aspect of the greater desire for spiritual growth and evolution. This led me to investigate much to do with shamanism, something that, from the books at least, I felt an inner resonance with. What happens when you begin to explore these different fields is that you have immediately left one school and entered another; it is not intentional but nevertheless it is a fact. Your evolution and education has evolved beyond the merely obviously useful subjects that you may be able to earn a living by, and has

37

become something that is directly related to your inner growth. It doesn't seem much, but is in fact a huge leap in your reasons for investigating these more remote teachings. I found, as I usually did, a group of interested and interesting people who were fully engrossed with the subject and were sincere in their attention. This was the first time I had known such people for any length of time during a training, usually I had been taught alone. I liked them. Our teacher was well known and yet to meet this person in the flesh was something of a shock. Unlike my previous "huge" human, this person was someone who obviously hadn't integrated the different aspects of himself. He could occasionally be absent minded, distracted and repetitive, and yet at other times there were glimpses of someone who did have knowledge and presence. His instruction was a strange mixture of the banal and the too infrequently insightful and inspired. Yet I did learn one invaluable teaching from him: that of the return of consciousness to the elements.

He instructed us on the idea that to set up any kind of awareness or consciousness of the elements, of nature, we must first humbly give thanks for the support of our life. It matters not whether they actively or passively facilitate our existence, but it is absolutely essential—if you are to evolve on an individual basis—to recognise that your very breath is absolutely and utterly dependent on the earth and its fellow brothers and sisters which hold it in place; on the physical and spiritual forces of the air; of the waters; of the earth itself; on the plants and animals which are our fellow travellers. They often don't have anything to do with us per se—theirs is a separate consciousness and their path of evolution may have nothing to do with humans whatever—but the simple fact is that without them you would not be alive. Like it or not they facilitate your aliveness in a physical body. The first time I asked if I could take something; the first time I threw my offering onto the ground or plucked a hair from my head to leave on a tree, was yet another opening along the constant path of growth. It still is. I felt this sudden sense of belonging and support. Even if every other human rejected me, there would always be air to breath and water to drink. The elements did not judge me, nor did they actively decide if I lived or died. That is a fact: saint or sinner is supported or destroyed in just the same way. The act of returning consciousness is not so much for the elements' sake but for ones own.

With it comes the humbling; and without the humbling a seeker cannot progress. Always and always and always you realise that your physical life is dependent on forces far greater than we can imagine. Without a second thought the wind can crush the largest tree; the rain can drown the strongest man; the earth can swallow buildings whole; and we can so easily be burned to death that it makes one wonder if there must be some huge force of equilibrium which, as soon as one element moves too far out of line, brings it forcefully yet subtly back into harmony again. As if there is more controlling this puppet show than meets the eye. Yet the consequences of these occasional incursions are dramatic and often tragic. We are absolutely at their mercy. Understanding the purpose behind this return of consciousness was an important step for me, and one which I have never forgotten. Even if these ancient powers couldn't care less about my life, there is one huge benefit for me personally: humbleness. When I lose my sense of proportion I need only to remember this fact and I am returned closer to my true place amongst life: I could be crushed at any moment, yet I am supported with every breath.

Concurrent with this instruction arose an interest in Taoism. I had often used the I Ching with some obscure success, but I now began to use its lessons as instruction in themselves: it is my belief that it's a far more important book for personal and spiritual guidance rather than as a divinatory tool. From Taoism came the utter belief in the invisible; that which cannot be named but is known; an unspoken sense of harmony and flow, of endurance. Again and again endurance and adapting. Change and more change. One particular incident showed me that I too was changing. I went for a long walk along a canal in order to collect some blackberries for making jam. I walked on and on during a very hot day but found so few blackberry bushes I believed I couldn't have taken a more unsuitable route. On my return along the path I came upon one bush fully laden with blackberries and I eagerly began to pluck and search out each and every fruit. Then out of the clear blue of my mind there came this thought "I should leave some for the birds and animals; some for other humans to collect; some for the bush itself to reproduce with; and some for the sake of it fulfilling its nature. I could of course take some fruit, but I could by no means strip the bush bare." I heeded this thought and noticed an up welling of great peace. I had leapt from knowing something to putting it into action: a leap that has to be constantly made otherwise any knowledge we have is mere useless theory and supposition. I only had enough berries to make a sorbet with. It was the sweetest most delightful sorbet I have ever tasted, and its taste still lingers in my nature.

This period in my life was truly like climbing from a dark hole into the daylight. Ever since I'd taken my fearless leap into life—by choosing to leave my work in the first place—I'd had nothing but new experiences; some of which were good; some bad. I wasn't only learning of things I hadn't already known consciously, but also I'd taken the very difficult step of beginning to confront much about myself that needed to adapt or change. It wasn't as if I was a terrible person—most people are not—but it was a case that I could no longer simply learn facts: I must, if I was to find the real truth in life, put them into action. I must test them against the reality that was all around me.

My love life had always been rather treacherous. I fell in love easily and was equally hurt—quite brutally sometimes—by the actions of my so called lovers. I would swim for a while in the sea of love. It was warm and startling. It was scary and full of trepidation. It was aliveness in its most sensitive arena. It was vulnerability beyond what should have to be endured. But it was, occasionally, sweeter by far than anything I had ever tasted. It was, however, always inevitable that I would be unceremoniously cast upon the rocks. Cut and bruised, aching and lonely, I would make my way home. But still I believed in love. Still I looked. Still I was open to the possibility of success and an end to my longing.

During the period of my shamanic training I was befriended by someone who I thought could prove to be a real and lasting soulmate for me, and vice versa. We enjoyed each others company very much, communicated frequently and became close. We planned a trip around the world together; a huge leap of faith for me. However it was not to be. Quite brutally, one day this person said "I am not in love with you, I never will be, so don't even think about it ever happening." I was devastated. Not only because I had imagined that very outcome so clearly, but also because in my heart I knew it was not a mistake on my behalf. I checked this out with friends and colleagues, trying my best to relay the facts and incidents as clearly and as honestly as is possible for one man. They, like me, came to the same conclusion. Not only was I deeply hurt but I also had serious doubts about my perceptions of others. How could I misread another's nature so wrongly? Years later I came to the conclusion that what I had interpreted as friendship—as the actions of one who genuinely cared for and even treasured another—were in fact nothing of the sort. It was a clever act—very clever—which I would never have dreamt of perpetrating on another. It was a skill I was not the least bit interested in acquiring: honesty in personal relationships was very important to me and still is. What this incident pointed out to me, more clearly than I would admit at the time, was that I had the habit of seeing the best of the people in front of me. I talked, reacted and responded to that part of a person I felt was their inner light—who they really were. In some instances this is not a mistake; but in others, as in this case, if that person doesn't see it themselves, it is more than useless. It can lead one into dire and disastrous circumstances in which you not only suffer emotional pain and trauma, but which can easily set back your personal growth to a disheartening degree. It can even sever your connection with the spiritual: a dreadful consequence for having seen and loved the light in another. Dreadful but quite possible. There seem to me to be many such damaged individuals walking this Earth, those who have inadvertently believed in another when it would have been wiser to exercise restraint. Far too often during life there are times when we absolutely must see the actual physical and mental individual before our eyes; see what is before you with utter clarity, as disappointing as that may be. Then you begin from a space of honest perception, and your own integrity and wholeness are less endangered by what may come. This is a vital lesson and became an aspect of what I would later call "the light." Clear perception must go hand in hand with the power of love: one without the other is cold and calculating or else so dreadfully disappointing that it can take years to heal. Love and light: the warrior's sword and shield.

I was in a quandary. My reasons for training in shamanism seemed to diminish by the hour. I felt I'd obtained the valuable teaching that I'd sought, and staying in this place any longer was not only of little purpose but could stall my search for knowledge. Of course there was also bitterness over the broken hope of a love lost. I knew not where to turn. The teacher would be of no use in this instance for we hadn't developed a great bond; I think we were of very different natures and there were others in the same group with whom he had a better relationship. Also I didn't feel that his character personified his teaching, because problems would be solved in an intellectual way and not from putting his knowledge into practice in the substance of his being. I hadn't a sense that any answer I received could possibly help me. I wrote a letter of apology for finishing my attendance and never saw him again. I wish him well.

With this ending I was at a loss concerning my immediate future. Although I had travelled quite a distance along my path within a few short years, I needed—yes absolutely needed—advice about how I should now proceed. I felt like a man who was just one millimetre from discovering the truth: only the thinnest skein separated me from the light I sought. Inside I could feel it and observe it, but I just couldn't advance any further on my own. I needed another's assistance and guidance. There were others out there who knew more than I, but how could I find them. I felt that I'd drunk fully from all that was commonly available and was still thirsty; in fact I was thirstier than ever as I walked on into the desert.

One day I was pondering this problem again. Suddenly there was a picture in my mind: my magnificent friend. Of course, she could surely help. After all, she'd been the only human I'd ever met who definitely knew far more than she let on and, even more importantly, she had manifested in her nature the truths that she held. 'I must go to see her,' I thought. It was to be a dramatic decision with life changing consequences.

After travelling all day I knocked on the door to her home.

"Ah", she said, "so this is the time."

I entered. She went into the kitchen to make tea. Then we sat down. As we sipped our drinks she listened to what had happened to me during the intervening years since we had last seen each other.

"I knew you would come back, I just didn't know when. There is no predicting how long it takes for the ripening. Even in the talented it may be put off for good. Just the odd one makes it." Then she was quiet.

"It's just that I have nowhere else to go," I said. "They're all teaching something that I already know. They're all keeping their power. I want to be a master and I'm not sure in which direction to travel. I don't know, but I think you have something which I need, I just don't know..."

"Perfect." Under her breath she said "perfect." She stood up and opened a box that lay hidden amongst some books. She picked out a folded piece of paper.

"This is a map," she said, "you'll have to travel in order to follow it. On this beach," she pointed to a section of the map, "there is a man who will teach you. Tell him Kanaka Nui sent you. Don't be afraid of him, just be yourself, don't pretend anything because he'll see straight through you."

That night, as I slept in her house, I had a dream. Forest foliage parted to reveal a tiger's face. I couldn't judge whether it was friend or foe. I stood transfixed, not knowing whether to advance or retreat. Neither seemed the right decision so, unexpectedly, I sat down where I was. I closed my eyes. The next minute I awoke in my bed and it was the middle of the night. Traffic passed by the window. Outside it was just an ordinary night, like any other, but I was not the same as I had been: I was beginning to be changed forever. Later I looked upon this night as the ending of my search and the beginning of knowledge. I had set forth upon the narrow path—a path that narrows to accommodate you, because it can only be travelled alone; so narrow that it's easy to fall off. That is why we need a guide: someone who knows the twists, turns and pitfalls that lie ahead. A rare individual indeed.

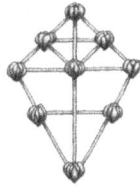

THE SEEING

I took a leave of absence from work for a few weeks and found myself—after a lot of travelling—in a forest. It was the end of a beautiful, if hot, afternoon. I sat down and leant against a tree. To all intents and purposes I was lost. The tree canopy was dense above my head, there was lush growth all around, and somewhere in the distance I could hear the sound of the sea. That is where I was supposed to be heading, but somehow I no longer knew which direction to walk towards. At once the sound of the sea played together with the sound of the wind in the leaves. I closed my eyes. I was tired and hot, and my skin was itching as it always did when I sweated. I sat there, fanning myself with the ridiculous but effective hat I'd bought for the occasion. Suddenly I realised how far I had travelled in a relatively short time. Why had I even considered this ridiculous journey? After all, didn't the texts say that the answer lay inside, not externally? Little did I know then that guidance on the journey to the heart of oneself always comes from an external force: for the way is full of pitfalls and enticements that can quickly and invisibly lead one away from the path. Without this external guidance it may be years later before it is possible to see where it was that you took a wrong turning. By that time it might take an almost insurmountable effort to struggle through the undergrowth that surrounds one in order to get back to the overgrown path of knowledge and truth. Overgrown because so few travel this way now. Then again, perhaps it has always been so.

Having lost my direction, and overcome with tiredness, I began to snooze. I dreamt of that tiger again. First of all his face filled the scene. He looked at me, then at the ground in front of him. There was a snake making its way towards me, but I wasn't scared. It curled into a spiral in my lap and suddenly shot into my body through my nose. I awoke with a start and gasped for breath. The forest was now utterly silent. Then in the distance I heard a sound, like a horn being blown. Time and time again it blew. What had I to lose, I was lost anyway. It was consistently coming from one direction which I began to follow. Because daylight was beginning to diminish, I walked as quickly as possible through the undergrowth towards the sound. Then it stopped. Still it was a distance away. I looked up desperately searching for anything that would guide me. Through the trees I could just about see a mountain top jutting into the sky. It was in the right direction so I walked on, keeping my eyes fixed to its distinctive peak; shaped, presumably by the weather, into a flat plateau with a short, very roughly shaped, obelisk-like pinnacle pointing upwards. It was about another three-quarters of an hour before the forest began to thin and the sand became more obvious. Then, all of a sudden, I was on the beach.

The sun sat across the bay, resting on the gentle sea's surface with its glorious orange rays skimming the water and bathing me in light. I took my shoes off and felt the residual warmth in the sand as I stood there, kissed by the sunset and the warm wind whispering to my body. It was a magnificent moment and suddenly I was lost in no-thought. I was swimming in the vast void, expanded beyond everything in existence and smaller than the smallest creature alive. An internal warmth spread through my body, in every cell there was this speaking "at last—now is the beginning, now is the quickening, now is the change." I felt better than I had ever felt before. Perhaps that's not quite the phrase: I felt more alive than I ever had before. It was a totally unexpected and unprecedented experience. And, just as suddenly, I came back to my ordinary consciousness with that sweet taste still on my tongue.

I looked around the bay. It was formed between the mountain I had seen through the forest—which was across the other side of the bay in front and to the right of me—a semi-circle of beach surrounded by the forest and hills, and to my left another small hill, which I presumed led to the next bay. There was a cabin on the beach in the distance with a small fire outside. I walked towards it. Actually it seemed closer than it was and the walk took longer than I expected.

The sun had begun to set, and as I reached the cabin I was surrounded by increasing darkness.

"Hello," I shouted a little reticently, "anyone home?" I knocked on the cabin door "Hello." No answer.

I sat outside by the fire. There were a few branches of dried wood by the side of the cabin; I put them on the fire to rekindle the flames which were beginning to fade. Looking out onto the now darkening sea, illuminated by a stately bright moon, I could hear the waves on the beach, the gentle rustling of the forest behind me and nothing more. It was very peaceful. I became aware of my breathing and was overcome by tiredness. I lay down on the sand by the fire with my backpack behind my head. Then a friendly cat rubbed my legs and waved up my body until it purred into a cat curl between my arm and chest. I fell into a deep sleep.

I was awoken by the sound of activity inside the cabin. There was the smell of fish cooking over the fire. A face looked around the door.

"Oh you're awake then, I wondered when you'd arrive, blew my conch for you but you aren't half slow, so I went for some food. You've met Chai then." as the cat wound around his legs.

He went back into the cabin. "Ah, there it is." He came out again holding two tin plates. "Couldn't find the other, not many visitors..." He laughed. "Come on then, sit up. Here's some tea. No sugar, don't have any, you'll have to bring your own if you want some in future."

He divided up the fish and we sat there eating in silence. Occasionally he would search through a piece of fish for any bones and then feed it to Chai.

I didn't know what to say, so I said nothing for the moment. I looked at him. He looked like one of those people who have no age. His face gave away little other than the fact that he was older rather than younger. His hair was receding but was cut short anyway. His clothes were kind of worn, comfortable but not in any way fashionable. I guessed that fashionable would be a word he would laugh at. He had baggy shorts and his skin was lightly tanned. He moved rather smoothly and used his body differently than I did. Perhaps he seemed to move consciously, deliberately, with awareness.

I finished my fish and drank some tea.

"Well?" he said, when he'd finished his tea,

"Er...thanks for the food."

"You're welcome."

Silence.

"Well?" he said again, a little impatiently.

"Well what?" I said.

"Well, why are you here?"

"Oh." somehow I expected him to know.

"I want to know more and I hadn't any idea who to turn to. Kanaka Nui suggested I come to visit you."

"Right: know more about what?"

"I don't really know, I thought I did but I'm not sure. I suppose it's about life and stuff, what we're here for, what's behind it all."

"Oh is that all," he said. "I can tell you that in a few minutes, that's the boring bit...nothing else?"

"Like what?"

He remained silent.

I thought and searched—why was I actually here? Was it really about what I'd said? Suppose he gave me the answers to all my questions during the next few minutes. Surely, if it was so quick and easy, that couldn't be what I had searched for all this time. Would I, in any way, be content? No, I don't think so. There has to be more to it than that.

"I think what I'm after is some instruction on living my life. What to do, how to live life but to always walk on. Something like that anyway. How do I become a good human being. Not good in the..."

He stopped me with his hand.

"That's better; I'm surprised you got this far without realising that's what you're searching for." He laughed.

I was a little taken aback. He seemed curt and a little patronising. I'm sure he was laughing at me. But where else could I go, who else had the knowledge I sought? I was confused, tired and crestfallen and took offence to his comments.

"Listen, perhaps I'm not so sure, maybe this isn't the place for me. We're obviously not going to get on if you're this impatient with me already. If I can sleep here tonight I'll leave tomorrow."

"My, my, my, you don't want it much do you?"

"Yes I do, but you're so sharp with me, obviously I'm not up to the standard you expect."

"So you're saying that if I'm nice and lovely and kind and wipe the tears away from your face you're prepared to give me the honour of teaching you?"

I felt like a fool. A small minded seeker. That's the last thing I was, at least I knew that.

"Sorry. It's just such a big thing. I can't put it into words. I'm sorry..." I said. My spirits sank. What a wonderful first impression I'd made. He looked at me. I was afraid to hold his gaze. He shuffled around the fire and put his hand on my back.

"It's OK," he said. His touch was not like his words. It was so gentle, light and warm. It reminded me of how long it had been since I'd been touched in such a way. It felt good. "We all make fools of ourselves when we're at our most earnest. Your bed is made up in the cabin. I'm going for a little walk—sleep well." And with that he stood up, grabbed his staff, and walked away. Chai followed him.

I was tired. I picked up the dishes and walked through the doorway into the cabin. It was much more than the word cabin implies. A couple of rooms off at the end and a small but adequate square living space with a little basin, bucket of water, three chairs, cupboards. I couldn't see a toilet though. I dropped the plates and cups into the basin and washed the dishes. Then I went up to the forest edge for a pee. That done, I carried my rucksack into the emptier of the two rooms and fell onto the bed utterly exhausted. Soon I was deeply asleep.

Watching this now, as an older man, I laugh at myself. And then I see my teacher returning and popping his head around the door. He sees that I am half on the bed and half hanging off. Gently he eases me onto the bed and covers me up, smiling to himself. There are many reasons behind him smiling. I know all of this now. I knew none of this then. He walks into his bedroom and sits on the edge of the bed, very thoughtful and serious. I also know now why he is so serious. Under his breath he says "must be careful with this one...must be careful..."

"Wake up sleepy head..."

I rouse myself from a heavy, deep, sleep. There is the sound of the sea, the wind in the trees behind the cabin and the smell of something cooking. I walk into the main room.

"Wash your face with seawater, it'll wake you up."

Like an automaton I do exactly as told. I run down the cool beach and scoop handfuls of water on to my face. Wow, this is what I call waking up. I look out over an expanse of never ending blue; the water and the sky, that's all there seems to be in the whole world. A large wave crashes up my legs and brings me back to the present. I walk back to the cabin.

"Ah, that's better, you look half human now. Eat up."

I sit down at the table by the cabin window which looks out to the sea. He sits on the other side of the table. Chai eats his meal from a saucer on the floor.

"What's your name by the way?" I ask.

He looks through the window.

"Call me Nohona," he said. "My name is Nohona."

"Is that your real name?"

He just smiles.

"Does it mean anything, your name?"

He laughs and keeps on eating. It doesn't take long to finish breakfast. I go to wash up.

"I'll do that," he says. "Go and look out at the sea, she's looking good today."

I walk outside the cabin. How different the scenery seems compared to last night. I suppose this is how you would imagine paradise: lush forest behind and to the sides of me and the blue water and surf in front. I breathe-in the salty air and realise how long it is since I last saw and smelled the sea. It feels really good to be here and I think to myself that it's far too long since I last looked on such a scene.

Nohana joins me.

"Well," he says, "let's get on. You'll need your walking shoes and water, I'll take some food."

In a few minutes we are ready. He takes his staff and we walk to the right, along the beach.

"We're going over that ridge," he says.

It looks a bit daunting to me.

"I forgot to ask you about your skin—does it cause you any problems?"

"Well, when I sweat," I say. "Got kind of used to it now, its only taken thirty odd years."

"Is this pace alright?"

"Yes, it's fine." Actually it's a bit fast and I'm sweating, but I don't want to appear weak or helpless or feeling sorry for myself.

"Just say." he says.

We reach the end of the beach and begin a steady climb up a rocky path. Slowly we climb and I quickly begin to lose my breath. He's started panting as well so I don't feel too bad about my fitness. Up and up we climb. Soon there is nothing else occupying my thoughts other than the climbing, making sure my footing is secure: I'm not particularly brave when it comes to climbing and descending unfamiliar terrain. He moves upward, quite sure footed, and is leaving me behind. He looks back and stops.

"Sure you're OK?" he asks.

"Yes." I say between my huffing and puffing.

He walks on. It's a long walk up, but when he finally reaches the top he sits down and I join him a few minutes later. I'm absolutely out of breath, he's just sitting calmly.

"Drink some water." Between my heavy breathing I gulp water.

"Sit down for a minute," he says.

"You're not out of breath at all," I comment.

"I was. I'm not now. It's not how quickly you get out of breath, its how quickly you recover," he says, still looking out at the sea.

Only now do I notice the view. To the left is the bay and to the right countless other bays and inlets, all separated by higher or lower ridges. The land is beautiful here; ancient and beautiful. The sea extends for more than half the horizon.

"It's nice here," I say.

"Yes," he replies.

"Where are we going?"

He turns around and nods his head. "Behind us there are some old temples I think you'll enjoy visiting."

I hadn't looked behind me. Through a small break in the dense forest canopy there seems to be green grass and some walls of rocks in the forest. I can't see much though.

"How's your breath?" he asks.

"Oh it's back to normal." For some reason I ask "How old are you?"

He laughs. "One day, a million years, and probably neither."

"Right" I say, "thanks for the clear answer."

He looks directly into my eyes, "I gave you an honest answer. Come on, let's get going."

The walk is slowly downhill, through shrubs around head height. The closer to the temples we walk the taller the trees are. It takes about half an hour at an easy pace. I look to either side, we are hidden from the bays by foliage and I am unable to see the temples from here. During this walk I feel more peaceful than I have felt for a long time. My other life seems a long way away from here; yet it wouldn't be too long before I had to return. However, not wanting to spoil the moment, I tried to forget the fact and concentrate on the present. I had to smell the foliage as well as see its vivid greens and browns; hear the sea; feel the heat.

Soon we arrived. The forest suddenly disappeared and in front of us there is grass in a huge circular clearing, surrounded on all sides by the forest.

Nohona said, "Walk around, get your bearings. It's OK to touch the rocks but don't move them or take any away." He walked off on his own and stood still, then he closed his eyes. I left him and walked forward. In front of me there was one larger structure, somewhat in the centre of the clearing. Scattered around the outside were one or two other temples. They were much smaller. Also there were a couple of very large rocks, the height of a human with sloping sides. They looked very old.

To use the word temple seemed strange to me. When I thought of a temple it bought to mind a magnificent building;

resplendent with luxury and craftsmanship. These were round enclosures, built to just above waist height, with huge and medium sized dark stone. I walked in-between the rocks of the two isolated stones and gradually became entranced by their age. They must be very old: the rocks were covered in lichen. Here and there were single specimens of a certain type of plant which had large green leaves and a long stem. The air around the whole of the clearing was still. I wondered what these stone spaces were used for. I spotted the entrance to the central temple but felt reluctant to walk inside it and just leaned on the outer wall looking in. It gave me a strange feeling. When confronted by something we haven't experienced before it can give as a jolt, not only mentally but physically. Standing there at the entrance I was trying to fit these strange spaces—so unlike anything I had encountered before—into other teachings or ideas I had come across. They would not fit in. You see, the fact is that these temples were so understated in their appearance that I wasn't quite sure what they were about. Funnily enough I experienced a mixture of mystery and disappointment at their austerity. I was still at a level of spiritual maturing that the invisible could not quite overwhelm my expectations of the material. I cannot believe this of me now; however it was true at the time. It would be a remarkably short time before my perception attained more of an equilibrium.

I felt a hand on my shoulder. I jumped, not realising how absorbed I had become looking at the rocks.

"What do you think?" he asked me.

"It's a strange space." I answered. That was enough for the moment, I had often said too much in the past about how I felt. He beckoned me away and we began to walk towards the forest.

He said, "This is the last time you will leave a space like this in such a way." He wasn't angry or disappointed, but said it almost under his breath. I realised what I had done immediately and went to turn back in order to correct my error.

"Don't go back, it's done."

The walk through the forest was quiet. We walked back on a different path. There was a tension between us; but I think it was really my guilt and disappointment at forgetting my previous training. However, this was the difference between training and being. Nohona taught being; until a point, only slightly in the future, I hadn't put into practice much of my mental knowledge. Perhaps it was my all too human nature: it's easy to say and think one thing yet do another—it could have been fear, ineptitude, inability. There were many reasons. The truth contained an element of all three probably; yet none of these is a sufficient excuse. I've since found it an all too common trait in many who tread the path. For myself I can only say that the weight of my learning wasn't sufficient to tip the scales of my consciousness onto the next stage. Soon, that would all change.

Nohona prepared our evening meal in silence.

"Are you really angry or disappointed with me?" I asked.

He turned around, "No, not at all, I'm just thinking, sorting something out which is to do with you, but it's not a judgement or anything like that," and he carried on cooking.

I walked out of the cabin and looked out at the world in front of me. Nohona shouted "I'll be a good half-an-hour here, go down to the sea but don't go swimming, it's dangerous in places." I headed towards the sea.

Small waves gently lapped the sand, in the lazy way that only a master force can. It is a strongly soothing sound. Even though I was born inland, the sound of the sea is very calming to me. I closed my eyes in order to simply listen to its freestyle rhythm. For a moment there were no edges to my perception; or rather there were no hard edges for my perception to brush against, and I felt as if I was standing isolated in a sea that went on forever. All around me, for ever and ever, there was this lapping sea without a shore, and I was standing on the only circle of sand where the sea could contact another substance in order to define itself. Just me and the sea and this little mound of sand. The sky above my head extended forever, into infinity, with an infinite number of stars set in an infinite blackness. Inside me there was only perception—nothing as crude as thought— only the dissolution of barriers and an ever extending, flowering attention. I acknowledged the infinite.

Nohona had begun to eat his meal as I entered the cabin.

"Help yourself," he said.

I sat down.

"From here you looked utterly still and calm," he commented.

"Yes it was amazing. Sometimes it happens to me but it's fleeting and moves on. It's as if bubbles of consciousness travel around the earth, and just occasionally and by chance we're enclosed by one as it moves ever onward; and it stays for a while, initiating us into its nature." I began to eat.

"I like that," he said.

We carried on eating in silence, looking out of the window into the black night. The reflections from inside the cabin and the view of the outside world all mixed together in the inky depths of the glass.

The next morning was fresh and overcast.

"I need to go into the local town for food," Nohona said. "I'll be back this afternoon so you can do what you want. Remember what I said about the swimming. See you later." He walked into the forest.

So here I was, alone, on a beach that looked like paradise. However much I tried to remember why I was here, it was lost only a few minutes later, as I became absorbed in the scenery all around me. I decided to walk towards the opposite end of the bay.

It took about ten minutes of slow walking to reach the base of the hill that enclosed the bay to the left. I wanted to walk up and over into the next bay but preferred to wait for Nohona to show me what was there. He was obviously at home here and knew every place that was worth visiting.

I sat down on the sand. The sun was beginning to peep out from behind the clouds and its warmth caressed my skin. There was a gentle sea breeze. I decided to spend some time here and relax on the white sand, so I dug a little body hollow to lie in, and raised the sand at the edges just to keep the wind off me. I lay down on the dry fine sand and snuggled into it, just as the clouds began to clear and the sun shone warm and bright onto my pale skin. Occasionally an odd cloud would drift across the sun and I'd lie still until the next wave of warmth flooded my body. Sometimes the breeze ceased and everything was still, apart from the distant sound of the waves. I began to relax. I realised how tense I'd been over the last day or two, as if I was trying not to put a foot wrong in front of Nohona. I was making the mistake of trying to impress him; to show what a great knowledge and wisdom I had. It was nonsense. If that had been the case, then there was no reason for me to approach him in the first place. There would be no need for instruction and guidance. I realised that what he was interested in were my qualities: the nature of my self and how much of it was accessible to him in order to bring out that which was already inside me. Watching him over the last few days I realised that he had a depth of knowledge I definitely didn't have. I needed to be more humble and willing to follow; not easy for me by any means as I had a naturally argumentative and headstrong nature. I liked the sound of my own voice a little too much.

Having realised what had been troubling me over the last few days—my pride—I could relax again. All of a sudden, as I drifted within the warmth of my body, I began to remember something that for many years I had completely forgotten. It was a memory from my youth. I'd travelled with my parents and sisters to an isolated bay on the coast. There was a steep descent down the sides of the cliffs via some steps cut into the rock. At the bottom we were greeted by a small but perfect bay; smaller than this one, with white warm sand underfoot. There were only a few visitors. The remarkable aspect of this particular memory was that, out of all the holidays we'd had as youngsters, it was this one that always stuck in my mind. After my family had settled by the rocks I walked down the beach and into the sea, with the water lapping my knees, stinging but bearable; and suddenly, almost magically, everything changed. I was standing there with little fish fry swimming around my legs in the beautiful blue water; the sun; the warmth; on my own; and something happened to the atmosphere. Looking back now at this isolated experience it is almost as if there was a little insert in the fabric of time; as if I'd been driven all these years to reproduce this feeling of utter pleasure. The water was bluer; the sky somehow vibrated; the utter safety and pleasure of standing in the sea—in a place that was a lifetime away from a tropical beach and yet exuded the same quality—was overwhelming. As a child my father and I kept tropical fish so there was a great pleasure for me in standing amongst them in the sea, in their natural state. I saw now how my life had left that carefreeness and I could no longer be as I had been; however, perhaps I could try to regain that feeling of simple joy that once ran through my body on that distant beach.

I stood up and walked down the beach into the gently rolling sea. Yes; there were fish fry in the water; it was blue and warm and I had that same feeling of pleasure. I'd completed a spiral of evolution—onward and upward—re-visiting an exact same circumstance yet at a higher level. This was my first concrete example of something that I'd once been taught and had yet to appreciate: that often, during our life, we encounter the same circumstances time and time again, but are asked to deal with them in a more mature, a more spiritually evolved, way. At other times they occur in order to graphically point out to us that we have moved on. I felt real gratitude for this clear elucidation of a profound truth. When a teaching is made real there is a deep resonance which sings, seemingly, through the universe of one's nature. So often it is not the case and only faith drives us along.

The rest of the morning and early afternoon were spent sunbathing. Finally I'd begun to relax and fall into a time frame that's so different from our normal life in cities and towns. Little did I know that this was only a prelude to the relaxing change that's possible and especially effected by such places. This relaxation facilitates changes so much easier and more subtly than the normal tension of living that is our constant companion. Relaxation doesn't exactly describe the process: rather it's a releasing; a freeing; an easing; an expansion. It is a flowering. Later on I would experience this fully.

I meandered back to the cabin. Nohona had arrived and was sitting outside. He was friendly and open.

"Come and sit down. No, get yourself a cup of tea and then sit down with me."

I did so.

"Where do you get the food from, the nearest town is miles away?" I asked.

"No, there's somewhere nearer by, with a great little food shop full of stuff. I'll show you one day." Then he paused. "Oh, that's why it took you so long to arrive is it?"

"So do you live here all the time?" I asked.

"No," he replied, "Chai and I come here when I want to, or if there's a need, as there is at the moment."

"What...me?"

"Yes, of course you."

"Oh." What could I say to that? I decided to change the subject. "So what do you do for work?"

He looked up to the sky and sighed. "I wonder if I should tell you, I'm not sure what preconceptions you have of me..."

I was about to lie—unknowingly—that I hadn't any, when he held up his hand.

"My job is very ordinary, very simple, it takes little skill and most of the time is unchallenging. Does that disappoint you? Don't let it. This..." and here he moved his hand between us and around the scene in front "...is what it's all about for me. As long as I can retain my integrity, evolve and progress without too much hindrance from my job; as long as it doesn't compromise my being; then it's enough that it supplies me with money to keep body and soul together. Unless you're lucky in life and find a field of work that doesn't hinder or compromise you and actually furthers your growth, then what I've described is enough. Although it doesn't seem so, sometimes the freedom of development provided by an ordinary and non-challenging job can be very valuable."

Somehow I couldn't accept this as true, even after my earlier experience of failed self-employment. However it was clearly something I needed to consider in depth. This didn't feel like the time to challenge and argue with him about the matter.

"Do you feel differently about me now?" he asked.

I sat there looking out at the sea. My immediate response would have been "Yes, I'm looking for a magician, a sorcerer, someone who can make lightning come out of his or her fingertips." It's childish I know, but which seeker hadn't at some time imagined being an apprentice to a wizard; a truly mysterious human with a staff and a living vine winding up its rich wood. Who hadn't imagined taking magical trips to far off dimensions or lands, to meet mysterious forces in struggles of good and evil? Every single seeker wanted that at some point or other. You see I hadn't yet grown out of the adolescent fantasies that for some reason can pollute our development for ever if we aren't careful. The truth is that I hadn't the least conception of what true spiritual development meant. There I was, thinking that I had a sophisticated and in depth understanding of what a "developed" human would act and appear like. I did, somewhere hidden inside me, have a good knowledge of the truth; but at this time of my life its secret deep calling sound could not be heard above the enticing and cheaply alluring images that, like all seekers, I carried around with me. It would be years before these imaginings left me for good. Often, in difficult times—of which there were many—they reappeared to feed my impatience with sweet and seductive promises of untold power and impressiveness. Sometimes it became really hard to resist them, as it does for all path walkers. I have to admit that their worse than empty promises caused me to tread perhaps one or two steps in the wrong direction once or twice. Nohona's art was to gently and unmovingly call me back by his strength of character; by the magnetic attraction that called to the deep part of me which could not be persuaded by any argument or inducement to change. That is because it was, in itself, the truth; and the truth cannot bend one millimetre to accommodate anything. Often, when we find the truth, it's so different to what we'd imagined it to be that it's actually difficult for us to even appreciate its qualities, because they do not reference themselves by the parameters we had assumed they would. Instead, the truth is so subtle that we miss its message completely. Rather as if we had to tune our radio into a totally new frequency, before we can hear the words and music clearly. Only then can its clarity move our intransigent mental identity towards the light of true growth and selfhood.

"I presume your silence means that you do."

I came back to the present "Oh...sorry, I was wondering how to answer you. The fact is that I'm not sure exactly what to say. In all honesty I really would like to be apprenticed to a wizard who changes into an animal or plant or rock at will."

"So would I," he interrupted with a laugh.

I carried on, "but maybe I've got it wrong; perhaps what I'm really looking for is something that I'm not able to appreciate yet; perhaps it's much much less obvious and yet all the more legitimate because of that. And perhaps that's why so few people get it; so few people teach it: simply because it's not obvious and it's only the obvious that really attracts people.

"Yes...I suppose so. Out of all the people I've met—some who were well respected, well educated and knowledgeable—I only met one person who I realised was really different; someone whose special qualities I only just about managed to tune into but which left me with an indelible impression that there's a secret way to behave, which only those tuned in to it can appreciate. And the more I tuned in to it the more it became obvious that there was a whole other world waiting for me to visit; but I don't know how to get there and I want to."

"Listen," Nohona said, "Listen to me now because I'm only going to give you this talk once, but it's probably the most important one I shall ever give you."

Believe me I was listening.

"Before you can learn the little that I have to teach you, there's a kind of prerequisite that has to be addressed. Believe me when I tell you that I do know exactly where you're coming from, why you are here, it was the same for me, and it's probably the same for all of us. But before you can learn this way of life—and here and now I have to tell you that you need not accept blindly anything I say ever, if you disagree you must argue and debate until it is clear—before you can learn you must know that this path of truth, of light and of love is a very hard path to follow, for it is entirely dependent on your commitment to your own evolution and growth. I can't do it for you; I can only give you various pieces of the puzzle which aren't generally known, but which aren't secret either: it's just that they aren't wanted. With these vital pieces of the puzzle—together with some of the other truer pieces that you've learned both yourself and from others—there will suddenly arise an understanding: a posture which will resonate with the great truth, the great light, and you'll swoon at this image; it will literally transform your life. But that transformation won't be as you expect it: it's about your internal life, that's the place where there has to be change. No longer will there be places within your self that you can ignore; you'll only be content with the highest manifestation of your true nature; and you'll always be dissatisfied with your development. However, that's how it should be. The trail moves on forever, and the further you travel the more undergrowth there is. Sometimes the path disappears completely because it's so rarely travelled, and much of this walk of yours will be done alone. And, of course, you can never return; you can never go back to a less enlightened state which, as strange as it may seem to you now, you will often wish. You will yearn for the ignorance of yesterday. You will ask for the life that others have: content in their ignorance, not even recognising the odd piece of the jigsaw that's part of this truth. You see, ironically, you will be living a life lived with simple truths and yet there is a more and more subtle evolution always beyond you." He paused and then, after a sigh "There's one final truth that I have to tell you, and it's the one that hardly anyone ever mentions. It is this: you'll almost certainly become lonelier as a result of walking this path." He paused again, as if he'd said something he didn't want anyone else to hear. "You will be more lonely than I can say.

Sometimes your only companions will be the plants and rocks; the sky and the sun; the stars; the invisible gods; sometimes your little pet, like Chai here. The tears of the immortals watching over you will drop down like rain, in empathy and remembrance. You will cuddle your arms around yourself at night; wondering how it can be that to make an effort to raise your spiritual self to encompass the wonderful star like brilliance of your true nature can result in so much aloneness. I have no answer for you that will make sense at this moment other than to state that what I can teach you is the way, and it is the brave way. Make no mistake, it is the true way of a warrior. The way of a warrior of love and light. You may be lucky enough to find a companion along the way; I did, and I hope you do, but there's a possibility that you will be alone for the rest of your life on Earth.

"Finally I can assure you that it is the truth; I have never found it to be anything other than the truth, and if that's what you seek then I can lead you towards it."

Everything had fallen silent whilst Nohona spoke. It was as if he were addressing the entire universe with his words. Even the sound of the sea seemed distant and muffled in recognition of the truths uttered from a totally unrelated life form; yet because it was the truth it was acknowledged. Gradually the sounds came back. Perhaps it was simply that I'd entered an unknown state and was readjusting to the familiar again.

"I'll make us a cup of tea," he said, and went into the cabin.

Chai walked over to me and rested on my lap. He purred as I unconsciously scratched his soft belly. I sat there, looking out at the sea. How often had the waves heard that speech? Perhaps the reason why everything became quiet was because it was so rarely heard by humans, let alone by the world. I realised he'd told me everything in honesty, and I thought it would be a while before I could ally myself to him and what he had to teach. The reasons were many and complex. Firstly—with my natural reluctance to formally join with anyone—there was a reticence that had to be broken through; not by reasoning, because in all reality reasoning about something of which you know nothing is impossible. No, it would have to be the sheer weight of my desire to know which would tip the balance and fuel the courageous leap I had to take. In order to endure what was to come I had to really want, and need, to follow through to the end. How much did I want to know? Reflecting on my life so far, it was obvious to me that the golden thread which I'd often lost sight of—but which I had always strove to catch and grasp tightly, no matter where it took me—had reappeared; and it was pulling me towards the instigator behind its movement and direction. Was Nohona the weaver who would bring everything together for me? Perhaps he was simply the man who would teach me to weave my life together into one individual, magnificent, golden and sparkling cloth. But the special qualities of that cloth could only be identified by others who were beginning to weave in such a way themselves, using the secret power of the same irresistible desire. To live this way—when viewed by others—seemed such a little thing, so insignificant as to be totally worthless; and yet the desire to do so is but a natural reaction to your reawakened awareness of the life and death of stars, the falling rain, and the impression that the staggering, startling, frightening and confusing life we see before us must leave. Without obstruction it is a natural consequence. There wasn't the distorted power struggle of many humans to attain the ultimately unattainable—the control of the world around us to serve our own, and only our own, purposes. I was to learn later that what was to be taught to me should have been a natural consequence of living as a human being on this earth; it is only our distorted perceptual framework that has arisen out of the society we've created that stops dead this natural process; this gift.

As for the truth about the other matters Nohona mentioned I could neither agree nor disagree—at this level I was simply too inexperienced to offer an opinion. But there is a part of me—all these years later—that wonders what would have happened if I hadn't gone forward, because I couldn't confirm the full truth of his words at that time. Would life have been better, banging around in the fully visible space that I had access to then; not realising that if only I'd left that restricting and inhibiting place there was a whole new world waiting for me? Or, in truth, was it inevitable that I would move forward: inevitable because that was my nature; inevitable because I hated the fact that someone else knew something that I didn't. Pride has its place; and the delicate manipulation of our eccentricities by a master can lead us along a path we might not have taken otherwise. I didn't know myself well enough then to realise my desire for knowledge could so easily bring about my fall: a fall from a false pedestal upon which real masters look and smile with that secret internal knowingness, born from the inner light. A fall to the ground on which I could walk, as other flamekeepers do, one foot in front of the other.

What lay ahead for me, if I said yes, I couldn't predict. But if I'd said no there would only have lain before me years and years of wandering in the wilderness, and I realised I'd spent long enough in that place already. So, in this way, I decided to say "yes" but these thoughts were not so clear to me at that instant. It was a feeling that invaded me: the frightening apprehension of a decision that would change everything, but one that was inevitable all the same. Rather as we know inside that a relationship is over and it is time to move on—with the only issue left being when the separation should take place—I decided to grasp the thread that had been offered, because my life as it had been lived until that point had come to its natural end. That is why I was here.

Nohona sat back down beside me and handed me a mug of tea.

"I have decided..." I began to say, but before I could finish the sentence he interrupted.

"Quiet," he said, "you can't possibly answer now, you need to go home and think about this very seriously. It's the most important decision you will ever make, surely it deserves more than five minutes of reflection." He began to drink his tea.

I felt so sure and yet, of course, it was good advice. It was the most important decision of my life; it was ridiculous to make that decision so quickly. At that age I didn't know how it would all turn out. My life would take such a penetrating and deep turn inward as a consequence, that I could only guess poorly at the real implications. After all, there was a possibility that this was my one and only life— that is a possibility that is often forgotten – and, therefore, did I want to spend it on a path that, if what Nohona had said was correct, would bring me little if any material reward and whose benefits would be elusive, gentle, subtle and yet utterly profound for all their whispering secretness?

Nohona suggested that I make my way home the following morning. My stay had been short and sweet; much shorter than I had originally intended. I presumed—should I decide to accept his offer— that he would accept me as a student, an apprentice, from his talk the previous evening. When I left he hugged me, and with his hands on my shoulders he said:

"Take as long as you want to. Even if it takes five years and the answer is no, that's fine. Thank you for visiting. Have a safe journey home."

"Thank you," I said, and I began to walk into the forest.

He shouted to me "You'd better walk fast, its going to rain in about half an hour."

I waved and embarked on my way home via a winding path that started just behind the cabin; much easier than the laborious way I used when I arrived. It didn't take long for the sound of the sea to pass into the distance and then to mix again with the leaves chattering in the gathering wind. I was moving away from the promise of new life, adventure and challenge, to the already known and bland, as if I had awakened from a lovely dream to the prospect of yet another day at work. Such is life.

Ordinary life gradually reasserted itself during the following few weeks. Each evening I'd prepare my meal and deliberately spend a while reflecting on what I wanted for myself during my life. Time and time again I came back to the same conclusion: that it would be absolutely impossible for me to look back on my life from old age and to feel that if I hadn't taken the offer that was before me now, then my life would be just as fulfilled as if I had. I knew that couldn't be true. All I needed to do was to look at how my life would be if I didn't take this chance. There would seem to be nothing but a perpetuation of the known; a never ending search for a treasure of knowledge which constantly eluded me for one main reason: I was looking at a worn and tattered map made by men and women from the past which had been copied time and time again, polluted with its confusing inevitably-human mistakes. Like everyone else, I was unsure where the cross was marked. Now I had the chance to set myself down in a very definite place, and begin to dig with the real promise that although the treasure I found might not be exactly as I expected, it was, nevertheless, the treasure I had always sought.

When such a decision has to be made it must be thought about long and hard. It was in my nature not to make a commitment without meaning it literally—a commitment; and for me to make a commitment was to go against my nature. I liked to think of myself as a free spirit; free to roam and investigate; free not to be held in place but to move at a pace that suited me and only me. But the fact is that as much as it's possible to gather information from the surface of the sea—and there is a huge amount that can be gathered—ultimately one had to dive into those deep waters to actually know. I had to know. I had a yearning to know; and, to the best of my knowledge, I'd only ever met one person who was prepared to teach me to swim down to the deep unsuspected depths of my being. Of course, because I'd never been there, I could only guess at what it would look like. Later it emerged that it wasn't how I expected it to be, and yet I was not disappointed with what I did discover: how could I be, the treasure was closer to me than my own breath.

It was about one month later when I next went to meet Nohona. This time the travelling was much easier as I was prepared for the long haul and, since I also knew the much shorter route to the cabin, my journey seemed less tedious. Besides, I realised that I could use the travelling time constructively to provide a necessary buffer zone between my ordinary life and my extraordinary life. Rather like warming up for a race or competition, the time spent travelling helped me to leave the familiar behind and anticipate the new.

When I approached the cabin, about one or two o'clock in the afternoon, Nohona was preparing some food.

"Ah, welcome, come in." he said. "A good journey?"

"Yes thanks, not too bad; am I in the room I was in before?"

'No, I tend to sleep in that one."

"Oh, I'm sorry, I thought with it being the barer of the two that it was meant for guests".

"No, the spartan one is mine. I like it that way."

His manner was much friendlier and more open than before. He later told me that his relief at finding someone suitable who wanted to tread the narrow path filled him with joy: so many times he'd listened to entreaties and supplications for tuition and yet they'd all been unsuitable. "What is necessary" he once told me "is that the apprentice has a sufficiently open mind to the new and sometimes unpleasant, and that their previous grounding doesn't embed their feet in concrete: that they can fly if need be, free from previous constraints. People," he continued, "love the familiar, even if it doesn't serve them; they are so afraid to venture into the unknown land because enjoying the new would seem to invalidate the time they've spent in that other place. They don't realise that not only is it the past that's brought them to this point, but also that the more they procrastinate the less time there is to establish themselves in the new. It need only take an instant to change, to make the decision, but that instant can last a lifetime. In the end it's all down to foolish pride again: an inability to accept that we are occasionally utterly and totally wrong!" He chuckled.

Over the meal we chatted about ordinary things, much more about my life than his. I think he was deliberately obscure, but of course there was the remote possibility he was actually interested in me. As the conversation dwindled I said:

"Listen, I've come to a decision."

He nodded for me to carry on. His face was serious, patient, and a little apprehensive.

"I want to become your apprentice, if you'll accept me."

He didn't immediately smile but, I suppose, was secretly weighing up the fact that it was time for him as well. Then:

"That's wonderful news. I'm pleased for you and I'm pleased for me." He smiled.

He rounded the table and gave me a hug. It was full of relief, and he let free a big sigh as he did so. It was only the second physical contact between us. It's strange when you touch someone: perhaps they appear hard or distant; perhaps there's resentment or bitterness; perhaps there are any number of confused issues between you; but as soon as you touch each other there is only warm skin and flesh; a human body which breathes like yours; whose heart beats like yours; whose inner fire, no matter how low, burns inside. When Nohona hugged me it was the first hug I'd had since his last one. Funny how we can live without physical contact for so long and yet immediately know, as soon as we encounter it, how important it is to us. One human embracing another is a secret path to peace.

"Well, we have some preparation to do, so we'll wash up and then go for a walk.

We walked up to the temples again. It was a very simple ceremony. A few words, a few movements, and intense awareness of what was going on. He told me that if I accepted my staff I would have to follow the path until its end, no matter how long that took me. And although that commitment could only be spoken by me, it would be said before both Nohona and the gods. Despite the fact that I couldn't feel their presence he assured me that they were watching. And, indeed, the forest did quieten; the sea sounds disappear from my consciousness; the birds in the forest were silent. I felt as if the whole of the invisible world was watching. Before I said yes and accepted the staff I thought long and hard about my decision. Perhaps five minutes passed as I anticipated and weighed up the implications. I think even Nohona suspected that I might walk away: but in the end it would have to be my clear and honest decision. Made in the same way as any true warrior—bravely, soberly, and with the full commitment of my whole being to my words and actions. There would be no going back for me; I would never be the same again. And, indeed, everything did change as a result of that simple statement; yet intrinsically my centre would remain as it always had been.

During my sleep that night I had a peculiar dream in which I was viciously attacked by some dreadful and negative force; however, I was protected by an unknown yet protective being who had temporarily entered my body. I awoke with real fear running through my veins, and yet marvelled at the pure feeling of this experience: it seemed more real than reality itself. Obviously my declaration that evening was by no means an empty gesture; and this experience proved that I had truly made a commitment which had also been observed by those who normally insinuate themselves malevolently into our lives; however, they can make a determined lunge at the light that blinds them should they feel it necessary. Their desire is to remain unseen and unsuspected in this universe.

The following day we walked into the forest, on a path I hadn't used before. The forest appeared in places to be managed; in others it was wild and difficult to walk through. There always seemed to be a purpose when walking in this way, but it was only now that I was beginning to relax into it, to allow it to have its effect. Journeys such as these seemed to facilitate a shift in consciousness in order that I better comprehend what was to be taught.

All of a sudden we came upon a clearing. It was roughly circular and covered in short grass. On the opposite side to us there was a waterfall which fell into a stream, formed a pool in the middle, then wound around the clearing and ran away past us into the forest. The water trickled softly and the sound was restful and refreshing to listen to. There was a large slab of irregularly shaped rock on the other side of the stream; it was smooth and of sufficient size for two or three people to lie flat upon. The whole scene seemed surreal: for the combined effects of the sound of the falling water, the warmth of the sun as it shone down into the clearing, and the distant sound of the sea, produced a feeling of utter tranquillity—as if we had stumbled upon some secret and enchanted glade, undiscovered for aeons.

"My teacher bought me here as I bring you now," Nohona said. "First of all we must announce ourselves to the area and to the spirits of this place, tell them why we are here." He looked at me.

"I'm not really sure." I said hesitantly.

He smiled, "No, I know you're not; I'll do that bit for you."

In a gentle but firm voice Nohona said "My name is Nohona. I bring my apprentice Kawowo here to this revered place, in order for us to learn and understand better our true nature. We ask for your blessing and permission to enter."

I looked at him. He looked all around. The breeze dropped and all that could be heard was the splashing of the waterfall. I was barely aware of the forest, but now I noticed how its sounds disappeared and the reverberating stillness echoed all around us with its own silent note.

Nohona smiled "It is good. Say thank you."

I bowed my head and said "Thank you."

"Drop your rucksack here," he said.

We walked towards the centre and sat down by the pool.

"This, as you can tell, is a special place. It was not created for us, but can be used by humans in order to understand their true nature better. There are certain places that are conducive to your development and others that are not. It's not that they were specially made for us, but that we find the confluence of energies at such a spot beneficial to our evolution. It is possible to make such a place, but it's a valuable gift to find them in the natural world. This is one of them."

His nature had become calm and authoritative; somehow it made me want to listen. To be quite honest I felt excited and special to be receiving this knowledge. I knew I had begun.

"We will come to this place a few times during your training because it is here that I shall teach you the most important, the most utterly important fact of this whole teaching. As a statement of fact it will not take long to tell you, yet the rest of your life will be spent putting it into practice. The subtle anatomy of humans is a lost knowledge that very few people understand now and you will be one of them. Humans have four possible bodies which exist all in the same space but within different dimensions. They all connect through the physical body, which is most important and special, more special than you know at this moment. There is a mental body which connects to the physical, which we shall talk about later. There is a soul body, your body of life energy—mana—which is created before this physical life, but also connects directly to the physical body.

71

He stopped. The silence bounced back. He sat as if waiting for something. Finally I said:

"You've told me of three, what about the fourth?"

"When all three are aligned; when all three are integrated; when the three begin to act as one, then the fourth body is formed. It is like an imprint on the nature of the universe; on spirit itself; on the void. It is what survives after physical, mental and soul death. For, make no mistake about it, they will all die and only your spirit body will survive; and only then if you have created it by integrating the other three bodies."

Again he stopped. I had nothing to say and yet a thousand questions swirling around my head. I hadn't heard of this before, but felt I knew parts of it already on a deep and instinctive level. Most of the questions were "yes—but" questions. I opened my mouth to speak but he put his hand up.

"No questions here. Experience first, questions come later and away from here. Always the same. Always. Now, take all your clothes off."

"Really?"

"Yes really."

I felt a little embarrassed, but did so.

He led me over to the pool in the middle of the clearing.

"Now I want you to lie in the water, rest your head on the edge."

The water was warm and comforting as I stepped in. It was about two feet deep so my body could float as the water flowed gently, but still noticeably, over my skin.

"Just breathe deeply to start with; I'm sure you're quite an old hand at relaxation so I don't need to go over that. Breathe deeply and float. Close your eyes. Now notice how the water touches every part of your skin; there isn't a single part of your body that isn't touched; all of your skin is stimulated by the water flow. That's why we use this pool. Look down with your internal consciousness at your toes and follow your body up slowly to the top of your head. I want you to notice the internal sensations of your body as well. Don't forget your arms and hands; your fingers; don't forget the back of your body; or your genitals. Try to become conscious of all this at once. Just try your best, you won't get it completely to begin with; you're going to do this every so often for years, so just do what you can. Now go deeper. Try to be conscious of your muscles and tendons; all your internal organs; your heart and circulatory system; brain and nervous system; lymph; digestive organs; the senses. If you like you could describe it as becoming conscious of the inside of your body and what it does for you: even if it's only acknowledging or remembering that all of it enables you to function and live. Think about what your body allows you to feel. What about the wonderful and amazing sexual feelings you can enjoy. Sex is a gift, a tremendous and exhilarating enjoyment and the feelings all come from, and are experienced in, your body. There are your senses; the magic of sight; the joy of hearing, touch, smell, taste, kinaesthesia.

"Now comes something important: the skeleton. Very, very important. Try to become aware of your skeleton. You've got a good idea of what it should look like, but remember it's living, not bleached white; but I want you to really feel it inside you. Try to become aware of your skull and spine, down to your pelvis; don't forget ribs, legs and feet; shoulder blades, arms and hands." He paused. "Try to hold everything now, everything we've been looking at in one go. One whole. This is physical consciousness. Just move your body a little, wave it in the water. Now be conscious of your physical body as you move it. Don't think about it, don't reflect on what it could or should be like, just be aware. Let your consciousness expand into it. Be your body."

I followed his instructions perfectly, but this was new to me. No one had told me this before; it was difficult to work at his pace. Even though it took longer than I have remembered it, still it was too fast to perform correctly. However, I was aware of more than I had been before. Nohona told me that body consciousness resembled the qualities of water: fluid, streaming, adaptable; it could be still or fast, solidified and cold, warm and flowing, soft, hard, yielding, active. "Think on this." he said. And there I was, for nearly all my years, concentrating on my mind: learning, refining, quickening. That was me. Now I had to deal with the fact that this was only a part of the truth. The idea that much of what I had been told by others was only a fraction of the whole and that it was not—as people had told me— the path to truth, surprised me. It was as if a blind man had asked how to regain his sight and was mistakenly led by others who believed that the images they see in front of their own eyes are real; yet they are themselves blind. Everything they see is in their own imagination. Quite conceivably they could cause him to wander in a desert for ever; or to drown in unseen waters; to believe that the beautiful sounds assailing his ears were only benevolent and must issue from the cure for his disablement. How many infinite possibilities are there for deception; how many times did he have to leave one group and yet try to integrate into another just as deceived, just as eager to lead him towards sight. How could they? They have no true sight themselves. In Nohona's words "the beginning of that true sight is the physical body: it is the communicating hub of your bodies; it transfers and translates all that enters it."

Later, back at the cabin, Nohona couldn't emphasise enough the importance of the physical body.

"Because of the nature of humans beings we have, over recent time—but in the past less so—transferred our consciousness to the mental body; yet this is one, and only one, aspect of your nature. The first and most important piece of truth I want you to understand is that life is multi-dimensional, and as far as humans are concerned we all have three dimensions to our being. It is these dimensions that have been ignored by many teachers and seekers. Sometimes these facts were known and yet were misinterpreted, or the metaphors and similes used were taken as reality, not a means to better illustrate the truth. You see, there is this constant desire to glamorise and embellish the nature of things. Sometimes it was done to maintain power, but mostly it was done to entice. Which do you prefer, the paint in the tube, the hair and wood of a brush, the plant material used to weave a canvas, the wood for the frame; or do you prefer the picture? And yet the picture is only made up of its components. Infinite possibilities from elementary origins. It's only a metaphor, but it does illustrate how it's possible to misinterpret the message in any number of ways. Whatever happens, do not forget your physical body, ever. It is all important. It is a wonderful and marvellous creation."

That night I slept fitfully: I had many arguments and yet could not formulate them into well structured questions. It felt so obvious and so simple, but that simplicity took away much of the romance that I, and others, seek on the spiritual path. It did come—the romance and the magic—but in ways that are subtle and perhaps mystical; more in retrospect than immediately. Real magic is the transformation of oneself into the full, marvellous, sparkling creation that is at the centre of the human heart; and if you persist with the work it will manifest in very real ways.

I came to the uncomfortable conclusion that the enticement of the infinite images, beliefs, and games that were possible in my mind interested me much more than the somewhat ordinary sensations of my physical body. I suspect that this is the case for many aspirants. It's so much more interesting and deceiving to deal with the language and images of our minds than to learn to appreciate and become absorbed in our physical body. Perhaps it's a result of how we have been led to believe the process of spiritual growth must proceed.

This was graphically brought to my attention the next day. We once again visited the clearing in the forest. This time he instructed me to stand on the stone itself. After muttering something under his breath I became aware of the rising wind moving around me. Nohona spoke:

"The easiest way to become aware of the mental body is to first of all become aware of where you think your physical body is. Think about where your legs and arms are; your torso; your head; your whole body. Now you have to differentiate between where you feel your legs are and where they actually are. Sounds weird doesn't it, but that's the easiest way. Become aware of where the whole of your body is. It's very common to think that certain parts of your body are in slightly different positions to where they actually are. Now try this: think of a part of your body, its size and where you think it is. When you have a good idea, touch it with one of your hands. That's it. Now is your upper arm and shoulder how you thought it was?"

"Not quite, no."

"One of the best ways to create a perfect mental body is to touch your own body, or have it touched, when you are in full consciousness; conscious of the physical and conscious of the mental. Switch between them.

"Now of course that isn't all there is to it. In the physical world there is the rest of the physical world and—apart from in exceptional circumstances—it is a common experience to us all. However, in the mental dimension, there is your own mental world and every other mental world belonging to every other human.

Frightening eh? You see, how you create the rest of your mental world is entirely up to you. It is usually the case that no thought goes into the construction of a persons mental world whatsoever, so the truth is that the concepts that we talk about to each other bear only the slightest resemblance: enough for communication to take place, but nowhere near enough for the words we speak to have real resonance with the other person's world. Only if we have predefined our use of certain terms can we hope to communicate efficiently and comprehensively. That's part of what I'm doing with you now. This is why, as I'm sure you're aware, there are some weird and plain bizarre creations out there; take my advice and don't ever get embroiled in them."

I could hear him talk with a smile at this last remark.

"So you see, its up to you, your mental world. My suggestion is that you enclose yourself in some form of shape that suits you; as big or as small as you want. You can install any number of protective mechanisms in or around you, literally anything goes, but you do need to do so. However, it's very important that you feel fine with it. You need to find out for yourself how it's created at the moment and then alter it to what you want. In the future, when what you feel better with becomes clearer, then you can change it to suit you as many times as you want. For many people on the path, simple is definitely better. Like I said it's up to you. We'll talk about this again."

I had become absolutely absorbed with his words and his voice. As Nohona told me, this absorption was a trance state; an example of the wide variety of trances we enter into and leave all the time. As I came back to my everyday awareness it was like surfacing from a dream. He led me over to the pool. I took my clothes off and sank into the water as he cautioned me not to become absorbed in my mental world but to try my best to maintain and become fully absorbed in my physical consciousness once again. In order to facilitate this I had to keep my eyes open, it would be easier this way.

As I stood up the breeze made me shiver and I became suddenly aware that I was definitely back in my physical body.

"It's always best," Nohona continued, "to return to the physical after any other dimensional awareness. As much as it's really disappointing for you to try grounding your experience in the physical again, the truth is that in this way your progress is much more certain."

The mental world proved to be a slippery customer. To become enthralled in its machinations was all too easy for me. Now I began to recognise how—even though I might protest that this wasn't the case—I actually spent almost all my conscious time in the mental dimension. Because this was such a large part of my everyday experience it became increasingly important for me to spend some time, daily, in my physical body; simply being conscious and aware of its movement. It wasn't that I disliked physical consciousness, just that my mental world was so enticing: arguments, wishes, justifications, desires, the whole galaxy of possibilities proved all too tempting. No sooner had I grounded myself than, imperceptibly, I had once again become enmeshed in the infinite variety of cloud like impressions that drift within. The practice of awareness meditation proved useful, although it was all too easy to become far too serious in my manner as I became engrossed in this constant watching of myself. Ultimately, simple, brief, self-reflective awareness of the state of my consciousness—where it was actively engaged at a moment— proved more useful. This spontaneous act proved to be one of the great gifts of being fully alive.

Nohona talked often about the mental realm. He indicated that it inevitably proved the downfall of many would be pathwalkers because of its nature. It had the quality of air: fast, changeable, ephemeral; easily moved yet difficult to grab hold of. Without differentiating it from the other bodies it was so easy to convince oneself of its omnipotence; to become caught, like a fish in a net which, during a struggle that could lead to a whole new life, only succeeds in entangling itself even more. Invariably, much of the mastery of the mental realm depended on the ability to change: to dissolve something that was no longer needed and replace it with something better, or more suitable. Humans dislike change unless it is ordered and brought about at our own behest. This is fine as long as you accept that you are willing to learn; that you are prepared to admit 'I don't know everything—teach me.' But how many people say this and really mean it. We are prey to programming from birth onwards; some of which is useful for ever, some only for a short time, and some not at all. It is beholden on each pathwalker to inspect their mental world for all its imperfections and incongruities, and to gradually release and dissolve them of their hold on that world; to stop accessing the rubbish that sticks to us as we walk through this life. We must replace, or cast out, old and unused prejudices, beliefs, opinions and thoughts which should no longer be part of our mental world; for, in reality, that world is not a separate aspect to the rest of us; its nature has to harmonise with, resonate and reinforce our true nature. Unfortunately it's so often the case that it only interferes with and disables our wonderful human potential and its amazing possibilities.

A few days later, as Nohona and I were walking through the forest to the clearing he said:

"Today we're going to look at the big one; something that you don't know of but which has been with you for ever. With this third body we complete the knowledge of the bodies that every human being has, and it's of the utmost importance that you understand one fact: to integrate the three is your main aim as a flamekeeper."

We reached the clearing. Nohona made his announcement and we walked forward. He said:

"I've never really found a specific place for this practice because it can be done anywhere in the clearing, so let's just stand here in the grass.

"Now, I want you to just relax your knees, let your body become still and your mind quiet. Close your eyes. Obviously you need to make sure that you're fully aware of your physical body. There is a gentle breeze now, use that. Listen to the wind in the trees and the sea in the distance, but don't reflect on them; just listen and feel. Now become aware as much as you can of any internal sensations, and come back to your skin again. Begin to feel the warm sun on your skin, heating your body, and gradually I want you to let the sensations of your skin disappear. Let its barrier dissolve, and expand your consciousness to the space around your body. Feel a large bright area around and within your chest area and let it expand outwards; above and below; all around you. Just feel this. Feel it, don't think it. Now, to help that feeling, forget your name. Imagine you had never been given a name. Imagine you had no specific skin colour, no religion, no beliefs, just the feeling of being you and being alive. Feel your radiance. This is your soul body, your body of life energy. Its radiance is like fire."

I felt warm all over. I felt connected. There was beauty. Love. No hate or anger, no impatience. There was personal power, but it was for me—nothing to do with needing or wanting to use it on or over another. Just the vitality of life, radiating and sparkling. My own original identity. Ah ha! At last, now I had a name for it.

After a short while I became absorbed, and lost all sense of time. Then Nohona said:

"Just open your eyes a little and walk towards the pool."

I staggered a bit and felt unsteady.

"Undress, then lie in the water."

I did so. Warm moving water stimulated my skin. It was as if my consciousness shrank back to the size of my body.

"Try your best to move your conscious awareness between the physical and the soul body. Let the boundaries disappear, let your identity shine through and then compact it into your physical body. Do it over and over; just switch."

This was easier said than done. Because the warm water was relaxing and pleasant it induced a pleasant sleepiness in me. The expanded state of consciousness was something I had enjoyed before but I hadn't known how to reproduce it. Certainly it had obviously been experienced by others and yet had been misinterpreted and misunderstood in uncountable ways.

"OK, time to get out, before you fall asleep. I think that on a hot day like this it wasn't the most helpful thing to do."

He helped me out of the pool and once again the breeze arose and caused me to shiver. I dressed.

"Ha! Now you're back in your body," Nohona laughed. "Let's try a bit of movement. Follow me."

He then proceeded to create a dance; just movements of his hands, legs, head; and the degree of concentration I required to follow his seemingly random but balanced movements soon brought my consciousness back into my body.

We stopped and then sat at the edge of the stream.

"Already you know more than huge numbers of pathwalkers. What I have laid out before you is the basic anatomy of humans, whatever their race, colour, religion, sexuality or level of spiritual maturity. All humans are born with a soul body and a physical body. During their early life the mental body gradually forms.

Unfortunately, what almost always happens is that the vast majority of their consciousness then moves over into the mental body, and stays there until death. This is not how it should be. You see the soul body, or your body of life energy—whatever you prefer to call it—is the intent and inspiration behind your physical body: it originated before your physical body was formed. It also exists out of time and, in some perplexing but still relevant way, knows about your life in the physical future. It is incredibly important that the soul body and its consciousness maintains a connection to the physical body—and infuses it—so that its communications can then be translated and moved into the mental body and back again. It also needs to be fully aware of what is going on in the physical world you live in. Do you see?"

"I think so. So does this all go on in the same space?"

"Yes that's it. In the same space, but in different dimensions. Like a sound contains different harmonics that can be separated but all together make a particular note."

"Ah...I see." My mind was racing.

"Don't get carried away for the moment, just let your awareness sit in your physical body."

"But I can feel waves in my body; different things."

"That's good; you're becoming aware of the transforming and translating ability of the body. That's why it's so vital to personal development."

"I've been thinking. Does this mean that all that mental thought is a waste of time?"

"Some of it is, some of it isn't."

"Well I'm glad you've made that clear then."

"Some of it is. Which part?" he asked.

"Well, from what you've told me, I suppose the thoughts that are resonating with the soul."

"Yes that's right. As you learn more of your soul, as you spend more time with it, there will be a gradual transformation of your mental body. That's the real magic of it. Once you shine the light of your soul on to all the mental quirks, prejudices, beliefs, all that stuff, there will be this process of change going on. Really it's a wonderful thing, there's very little that has to be rooted out as long as you are prepared to allow for change; many kinds of thought-forms shrivel

80

when the full light of the soul shines onto them: those outmoded and obsolete thoughts don't like the light of soul consciousness. But the connection between the two is the physical body. Like a homeostatic loop, the communication between them is self regulating as long as the doorways, or gateways, connecting them are clear.

"Don't think that the soul is this weak, snivelling, lacklustre, timorous, faint-hearted force. It is love; but again it isn't sentimental and dreamy. It is passionate, vital, radiating, pulsating, sparkling, energised, all these and more. Sometimes it's quiet, sometimes loud, active and then again receptive. Ultimately it is your absolute identity as given to you by the Creator, but it must, must, must shine into your body and into your mind or its true potential can never be realised."

Nohona had become very passionate and active whilst speaking. He looked at me directly.

"Yes, the way I'm talking to you now is with the full force of my soul behind me. It loves this kind of stuff. When physical, mental and soul are all unified there is a tremendous power available to you. We will talk about this later...that's enough for now."

Again I was reeling from all this information. Not because of the fact of it, but its implications. Instantly it made sense to me. Of course there were lots of arguments and questions but basically it did make sense. It was so beautifully simple and contained within it the foundations for human evolution. I was elated.

The final time that Nohona took me to the clearing was a few days later.

"This is the last time I need to bring you here formally, and perhaps it's the most riveting of all your lessons here." We were sitting on the rock. "I have told you about the desire of us flamekeepers to integrate and solidify the passage of consciousness throughout the three bodies. As this process becomes more and more real, as the reflection of your true nature echoes and resonates throughout your being, there is a very particular process that is almost automatically instigated. The very substance out of which all dimensions are manifested begins to get imprinted with that unified vibration. It's a process that has been misinterpreted, forgotten and misunderstood for hundreds of years; even longer than that in most parts of the world. The only real, living, truly functioning body that you can take with you after your physical death is this body; let us call it your spirit body. And, before you begin your mentally enjoyable excursions to the land of dispute and argument, let me tell you that it's quite possible to create a very strong mental body that does indeed survive your physical death; yet this is not a truly living body, it is a reflection of your mental self. It can survive for a certain time, which may be quite a long time in human terms, but ultimately it will dissipate and disintegrate into the void. Only your spirit body is truly immortal."

Although Nohona had given some hints about this process before, I hadn't understood it in this clear way.

"Do you mean that some people can simply die and that's that."

He looked serious. "Yes, that's exactly what I mean. I know it doesn't seem fair or right, but for whatever the reason—and I don't know the reason – this is the way that it is. You can have no doubt that the vast majority of people living on the earth at this moment will not survive their death, and even fewer will live on in their spirit body."

"But isn't that an exclusive belief? What if they haven't had the chance to understand it?"

"In a way you're right. The truth is that this is not about belief, it's about knowledge. As I've already told you, this should be the natural way for humans to evolve. There's no religion here; no powerful admonishments; simply an explanation of how things actually are. Yes, there are odd people who do make it, by chance and luck: a good upbringing; the freedom of thought that allows them to develop fully as human beings; the continuing connection with their soul; and an enjoyment of their physical body. On this coast, many years ago, life was orientated towards that goal. Can you imagine how such a life was lived: full of vitality, enjoyment, passion and of course a certain amount of dispute. That is inevitable. However, those in charge knew this path and always steered their fellow residents towards the goals of love and acceptance; of fulfilment during their life, whoever they were. The difference between then and now is that those in charge knew, or were advised and guided by those who knew. Now, sadly, that is not the case. Our society is not orientated towards or interested in this full life, only towards fulfilling the distorted and peculiar will of the mental world. That's why it is controlled and restricting. That's why it's so judgmental. That's why you have to travel so far to find someone who knows..."

His voice trailed off. He was obviously paying respect to a deep sadness within. Then, back in the present:

"Now, let's get going. Lie down on the rock. Just move your body so that your feet point towards the sound of the sea. Become aware of your physical body. Feel the heat of the rock on your back. Think about where your body is lying. Enter your mental body and as you drift back to awareness of the physical body maintain that peripheral awareness of the mental. Now let your boundaries disappear; let the warmth and vitality of your soul body flow. Again maintain that connection as you come back to the physical body. Now, as hard as this might be, try to keep all three in your awareness at once. Allow all three to be; without preference. It's not easy, I know; just follow what I'm saying whilst having some sense of these three bodies. Now the thing is, just like the mental body, this body also has to grow and mature, you are not born with it. Again, just as the moon relates to the mental body so does the sun with the spirit body. Unlike us, the sun has many more bodies than just our three; it occupies many more dimensions, it isn't just light and heat. What we can say about it, however, is that it's the most powerful imprinter that's available to us. What I want you to do is connect with the sun. Try contacting some of its emanations, seeing which one feeds your spirit body; which nourishes and illuminates your spirit—which one causes it to resonate and sing. You don't have to go out to it: those invisible forces are here and now. This is something you are going to have to work on, and I can assure you that it will take perseverance. The truth is that there is no real way in which I can describe what it feels like when done correctly, however you will know it when you feel it. You will just know. And as your spirit body begins to grow you have to give it access to your everyday life, especially to movement and consciousness. When you begin to create this body you will get a certain feeling of clarity, of clearness, and certainly of timelessness. You may well feel that you are one day and a thousand years old. I really can't describe it better than that. It seems to be different for everyone, but that's only because of a lack of suitable words to describe it specifically. I'm afraid that this part of the path is to do with trust until you begin to know. It's concerned with looking for and finding something because you've been told about it. Just make sure that you continue to differentiate between the sensations and feelings of the other three bodies, then you can be reasonably sure that what you are experiencing is the spirit body. If you remember that it's created with pure consciousness, with the integrated wholeness of your being, you won't go far wrong."

As you can imagine I had great difficulty with this exercise. In reality I hadn't the faintest idea what I should be feeling. It was more than enough just trying to gain an awareness of my three bodies all at the same time, and I didn't feel for one minute that I had achieved anything at all to do with my spirit body.

He bade me stand up. Then, once again, I tried to follow his seemingly random set of movements.

"Be conscious of the physical, be conscious of the physical," he repeated every so often in a whisper. It was as if he didn't want to awaken whatever had fallen asleep around us. Nothing stirred.

Gradually I fell into a trance-like state as we continued. The strangest thing began to happen: I followed his movements with balance and continuity. There was this peaceful, wave-like movement flowing through me; through the earth; from above. It was one of the most fundamental rhythms of life. I was in tune with far more than I knew. After a while we came to a natural still point and stood peaceful and at ease. Nohona said:

"Close your eyes and be conscious of your body."

I did so. There were waves and waves of movement flowing into my body. Not quick, but relaxed and full. From above my head to below my feet they seemed to come, one after another. As they began to calm and then disappear I felt marvellous—left with this impression of filled space. Whereas before I had no real sense of the inside of my body I now became conscious of its volume; not just of the outline but the inside; now it had real depth and substance. Somehow I felt more solid.

As I opened my eyes, the world was brighter, infused with life, vibrant and more beautiful than I'd ever experienced it. As we left the clearing I was filled with the source of livingness. This time my offering to that place—and to what had given me permission to be there—was sincere and heartfelt. Now, when I reflected on times before when I had made that same offering, in the same way, I realised that it had been an empty gesture. It became clear to me that there was certainly no objection to a habitual 'thank you' or one expressed with a sense of duty; but when performed in full consciousness, with a true sense of community and love there was this immediate rapport. The return came back simply as a sense of connection; not only to that place but also, in some mysterious way, to this ancient, human and spiritual teaching that integrated humans into the universe in which we live. With this same sense of genuine humbleness—one that would take many years to integrate into my everyday nature—there came a correct sense of my place in—and within—life: the grace by which our lives are supported and maintained; and a real sense of the knife-edge on which the beat of our human heart is balanced.

The following day I left for home with Nohona's request that I practice, if only for a few minutes each day, until we next met. We hugged goodbye. I was full of inspiration and revelation. Even as I travelled home I was amazed when previously obscure teachings either fell by the wayside of my consciousness or pocketed themselves perfectly into these new categories. I was genuinely taken by surprise at how quickly this happened.

At last I had been taken on a vivid walk along the path of human evolution and transformation. A few more footprints to prevent it becoming overgrown entirely.

The regular visits I had to make to Nohona made it impossible for me to maintain my permanent work. Instead, I took on various temporary jobs which, although leaving me short of money, allowed me the time I needed to secure my practice and training.

It is obvious to me that if we are to progress on the path we must at some point begin to spend an equal amount of time on our new practices as we do on our old and habitual ways. It takes many years for their desperate hold on us to loosen; at the same time it being necessary to replace that old and dying consciousness with this clear, bright, unrestricted and true awareness. Without this process of establishment, these experiences and this knowledge would give rise to structures which, although a definite improvement on the old, could only result in the same previous scenario: three bodies that hadn't integrated into one. I had to experience my real self, and then begin to manifest that real self in my physical life, in order for true transformation to take place. This is, in essence, the startling, needle-sharp light emanating from the centre of spiritual truth.

It proved difficult to regularly experience my different bodies with equal intensity; indeed on some days it seemed to me I was simply pretending to experience anything at all. Nohona had warned me that it would take a long time before I could move my consciousness between my bodies. I had also begun to experience, perhaps more consciously than ever before, how quickly this simple teaching could alter forever my relationship to the world at large. Almost immediately I felt I was walking around with a golden treasure, and my only desire was to give some of that treasure away to those I came into contact with. I wanted to share my new knowledge with others. It was self-evident that I was bursting to inform anyone, even remotely interested, of my discoveries. How strange to see the eyes of my listener glaze over, as they drifted off to their magical fairyland and the defence it provided against that which they least wanted to hear. They would walk away and I could see the freely shared treasure falling through the holes in their pockets. They could hear it hit the ground but chose not to pick it up. It took me a few years to realise that most people consider themselves sufficiently rich, in the spiritual aspects of their lives, to be able to throw away any nugget of truth that comes their way. I had never felt rich until now, always I considered myself impoverished and grateful for any wisdom that I was lucky enough to receive.

During this break, before I saw Nohona again, it also became apparent that my formal entry onto this path had affected me deeply. It was the first time that I had, with full consciousness, said yes to a teaching. This in itself sometimes proved, especially in future times, a burden. Although the teaching in itself would not prove in any way restrictive, the truth can both liberate and at the same time restrict. As my growing awareness made itself felt—and at this point it was only to me—I became acutely aware of the true commitment I had made that night at the temple. Who would have guessed that anyone had been listening in that remote place; somehow I imagined that only Nohona and I were present—insignificant in the warm blackness to all that lived—yet I now thought completely differently. My declaration to learn the true nature of man was not only made to humans but also to the earth and the wind and the sea, to those who had trod this path before me and those who came after; and to the gods, of whatever nature. Their eyes now looked down on me compassionately and sometimes oppressively. Not because they oppressed me specifically, but because I felt a sense of duty to keep my word: to follow through and to complete; and perhaps now I realised that it involved far more than I had originally anticipated. It truly was a declaration of intent to the universe. Then again there is a universe within that is equally as demanding.

When I next met Nohona he was in a cordial and friendly mood. I must admit that sometimes he seemed quite cold to me: efficient, comprehensive, informative and well directed. However, I was a person who tended to be friendly and outgoing, inclined to make quips, hardly ever missing a chance if there was laughter lying somewhere nearby to be picked up. It took me a long while to realise that his somewhat clinical manner was in no way an indication of how he felt about anything, let alone me. It was simply his nature and was evidence of how seriously he looked upon his task. His actions were his word. Inside he was a giant. I suspect that I must have seemed so small to him at the time.

He asked me how I was going on, and I answered honestly that I was finding it difficult and sometimes felt as if I wasn't getting it at all.

"What do you expect little one?" he answered. "Just because humans walk upright doesn't mean it's easy to learn to walk. It takes time; you need to go easy on yourself." He looked at me, top to bottom. "You look tired, how do you feel?"

"To be quite honest I am pretty tired. I'm eating OK, but there's this restlessness about me. Don't know really."

"Listen to me," he looked me directly in the eye, "you have begun to directly allow your soul body energy to enter the physical realm, you are now beginning to function almost on a higher vibratory level. It's very difficult to describe what is happening to you because I really couldn't tell you absolutely, but you will find that from now on there will be identifiable phases that seem to happen to all pathwalkers. You may, for instance, find yourself unaccountably pulled to a halt, fed up, depressed even, as though all the light in your life had gone out. In preparation for these times there is, above all, one quality that you must begin to exhibit now and forever: that quality is endurance. It seems to me that it's the main difference between flamekeepers and other people. Endurance is the willingness to go on in spite of the fact that everything in your life is pointing to another course of action; for you to bring a complete halt to proceedings. And yet your heart is still trying to force its light through the clouds of your life. In fact the interesting point is that as you endure through these difficult times, even though you can't feel anything, it strengthens the connection you have to your three bodies. In these times, because previously you have allowed your mental body to shape itself on the pattern of your soul, you can draw on what you have experienced, learned and imprinted on it, and it will not be wrong. I honestly don't know why they happen, these dark times, but it does seem that when the light flares up again it is as if you have made a giant leap in your understanding. It is one of the secret processes that take place."

As if to demonstrate the fact, Nohona took me on a long hike. I am sure he had in some way communicated with the weather, or perhaps the immortals looked down and decided to have a bit of fun. Whatever the reason, the walk was obviously a test of endurance. As we walked over the brow of the temple peak and continued onwards the sun shone down in all its glory; and its heat was terrible. The wind also decided to withdraw; in fact everything stilled to a point where I thought time itself had fallen asleep. The water we took with us was quickly consumed and after visiting a beautiful and isolated bay we began walking back. If it was at all possible, the day became even more still and tiredness gripped my legs, as if they were held by the earth to keep them from moving forward. This quickly became the nearest I had ever come to collapsing; I had to continually put myself into a light trance and believe that the next corner was the end of the trail. At each successive turn the winding path seemed ever longer. Nohona walked behind me for most of the way but towards the end came up to my side. He was also sweating.

"Wow, it's so hot," he said. He looked at me and I feigned a smile. "You do know that you are not going to die on this path: that isn't why you're here. You absolutely know that you are not going to die today, don't you?"

"No, I don't know that. I am at your mercy," I replied as we walked, one foot in front of the other.

"Rubbish; what I mean is look inside. You have more strength than you know. Search internally for the extra reserves of that strength that will easily keep you going beyond the point at which you think you must give up. Further on from tiredness is a whole inner world of reserved vitality. It will not fail you. I want you to know this fact physically and mentally, so look inside and discover that you will simply be tired at the end of the trail. Your heart will still be beating away; all of your marvellous body will function and cope and repair as it has done all of your life. You simply have to endure this unpleasant state of tiredness and let your body support your failing mental resolve."

And, with that ringing in my ears, he walked in front of me at a good speed; much faster than I could keep up with, and he disappeared around the next bend. To be truthful I didn't even want to follow. I was simply feeling sorry for myself. At the time I was, I thought, exhausted. However, since that time, I have occasionally found myself in the same position and with these words I mustered my reserves: "my body can absolutely accomplish this task; it does not need my failing mental resolve to drag it down." I always came through. Pure endurance. Sometimes it is indeed our body that cannot cope. At that point we have to stop and give as much assistance as possible. But there are many times in life when it is the mental body, our ideas about what is possible, that prohibits and inhibits the physical body before it needs or wants to give up. In the space of the chronic or even acute mental difficulties that can face us, does our heart stop beating, do our lungs deflate, our eyes stop seeing, or our sense of touch disappear? No. We can see the difference between our mental and physical bodies so clearly, but often choose to ignore the implications of this difference. What Nohona sought to teach me by such a hike was exactly this difference: I was much stronger than I thought I was; we all are.

At the end of the trail he was waiting for me, on top of the temple peak. He had water to drink and food to eat.

"Here, get your breath and then drink something."

I looked at him in disbelief, my anger arose. "Do you mean that all the time you had water and food?"

He just laughed to himself and carried on eating.

I was absolutely furious. I threw my rucksack down in temper and couldn't look at him.

"Come on, drink."

He offered me a cup. I turned around and hit the cup out of his hand. In response he just made that sound people do when they make fun of someone who is angry. I saw red; I was so angry that I couldn't face him and turned away from his eyes. I didn't want any human to see me like this.

He stood up behind me. I looked out at the sea.

"Let it out," he said, "no one is listening, let it all out."

I was so angry I just started to growl and pant. But then the strangest liberation came upon me. I shouted out. I shouted and shouted.

"That's it, let it all out," he whispered in my ear. "Close your eyes."

I did so as I carried on screaming and then spitting and there was this feeling of power surging upwards and out. I just let out all the pain. All that searching and pain and disappointment. All those broken love affairs and the desperate isolation and loneliness. And then it wasn't just for me but for all the injustice and the hurt and the pain I had witnessed; I had felt it for the others, my fellow humans, in this

91

sometimes utterly cruel and heartless world. And I began to cry. I began to sob jerky gasps as I surfed on those tears to the beach of aloneness and forgetting; the one inhabited only by ourselves and no one else. The one where you shout out and nobody hears. The one where you hit the sand in anger and desperateness and there's only the sounds of life carrying on as if nothing had happened. All you want is for someone or something to say "I acknowledge your pain, I pay respect to it." But nothing does. You have become invisible. There is just your breath and the wind; the emptiness of space, for ever and ever. And only you can swim out into the sea again to find the land you left; and walk on into it with red, tear stung eyes.

In this aloneness, as the waves began to smooth and leave me, I felt Nohona's hand on my back. I turned around and he hugged me, and it felt so human and warm and kind. And even now, at this liberated and tired point, there was still this phrase in my head: 'how long should I hug for, when is the natural point where this hug moves from kindness into desperateness.' Stupid thoughts. Thoughts of one who is still concerned at what he thought of me, how he appraised me.

He released me. "I only asked you if you wanted a drink..." he laughed, and then I smiled and laughed myself.

"But I wanted fizzy pop, not water," I answered.

We laughed again.

We both sat down on that beautiful peak, looking out at the sea as the sun began to sink in the sky. I felt drained but peaceful and realised I had released tears that had built up over such a long time. There had been this reservoir of unspilled tears amassing and waiting; waiting and waiting for a tiny leak to appear in the dam: a heavy insistence. One tiny fissure is all it takes and they race for freedom. Water should flow. That is its way. Everything was cleared away and, for the moment, I felt washed and clean.

Nohona spoke. "That was good, yes?" He looked at me as I nodded, "good, good. It's very important you know. One of the reasons I look much younger than I am is this: we have to live through emotions, be it happiness or sadness, anger or love. It's imperative that we walk bravely through them all. Don't ignore them. As you grow you will learn better ways of dealing with them but it is important that they are acknowledged, their origin sought, and then are liberated. Nothing in nature resists its nature; but we as humans have a choice how to direct and liberate these pent up charges. In anger we can try releasing that energy in various ways: like hitting the bed, running or exercising until we are exhausted; constructively channelling that energy in order to serve and support us and change our lives for the better. Of course you already know it would be wrong to hurt another living being of any kind as a means of liberating this fury; but you must not ignore the fact that it is indeed there. All emotions are like this. Acknowledgement is half the solution. Really, all I can teach you is to be utterly human. All I'm doing is introducing you back to yourself. All that people like me do is this; yet strangely it's a course beset with difficulties and deception. We start out as perfectly human, but somehow are corrupted in what we believe being human is: never do we achieve that elusive humanness. There is this idea that it's to do with impressive grandness, about pomposity or powerful manipulation but that isn't it at all, and the point is that most people secretly know this, they're just afraid to live it, this life of passion, of love and light. To be as human as you can, that's what it's about; to enjoy and revel in the blue sky and the warm rain; the wind, the battering downpour, the icy cold air; the sharp white light of a snowy morning; the silver moon hanging in a winter-star strewn black sky; a thirst quenching drink of cold water; the sweet drifting transience of a perfumed flower; the embrace of a lover; the explosion of a passionate and liberated orgasm; the thrill and anticipation of new love; the fondness and empathy for a life long friend; the unconditional affection of a beloved animal; the glittering and sparkling never ending grandeur of the earth and the heavens; all of it, all of this is absolutely magnificent. It is magical and magnificent and the exhalation of whatever created us and everything else. It is here, now, as are you and I; part of it, in it. Open up to it all, everything, and allow yourself to be..."

His voice trailed off. There were tears running down his cheeks. He was, at that moment, more glowing and loving, more passionate, more human, than anyone I had ever known. I felt it too. He'd vocalised what I'd felt before but not put into words. It was aliveness. Pure livingness.

After a while he turned to me, with his tear stained face and red eyes "There is nothing that can release humans more than the self-realisation that they are human: subject as we all are to the variety of pleasure and pain that makes up a life, be it passionate or dull, long or short. And it is the very fact that they are human which is in itself magnificent. People need to celebrate their humanness, not curse it, not dull it, not whisper it in the middle of the night, but in their every action; in eating it's the bite and taste; in sleeping the rest; in crying the emotion; in loving the dissolving; in seeing the perceiving. Consciously, with our every living breath, we are magnificent creations. As long as we don't let the fact have anything to do with arrogance or manipulating power over the rest of this amazing and frightening world, then it's right and proper that we acknowledge the gift, our luck, with gratitude: thanks, celebration, that we are human."

His speech had been elegant and effective. There were low, dark clouds racing in from the horizon but I was filled with warmth as we walked back to the cabin. My thoughts had expanded beyond thought into a chaotic melange of sparks and lights, just out of reach of my normal perception. Even as I went to sleep I was filled with this very real sense of awe at what it means to be human. Still today at this great age, I have not manifested this sheer breadth and depth to its utmost. It is deeper than the very depths of space.

That night I had a dream. I stood on the edge of a cliff looking out at the rolling sea below me. There was a storm; dark rumbling skies brooded overhead, the wind and the rain lashed against me. I was enthralled: I have always enjoyed the wind; it invigorates me with its powerful invisibleness. I put my arms out to the side as if to fly, and then behind me I heard someone say "go on...jump...you can do it." For some inexplicable reason I walked to the edge. "Just jump." I did so. At first I dropped like a stone. In horror I realised that I was going to die until, suddenly, the thought came in to my head, 'you can do anything here...you are free.' I simply imagined myself flying across the water's surface. It happened. I swooped down in a light curve and then skimmed the water as I sped over the waves. I was flying. The rain and sea spray hit my face. Then I raised my arms and moved higher. I climbed and climbed and now I could curve around and look down upon the cliff. Quickly I spiralled further upwards and then out to sea and into the clouds. There was this mist-water in front of my eyes. I couldn't see anything. Then, just as suddenly, I was above the clouds. Here there was sunlight. The peaks of the clouds drifted below me on all sides, and above there were only hues of blue with the sun low in the sky. Its rays silvered the edges of the clouds and warmed my body. Above me there were unknown currents travelling around the earth. In the distance were banks of clouds that looked like floating cities, with spires and towers and buildings resting on other skylands: unknown below, they were of this world, not ours. I dipped through the clouds and came once again upon the raging storm, then again up and down; a heady flux of air, water and fire mixed and melded into my experience as I curved and spiralled between those different domains. Then the experience became strangely homogeneous and I gradually surfaced from that place into the dark cabin and my warm bed. The wind and rain were raging against the roof and walls. Inside I cuddled under the sheets, cradled by the warmth, and sank back into sleep.

When I awoke, the rain still lashed against the cabin. It was the first bad weather I had experienced on my visits, and it certainly took the impetus away from proceedings. I felt lethargic and tired and sat eating my breakfast in a half sleep.

"Any questions about yesterday?" Nohona asked as he stroked Chai, who was purring away on his lap.

Many questions had crossed my mind the night before, but I didn't feel like talking just now.

"Come on, snap out of it. I know you're tired but we have a whole day ahead of us for lots of lovely discussion," he rubbed his hands in mock fun, "and I know how much you're going to enjoy that." He laughed.

"Very funny," I answered and kept on eating.

Then it came to me. "Actually there is one question."

"Ah, ha! Just one?"

"You know all you said yesterday about being human and the like, well I really understood it all, I kind of felt everything; but today I feel really low and fed up. That feeling of magnificence is absolutely and utterly gone." I continued with my breakfast.

"The fact is," he answered, "it's pretty well impossible to maintain that intensity all of the time. You just couldn't do it. Unfortunately we do have to walk across the road occasionally, to eat, to work—you know, all that living in the everyday stuff. No matter how great your spiritual development is, it won't necessarily pay the bills or put food in your mouth. So you see, what we did yesterday was special because it always should be special, not ordinary. When you experience such an appreciation of life it should be as a sublime refreshment to the everyday. That way the spirit is polished. Such a breath of spring air blows away any dust that's settled on the mirror of your being: its intense effulgence guarantees this. It's good to move into all these states of awareness freely and easily. Often people have the impression that they should constantly live in this sparkling light, but the trouble is that it's practically impossible to live our everyday, normal and sometimes very rewarding lives maintaining such a consciousness. Sometimes the very brilliance of that light blinds us to some very obvious and important pitfalls. How many supposed gurus and teachers have been found fundamentally flawed in recent and not so recent times? It's because they didn't understand the absolutely vital practice of bringing that consciousness back down to earth, to take part in the everyday. It's a difficult idea to understand but it's rather like letting the glorious and delicate feeling of a new love affair infuse your every action."

Involuntarily I laughed.

He looked at me sternly. "No, I don't mean in that sickly sweet way—even if it is enjoyable—I mean that its significance must be as real to you as the everyday. You see, what people always do is give all credibility over to the everyday, but assume that any of these exalted moments are mere delusion; joyful stardust in the desert sky of our lives. That is not the case; they are just as legitimate and just as essential and should colour the canvas of what you might call your ordinary life. It is by bringing back to the everyday the absolute certainty—not of the vision, but of the feeling—of what you've experienced, that the transformation of your being takes place. Bring it into the physical, just like you experienced back at the clearing, and then your body will know. That way it becomes easier to access when you again allow yourself to experience that divine refreshment. Gradually, over time, there'll be a permanent channel between—and confirming—the essential self of your true nature. So you see, it's OK to feel as you do now, in fact it often happens, so don't beat yourself up, miserable features."

He pushed me on the shoulders in a friendly way. I forced out a smile. Having an explanation was good but still I didn't feel any better, however it did encourage me to stop wallowing in my self pity.

"So how do I do to get out of this mood?" I asked.

"Well, you can start by washing up."

I just couldn't be bothered to argue with him. Then, after I'd washed the dishes, he joined me in moving the furniture as I brushed and scrubbed the floor, made the beds and prepared the food for lunch. Chai just sat there cleaning himself and occasionally watching us. He knew this already.

"Let's go for a walk," Nohona said. "We'll eat lunch when we come back."

The weather had cleared up and everywhere was fresh and cool. Sparkles of rain dropped from the leaves of the forest trees; tinkling glass star-diamonds flashing the inflorescence of the sun.

As we walked through the forest, on a seemingly random path, he would occasionally stop and point out a particular insect; talk about its life in minute detail, in a way that drew me into its mysterious and unknown lifecycle. Perhaps it was the bark of a tree used for medicine, or a plant which had a peculiarity all of its own. Once or twice he picked up a rock from the ground and could give me the history of how it was formed. Not only was I surprised at his depth of knowledge but also, again, he had entranced me with the complex diversity of life. However, this time it was not an explosion, but rather a steady fire simmering the water of my being. On returning to the cabin later in the day I had almost forgotten about my lunch and certainly my mood was utterly changed.

As we ate together he asked me "Do you get it?"

"Yes," I smiled as if in reflection to myself, "I'll give you that one."

We ate without another word.

I stayed for two more days although Nohona left the following day. He suggested I relax and let the atmosphere of the place invade me. On these short visits it took me a few days to wind down from my everyday life. Mentally it didn't prove too much of a problem, but physically I hadn't yet experienced the total forgetting that's possible in such a place. Over the next couple of days I found little to do other than walk and relax. During the second day I found myself sitting on the beach, with the breeze blowing gently off the sea and the water itself glittering and sparkling with deep blue shades of colour. My sight drifted off to the far horizon. I don't know how long

I sat there: time itself seemed to disappear. I swam out into space and floated away, looking up at the sky. How do I describe this state? It is something which creeps up on you as your attention dissolves and disappears—flying off to a rarely visited space. In retrospect it is absolutely inevitable in a place like this: no one can resist the pull of this intense longing. It is a better state; inherently available to us all. Only circumstances can break the shell within which it is protected from the onslaught of our everyday life; and its birth into light can only be as the seed's is: a willingness from within greeting the encouragement from without. It is, of course, love.

During the next few weeks I noticed that a change had taken place. It echoed many changes that were to take place during my life, in that they all had one fact in common: I didn't notice the transformation at the time it took place—only its effect. It was as if, unknown to me, secret burrowings and excavations were taking place. Only when the whole was finished was I allowed into the new construction. In this particular instance I noticed that some of my favourite music, some of my favourite films and television programmes, no longer interested me. Most of them had been favourites for many, many years; they were often old films and music which allowed me to access certain emotional states easily; however, the magic formulae they possessed no longer worked on me. I learned something else as a direct result of these specific changes: that often I had chosen, in a very subtle and practically subconscious way, to revel in these states somewhat indulgently. I decided that I had spent long enough wallowing in heart opening emotion; wishing for a better world to live in because I hadn't been made for this one. Just as I now looked upon my distant visit to that other place as a beautiful but long gone experience, I felt that my present state was echoing that same sense of goodbye. There arises a point in your development beyond which you have a conscious choice whether to take this or that action. When you travel a well trod path, the end result is already known and the same destination appears—all is well in the same old world. However, I was now experiencing exactly the same input but perceiving it at a different level; and, at this level, what had previously been fertile soil was now seen to be no more than arid desert. I suppose I was looking for true artistry: that which appeals to a number of levels of consciousness. It is rare. There is very little that feeds all aspects of us at the same time. Hence the cry of the true artist "how do I represent complete aliveness?"

A similar change took place concerning the relationships between myself and some of the people I knew. At first it was a surprise that such and such a person somehow moved out of my field of existence and activity; however it became more and more common.

I'd always had many acquaintances, but very few real friends; now I had fewer of both. It became apparent to me that there was a very obvious line between the two. Again and again and again I wished for a companion or lover to make this journey with, but it wasn't to happen for many years. As Nohona had warned me beforehand, I would 'feel alone; more alone than I had ever felt.' Sometimes it was so exquisitely painful that it was as if there were a sliver of cut glass embedded in my chest: to breathe was to become constantly aware of its cutting painfulness. All I could do was sit with it; be at one with it. I think it is the most painful feeling to have to endure. It didn't reach its peak until later in my life, but I was already climbing the steep approach. Try as I might, there was always a gulf between me and those I met: in the fact that my words meant what I felt and the sometimes carefree, even sloppy, way in which others often used them. Occasionally there was someone who walked a similar path to me and the connection and companionship was valuable; but their own search took up all their time and I had to respect that. Again, what Nohona had said rang out like a clearly struck bell: we had to practice and physically embody the truth that we discovered in and during our life. It was no use living in the clouds, for the fall to earth could be dangerous and oh so very disappointing. I wanted to manifest such a relationship based on what I had found to be true; but it was nothing complicated or mystical—it was simple: living love. However, finding another who sought to manifest such a hard won, challenging, real and evolving relationship was incredibly difficult; but perhaps this says more about others than myself.

On my next visit to the cabin it was as if I had returned to what I can only refer to as a sense of aliveness. Being here was becoming more and more real to me, and my everyday life, work and shopping, sleeping and eating, somehow felt like actions in a play.

"You must guard against this," Nohona told me. "It's important that you bring your newly birthing consciousness into these everyday activities. It is indeed true that often they seem of little consequence and are insignificant to the great turning of the universe, but still you have to acknowledge the fact that they do comprise a huge part of our lives. Try your best to keep the gateways to your other bodies open and clear; but the real fact that should underpin your practice is that at any moment—absent-mindedly crossing the road, eating badly prepared food, walking home late at night—your life could be in jeopardy. Your awareness is the armour that can defeat these insistent enemies. Only allow your consciousness to float into fantasy and imagination when it's safe to do so. Always come back to earth."

He was obviously serious about the point.

"Aren't you being a little bit dramatic," I commented.

He sighed "Come with me," he said.

We walked down to the sea and along to the base of the cliffs on the right, at the end of the bay below the temple peak.

"Climb up there for me," he said, pointing to the sheer cliff face. "Go on."

I looked at him aghast. I certainly wasn't an incredibly physical man and hadn't anywhere near sufficient skills to climb the rock.

"You know I haven't the skill to do that," I said.

"So you're saying that it's only a lack of skill that stops you from doing so?"

"Well...yes. I suppose it is."

"No it isn't," he responded sharply.

I was nonplussed.

"Suppose you had the skills, would you do it then?"

I thought about it: would I?

"Well, I'm not sure why I'd want to; and I wouldn't do it just because you told me to."

"Getting brave now are we?"

"Hey, you can't force me to do anything I don't want to do," I said.

"Did I ever say you had to? You've gone on the defensive for a very good reason but you haven't seen it yet. Just get on the bottom of the rocks and climb, say six feet up."

I walked to the bottom and made a pathetic attempt to hold onto the rock and pull myself upwards, but I really didn't want to.

"Come on," he said, "what's the real reason?"

I was scared, I had to admit it "I'm scared I suppose."

"Hallelujah!" he shouted in a sarcastic tone. "Oh, get down from there."

I was chastened and felt foolish as I jumped back onto the sand.

"Sit down," he ordered. We both sat down on the sand, but this time he sat directly in front of me, not to the side. He looked at me. "What was the fear," he asked.

"Well I suppose it was about injuring myself; hurting my skin; things like that."

"That's the surface; what's underneath?"

I searched. "Dying," I whispered.

"What? He asked.

"I said dying. I'm scared of dying as a result of doing something stupid like that." I sounded so melodramatic, even to myself.

"Ah ha!" he said. "At last. Now that wasn't too hard was it?"

I hung my head, almost in shame. Such a little task and I'd been scared to the point of being paralysed with fear.

"I'm sorry; I'll have another go in a minute, when I've got my courage up."

"What...No...It was an illustration not a task." Almost to himself he muttered, "I must be such a bad teacher."

"It's not you it's me," I said, "I'm not a very good student."

"Oh shut up," he said, "stop feeling sorry for yourself."

His comment only put me into a worse mood.

"Right," he started, "now a few minutes ago I was trying to point out to you—obviously very badly—that your life is balanced on a knife edge; all of your life, every minute of every day. It's something that everyone seems to know but very few pay real attention to. For practically all of us the most frightening thing that we can be told is that we are going to die: not at some distant and invisible time but at a specific and near date. However, for a pathwalker, what is needed is that you are generally conscious of the fact that your physical life is limited and finite, and specifically aware that there is only so much time left for you to do, achieve, be; to manifest the things that you want to. You see death is your great advisor. Now the truth about climbing that rock is that it isn't sufficiently important for you to lose your life over; and I agree with you, it isn't. So what is? Is there anything? What is really important to you?"

What a question to have to answer.

"Do I have to pull a knife out to scare you enough?" he said, rather menacingly.

"I think it's this actually: I want to find the truth before I die".

"Good. What else?"

"A love relationship worth its salt, but that's up to more than just me." I thought for a minute, "Oh yes...and I'd like to put my soul into my music."

"Good, I like those. So now you've sorted them out you have to direct your life generally in their direction. As long as the journey is rounded you've nothing to worry about. For those who are very specific about their goal and their journey there are two pitfalls. Firstly, there tends to be a lack of roundedness to their personality: obviously if you've spent all your time directed towards one specific destination there's little chance to take in the scenery. Secondly, and perhaps more importantly, there may well be paths and turnings along the way which prove very fruitful and actually augment the roundedness of them as individuals. This is all to the good. Besides the important achievements that your fulfilled life may manifest are other facets which will complete the cut of the jewel at the centre of your being." He stopped for a minute, as if to let his words sink in.

"You must remember one more very important thing: have some fun along the way. Ultimately there must be periods of joy and laughter. Pure pleasure is medicine to your body and your soul. Joy lets the soul flow easily into your physical body, and of course out into the world. Laughter is mysterious and intensely human; it is a great gift, enjoy it. Your body wasn't only made for toil, but also for pleasure and enjoyment. Consider your amazing senses, all of which can be utilised to the utmost to enjoy this physical life. Sometimes we can take ourselves and our ambitions far too seriously. Life should be full of enjoyment and fun. They are the stars in the night sky; the kisses of a lover; the chocolate chip cookies of life." He laughed out loud.

Then he became serious again.

"Follow me," he said.

He stood up and began to walk up to the peak. I followed.

We then trailed to the temple complex, skirted it, and came upon another clearing; probably only five hundred yards away, but not at all visible from the temples.

It was a graveyard. Just as if we had stumbled accidentally into a silent place, a sleeping place: even our breathing seemed too loud. Everything was quiet. But this quiet wasn't the mere absence of noise: it was the soundless space in the middle of the night as we slumber, dead to the world.

We separated and walked around, looking at the inscriptions on the stones, at least those we could read. Others were striking for their shape and appearance: moss and lichen had grown with their ageing and become one with the stone. They were very old. I was suddenly overcome by respect for these people and spontaneously began to tidy up each grave, removing twigs and leaves and placing a stone as I visited each one: just a sign that they were not forgotten. The old and the diseased; the broken and disheartened; the joyous children cut down before their time; the separated lovers; all of them lay here silent and, for the moment, remembered. I wondered what countless tales they had died with: secrets never shared with another human being; secret fears and loves; all the unfulfilled ambitions and the disillusionment of dashed hopes and wishes. The air was filled with words: unspoken words; sentiments that would never be expressed and never be heard by those they were intended for. How long ago they had lived; yet, in the life of this planet, it was but the blinking of an eye.

I felt as if we were watched. But they were silent eyes. They didn't say anything; I just felt their eyes. The eyes of those who wish to say so much but can only look: struck dumb by the distance; the time; by their death. I was deeply moved by this place and by those people. I wondered where I would be buried, or my ashes scattered. How long would it be before no human being remembered me or my life; when my body, my soul, my friends and lovers, my very bones, became food for the creatures of the earth. At once I was struck by a deep delicateness; a sensitiveness and vulnerability. Somehow, in that graveyard, I mourned us all, every one of us humans; brave or cowardly, truthful or deceitful, loved or hated; all of us were born from one source and in death our bones would be united as they mingled into the earth. Yet, at the same time, everyone of us; every creature and living thing; every rock and mountain top; every particle in the air and every piece of litter; every musical instrument and dab of paint; all of us are truly, absolutely made of stardust. Our physical bodies were made from the life and death of stars; the cosmic and the mundane is what binds us all together. In this, as in so many ways, we are all different facets of the single magnificent jewel that is creation.

We finished our visit and said a prayer of acknowledgment.

Nohona looked at me and, with his expression, asked me if I had finished.

We walked back to the cabin in silence.

As we drank our tea Nohona spoke:

"Let's take the idea of death one step further. Can you think of anything more you need to do before you leave this body?"

I thought for a few minutes. "Well, apart from what I've already said, I suppose, since the spirit body can live on after physical death, there isn't a huge amount that does need to be done. I mean the fact is that unless it's physical there's nothing that can't be achieved after this life. I think."

"Remember," Nohona said, "we're not just talking about achieving goals, it's about more than that. Perhaps that's the direction we need to walk in now. When you originally came to me, you asked 'how am I to live?' Now, I've told you about our basic anatomy and it's time to start to live your life according to it. In some ways you are definitely doing this or else you wouldn't be here. But there's a whole new world of action that you now need to manifest. It's a lifelong task to translate and integrate your true self into your physical life and, as we've discussed already, the prioritising of your life is now equally important. However, the true magic of this truth is the personal transformation that will take place as long as you stick to it. With the light of your soul radiating into your other bodies, that powerful love begins its innate capacity to dissolve and disintegrate all that's not your true nature. As I'm sure you already realise, when you leave this physical body you'll want your spirit to be a pure reflection of your true self and, of course, for it to have a nature which you would be proud to display to anyone that has eyes to see. Imagine your self scrutinised at this very moment by others who do not judge you, but who can see everything that you are; all those petty thoughts and judgements. What would you least like them to see in you? What would you be ashamed of?"

I listened to him and thought to myself 'there are definite things I wouldn't want others to see.' Perhaps my lack of courage; my fears; the times I'd been petty with others; judgements and opinions that would shame anyone should they be made known; but in that I was no different from most other humans. Then again, that was no defence.

"So you see, once you understand your anatomy, the rest of your maturing is about polishing your spirit: shining it to reflect your Creator given identity. Most of this is a gradual process. Sometimes there are life crises that precipitate a radical shift or affirm what you are not prepared to give up; rather like a testing or a refining. And there are yet other changes that we can facilitate ourselves. Some of these are very old and simple techniques that can radically cleanse the bodies of bound up waste and dross from our life. We all have this rubbish lying around. Only we can open the doors to these locked and dark rooms; only we can expose them to the light, and only we can constantly clean and refresh the places which have a propensity to collect the dust of our thoughts. You can, of course, enlist help; but there must, yet again, be a willingness within to greet and welcome this help. The doors can only be opened by our own hands."

With these words Nohona rose and walked out of the cabin. It was late afternoon. I looked through the window at the world outside. The sea exhibited its usual seaness, the sand its sandness. Was I being my humanness? Nohona's talk had definitely caught me unawares. Until this point I'd been directing my attention to the acquiring of pieces of knowledge. As it turned out this was much the easiest of the tasks. More difficult—the real difference between pathwalkers and others who simply wish to know about, but not become, flamekeepers—was the polishing of oneself. This was not dependent on knowledge—so many humans had made that very mistake—but on the personal maturing of our self-nature. It is a very private and personal affair. The truth is that it's a journey made alone because it is an inner quest; the search inside—where real secrets lie—for that which we really are. Then, as you touch that place, you also touch the true nature of everything. If you let this process continue, by providing it with the necessary conditions, your way of being in and with the world must also change. Externally, all that anyone can do to facilitate this process is to urge you onward into the dark cave that is your internal nature, and then to greet and encourage your new consciousness as it reappears in the outer world. They are rare beings, these enablers; those who, having been through this process themselves, radiate their self-realised nature, and can cause a similar resonance in another who has walked to the centre of their being and is now returning back again. Nohona created this effect within me; in retrospect I understand this as a major role of such a person in one's life. By their constant presence, input and vibration, their sole aim is to bring the seeker into harmony with themselves; and since all souls are in harmony, and the soul nature now shines throughout one's being, then we come into a natural progressing harmony with life. This is also why such people encounter animosity from others and usually prefer their own company: their very beingness radiates from the true centre, and not the illusorily created mental body. It's as if their light is fuelled by a different source of power. Behind their words and actions is more than the obvious: always, somewhere, there is a consciousness of the wider world; indeed not only the wider world of oneself, but the infinite variety of consciousness in the never ending space of our experience. The sun, the moon, the earth; the cat and dog and bird; the swaying tree; the silver sliver of lightning shot, from the sky above; awareness of their existence infuses the consciousness of oneself with its collectiveness. As I sat in that cabin I realised I was about to begin the real work of inner transformation: journeying to ignite the everlasting effulgent light of the flamekeeper with my very own consciousness. It is no less daunting or perpetual than melting snow water from the mountains weaving and descending to the shining sea. It is no less huge. No less natural.

Nohona returned to the cabin door "Tomorrow we'll visit the temples. I want you to think about forgiveness between now and then." That was all he said as he pottered around the rooms cleaning up, then he went outside with wood to light a fire. Chai watched silently from the cabin door as he walked to and fro, looking at both of us with eyes that were fuelled by the natural, marvellous and absolutely innate clarity and weight of consciousness that was his birth gift; honest and immense. It wasn't long before the wood crackled with fire. All conversation seemed to have come to a natural halt as the night quickly descended. It was a special pleasure to eat this fired food beneath the ever extending black sky: there was the moon glinting on the water, a gentle refreshing breeze, the rustle of leaves in the forest and the perpetual rhythm of the sea lapping on the beach. A perfect end to an important day.

The next morning the weather was clear and bright. We walked up to the temples via the cliff path. At the peak of the cliff Nohona stopped.

"Turn around and look down onto the temples. Imagine you're a god looking from above at someone standing in one of them. What would you see? What would you understand of their acts and words? How would you feel about them? Think about it as we walk down there."

We descended. His question affected me strangely. I split my consciousness between the part of me that would be humbling myself, and the part of me watching the whole process from above. How difficult it is to be totally involved and not split into observer and observed. Only years later would I be able to simply 'be awareness.' For the moment I was caught up in how I would appear. However, as we approached the temple complex, I began to fall into an unusual state of consciousness: not only had I become calmly centred on the task in hand, but also aware that there was a consciousness out there that I hadn't fully acknowledged before. I was being watched. I thought about what Nohona had said and it suddenly struck me that if I'd been watching another entering this arena, I would feel nothing other than love and compassion for their endeavour. How could I feel anything else: it was one of the most sacred acts a human being could perform.

After Nohona introduced us to the area we approached a small circle of stones, perhaps twenty feet in diameter and waist high.

"I'll leave you here," he said. "When you've finished I'll be sitting on the peak." He pushed something into my hand before he left me alone. It was a clear quartz crystal. I held it up to the sky. There were clouds inside its beautiful light; somehow they accentuated the clarity of its pure and clear invisibleness. I held it in my hand as I entered that sacred space.

Immediately I felt a shift: as if I'd walked through an invisible screen. Inside here there was a definite difference: not only in the atmosphere around me, but also in my body. I walked towards the large perpendicular stone at the opposite edge of the circle. It was positioned there for groundedness. As I approached I bowed my head and knelt on the floor.

I was overtaken by humbleness and reverence. How many serious-sincere-human-humans had knelt in exactly this same way? As I became just one of many in the long line weaving its way through human existence, I felt the weight of their genuineness and was instantly cleared of anything false—the door to my naked self was open and my infinite vulnerability exposed. I felt clear and still; no fear of inspection or imperfection because I realised my desire was genuine.

I asked to be forgiven for anything negative that I had done deliberately or unintentionally against others. I forgave anyone who had done anything against me. However, as I said this aloud, I realised that I had to mean all of it, or not say it at all. Fingers from my small self grasped and clung onto the petty pleasure I derived from holding to some past hurt or jealousy; that peculiar desire, common to most humans, for retribution or a wish for a person to suffer a similar pain as I myself had suffered. Believe it or not it hurt me to let them go; it actually proved much easier to ask forgiveness for my own errors rather than for me to forgive others. This letting go was hard: it left me in a strange no man's land where I came directly into the present moment. How easy we find it to define ourselves by the results of what has been done to us rather than what we actually are. By some mysterious means, when we remove our victimisation, there's this disconcerting—though temporary—void which, because of the vacuum it creates, ultimately fills with the present moment.

I left the crystal in that place, buried amongst the small pile of offerings at the base of the altarstone. I bowed my head in gratitude that I'd been granted this opportunity to make amends; to complete the circles of consciousness that should have been completed a long time ago. Also, I somehow understood my position: with my head bowed it meant to me that I acknowledged the superior knowledge of others; that I'd now begun the second and most difficult stage of human development—I had to put the teachings into practice.

I left the temple. In the future my offering always reminded me of my commitment to endeavour to forgive and be forgiven. Nohona later told me of a traditional belief implying that it was an offence not to forgive those who genuinely and absolutely asked for forgiveness. Who were we to say no: higher forces than ourselves were party to that decision.

Of course there were times in my life when that commitment was sorely tested. For certain periods I did not forgive: I just couldn't. I had to recognise that I was embroiled and entangled as soon as this became apparent to me. To forgive is to be free. However, this is easier said than done, and during my life there have occasionally been times when I found true forgiveness a difficult concept to manifest. I now believe that the most relevant aspect of this teaching for pathwalkers is that we should never hold on to a wrong after we have no use for it. If we choose not to forgive—and it is a choice—it serves us in some way or other, and that's the place we should attend to. What are we getting out of it? In fact, not forgiving only serves to obscure the clarity of our true nature; as a cloud passes in front of the sun.

I walked back to Nohona. "All done?" he asked.

"I think so," I answered.

"Yes, that's how it should be," he answered. "Now, let's go for a swim."

I followed him down the trail and onto the beach. We took our clothes off. As he was about to enter the water I said:

"I thought you said it was too dangerous to swim here?"

"It is," he said laughing, and then ran into the water. "Follow me, you'll be fine."

I entered very tentatively. The water was warm and pleasant. I needed to submerge completely. It was like some kind of rite: the cleansing after the ritual. Being in seawater wasn't my favourite sensation after all the trouble I'd had with my skin: seawater stung and hurt. However the urge was greater than the pain I'd feel, so I went ahead and it wasn't too bad. I swam around in the natural protection the curving rocks provided. It felt lovely to cleanse myself after the ritual. Pure recreation. Being totally naked, the water touched every part of my body and encouraged a whole body awareness that we only occasionally experience. Nohona seemed happy and relaxed. It was as if he felt more and more released as we progressed through various stages of the teaching. Perhaps it was the release of the obligation he felt to pass on his hard won knowledge. I know his life was not easy.

That night I slept soundly. The bed was warm and my body relaxed. My mind was peaceful. I wondered how many other rituals of a similar nature there could be which released and pacified our complicated and confused mind: for, after such a ritual, the chaos simply dissolves and all that's left is this peaceful contentment. What's done is done. The immediate result of this particular ritual was that consciousness from my soul flooded into my physical body and, because my mind was stilled, I felt love and warmth and contentment. Peace.

The next morning I awoke refreshed. As usual, Nohona was up before me preparing breakfast and Chai was sitting on a chair, taking in the sun.

"Sleep well?" Nohona asked.

"Yes, lovely," I answered.

Over breakfast he continued "Rituals can be very important. They don't have to be done in such a place, anywhere you've created or put aside is fine. It's the sincerity and integrity you bring to such a ritual that decides its power. Always perform rituals with sincerity and integrity. That's where their power is. Then at least you know they were heard. You see, the voice of one who has the whole weight of all his bodies behind him speaks with such penetration and clarity that it can't fail to be heard. Rather as if an opera singer began to sing a beautiful aria in a busy shopping centre. Gradually everything would become stilled. Everybody would listen. People would feel embarrassed to interrupt with their own concerns. That's how you can get your voice heard; and that's why true ritual is used only with issues that are hugely important to you: only the truly important can concern all of your bodies at the same time.

"Integrity is all in this teaching. To align yourself with your hard won, newly birthing, true nature is of the utmost importance. Then you need to try your best never to betray or deny what you are feeling as a result. You will of course: that's inevitable. But if you begin to practice assiduously then you'll notice very quickly when you're going against your true nature. This jarring is very obvious. It surfaces even if we don't want it to. That is why many flamekeepers are reluctant to interfere with the course of events using ritual. It isn't really so. They recognise that there's so much that it's possible to interfere in—that there are so many ways that a simple misunderstanding or manipulation to the flow of life can result in dramatic and absolutely unintentional effects—that they reserve their powerful interventions for very specific occasions. Or else such conscious acts are subtle and gentle; keeping watch on the effects of their actions, just as a chef would use herbs or spices carefully and subtly for a very specific purpose. In this instance, as in many others, the unification of your being is essential: you must stand on a firm foundation in order to make this kind of judgement. Try to extricate yourself from anything that offends or compromises that unity: work, relationships, religion, politics. If you have to compromise too much, the end results cannot possibly be worth it. Remember that many of the structures with which you are trying to compromise are very impermanent and over time will change radically from their original seed. Why then should you bear allegiance to something that is transient and whose ultimate purpose is in no way defined or definite? Much better to learn to differentiate between your mental world and its machinations and the lodestar of your soul; between the emotional and the feeling; between what is confused and what is certain. All of your life you'll be learning to do this more accurately, and you can be sure that there will be times when you get it wrong. Sometimes it's not in any way harmful and may lead you to a better understanding; other times you may pay dearly for your mistake. However, generally, your soul will try its best to support you on the path back to itself; to work in harmony with it; to radiate and facilitate its nature which, after all, is your true identity. Integrity is all."

I thought for a few minutes. Then I asked:

"So if you've done a ritual and you were integrated and sincere, does it assure you of a positive result, or is that a stupid question?"

He laughed.

"Well, that's the big one, isn't it. After all, that's the whole point of doing it in the first place. You've done everything you should have; assessed the consequences, the implications, and you even feel that it was heard. Then you wait; you wait and wait. Nothing happens. It's as if everyone suddenly left the universe and you've been talking to yourself. The sky is empty, the air is just air and the earth is nothing but brown and cold. What was the point?" He stopped and looked at me as if he expected an answer.

"I don't know. Perhaps just to assert your desires, to let them know you're here. Perhaps to set you free to pursue something else more productive. I don't know really."

"The only thing I can assume, because I don't really know either, is that at this moment in time it is not to be, or isn't possible. And the hardest thing to accept is that someone has your best interests at heart. Now, its up to you who you've addressed that ritual to; but even if you haven't anyone particular in mind you can be very sure that your soul has paid complete attention to what you've asked for. Your soul, as I've already said, is out of time: it can arrange things that you haven't the faintest idea about, and it only wishes to lead you to a more joyful, adventurous and fulfilled life. Don't forget that it's in touch with other souls out there as well; it's quite possible that it could take some time to arrange events in the physical world so that your request can manifest. But it must be said that if your ritual is not answered with the response you wanted, then you can only assume, even at this level, that it wasn't for you; perhaps at another time it may be.

"You see, what's relevant is that you do it in the first place. Rituals are performed and then finished and what will be will be. Do you see this? It's an important point. If you feel so very strongly about something then a ritual should be performed. The ritual has a beginning, a middle and an end. When it's finished, it's over. What happens, happens. That's all there is to it. The consequences may be lifelong but the ritual ends and you accept its effects as inevitable. And don't worry about what will manifest: in itself nothing can come about that is harmful to others or the world from your activities. If your motives were pure in the first place, and the seed sprouts, it can only produce something that is positive and evolving. As an integrated human you wouldn't dream of unleashing anything to harm others, because ultimately your true nature is about light and love. That has to be the beginning, always. It's funny, but as you grow you'll perform very few rituals, and even then they'll tend to be very private and personal affairs, so don't get embroiled or obsessed by them. What you did yesterday is a basic rite; there are a few of these, some of which you have already done, and a few you'll perform in the future at the right time for you."

He sipped his tea, waiting for my question.

"What are they? I asked.

He just laughed and tapped his nose. I took it that this particular conversation was over.

Mid-morning he asked me to accompany him to the nearest town. I hadn't visited it before so it was a good opportunity to see the local people.

We approached, out of the forest, down a bank of grass into a park. This led to a high street of shops and market stalls. Nohona obviously knew a lot of people. Everywhere people said hello and talked of this and that. He only introduced me to those who asked about me.

After buying some food we wandered over to a cafe. The sun shone through a clear sky; it was hot. We took refuge under the canopy of the nearest table. Nohona ordered some food and drinks.

I wasn't surprised to see him drinking beer: nothing much really surprised me anymore about Nohona. In fact it was generally only the thoughtless and selfish behaviour of others that constantly surprised me. It still does.

We ate a very pleasant meal under the shade, watching the world go by.

"Do you have any rules about what to eat and drink?" I asked.

"No, none at all. Obviously I prefer to eat food that's as natural and cruelty free as possible. Try to give thanks when you eat. After all it's true what they say: one day our own body will be food for the worms." He said this as he tucked into a large slice of chocolate cake. I burst out laughing, and this caught him off-guard. He sprayed cake out of his mouth. This reduced us both to one of those far too infrequent laughing fits. We laughed until our bodies ached. The waves of its pleasure washed over us at irregular intervals.

A lady walked up to the table. Nohona welcomed her:

"Ah, hello. Come, sit down. Join us." She smiled. They obviously knew each other well. "This is David...the student I've chatted to you about."

I said, "Hi..."

She looked upwards; I assumed she was thinking about my name. A minute later she said:

"Ah...right."

They talked about this and that. All the time I was wondering what the friendship or relationship was based around. How well did they know each other? Had he taught her? She was older than me. I felt a little like you do when your parents talk to their peers: eager to partake in the conversation but realising that I wasn't needed here. I stood up:

"I'm just going for a walk. It's nice to meet you. I'll be back in about half an hour."

They carried on talking as I walked away.

It suddenly dawned on me that Nohona knew many people that I hadn't any idea about. Only rarely did he talk about his life. He kept his private life private. Somehow I hadn't expected that: I expected complete sharing. After all, I told him about my life. Was that a mistake? I felt that this mutual sharing was important to secure trust between us. Later on I realised that he still had to be aware of appearing all too human to me, because I might mistake his humanness for a lack of skill or knowledge about how to run a perfect life. A shame to have to act like this, but I can see its worth. A teacher must give the impression of a slight aloofness until you, by your application and diligence, have warranted his or her confidence. It is and always will be true that the shallow and malevolent can often appear, on first inspection, to be worthy and good. Only later does that illusory shell break and the real person walk forth; with that first crack of the shell all hopes of a worthy and great human—which intrinsically all of us could be—fall away. Disappointment once again fuels the inevitable and erroneous feeling that we are always to be let down. I am not talking of human foibles and mistakes, but the sure knowledge, when another crosses us, that they work from a centre so small and petty that, should we choose to, they can only entangle us during our never ending struggle to lead them towards a better centre: that of light and love.

I returned back to the cafe. Nohona was sitting alone.

"Ah...welcome back."

I sat down.

"Has your friend gone?" I asked.

"Yes she has. Listen, you didn't have to leave you know."

"I just felt like I was intruding. Who was she?"

"She's a lady I treat every so often."

This came as a bit of a surprise. I never really thought of him treating people.

"So do you treat many people?" I asked.

"Oh...a few, every now and then. They ask me. I learned a long time ago that only when people really want you to help them help themselves is there any point in helping them."

"So is it based on what you've taught me, you know, about the three bodies?"

"Yes, not far off. Then there's trying to get them to move their centre back to where it should be. A lot of it is slow and hard work; you don't change people's attitudes overnight: their environment, people, lovers, friends, they all hold them back."

"Is she getting better?"

"Oh yes, much better."

It would be much later when Nohona taught me about healing. I was still too wounded to help others in the true way: re-lighting the flame that had been blown out by the hurricanes of life. Before I could embark on healing others my own flame needed to establish itself and be strengthened so that it would always shine, even in the strongest hurricane.

Nohona and I had been invited to a celebration that evening by the woman I'd met earlier. It was very light-hearted. Everyone seemed friendly and easygoing as we ate and drank. It was such a relief from the intensity of the teaching to simply enjoy Nohona's company as he relaxed and became a little drunk. Indeed everyone, including myself, was drinking. And we all seemed able to judge that fine line between levity and intoxication.

Nohona began dancing to the music. It was modern and I was surprised at his ability to move smoothly and rhythmically to it. He seemed to dance for ages. Often, as I watched him, he'd close his eyes as he moved his body.

He came over to me as everyone else carried on dancing.

"Don't just sit here, join in. Come on."

"Oh, I'm just watching you all. Taking it in."

"Nonsense. Come on. Movement, dancing, is one of the keys to the secrets. Give yourself up to it. Tonight there's good company, warmth, food and music. What more could any human want? Revel in it, it's one of the joys of living; it's the dance of life. Come on, dance yourself."

Since that glorious night I have never missed an opportunity to dance. Almost always the same exalted state of consciousness follows. Moving my body freely and expressively can do nothing but benefit me; not only the physical tissues of my body, but also the integrity of me as a human being. It is one of the great loves of my life. One of the joys of having a body.

I spent the following week at the beach and then made my way back home.

It was a strange return. Outwardly, there was little change; inwardly there was a profound shift. Again and again I found that it was only when returning to the everyday world that the real changes which had taken place became clear. It was a dissonance, a jarring, that alerted me to this shift. By feeling this strange vibration I could trace it back to its origin. It was something that became a regular occurrence, and as such was part of my life now; however, I was concentrating on trying to find a balancing point in my constantly shifting internal life, and therefore much less alert to the prevailing conditions around me.

A series of small disappointments befell me. If they had been isolated they would have been inconsequential. Unfortunately they came one after another; and over the period of a few weeks began to amount to much more than their individual weight. How quickly it is possible to move from a powerful feeling of completeness and wholeness, to surveying the shattered remnants of what we once, so recently, were. Although I was by no means concerned at the beginning, I certainly became obsessed and confused by these petty upsets as they began to mount up. I awoke with that dread phrase "I wonder what's going to go wrong today" echoing in my mind. Gradually, but surely, I lost most of my sense of integrity and quickly fragmented into someone at the mercy of the forces around me. It was a struggle that deepened. My skin condition worsened. All the shedding, bleeding and itching made me unable to cope on my own, and I became hospitalised. In the separate and safe space of a hospital ward I had at least escaped the difficulties of my life for a moment. It was a comfort when, after each daily bathing, the ointments and bandages were wrapped around my body by others: I was, for the moment, passive and cared for in a very practical way. There are times in life when every man and woman, whether they be saint or sinner, master or acolyte, ordinary or extraordinary, needs loving care and attention. When all our endeavours to support ourselves and our lives seem in vain: perhaps after shocking news; the sudden darkening after the light of love; the dissipating and disintegrating consequences as futility lays waste to our dreams and ambitions; whatever the cause there is great need of simple support whilst our bodies and mind readjust themselves and regain their strength and integrity. To admit to such setbacks can only benefit one with an essential realisation: that we are vulnerable and delicate beings; preserved not only by the natural forces of this planet but also by the perpetual shining light of life. Should either go out, then our life is lost.

�֎ �֎ ✖ ✖ ✖ ✖ ✖

It was a few months before I returned to that little cabin, which now symbolised the real light in my life.

I told Nohona of my experiences during my time away from him. I felt much better for just being in this place. He listened attentively and didn't comment until I had talked myself out.

"What's happened to you is really a symptom of the changes that are taking place within your bodies." He thought for a few moments. "Imagine that, for whatever reason, you are a being intent on maintaining the status quo as far as human beings are concerned. You are watching this world that, even with all its errors, manages to involve people in the struggles of life so well that only a few of them experience hints of the real possibilities and magnificence that is at the core of our creation; and even fewer actually spare the time from their brief lives to develop and investigate how to evolve into light. You are one of them. For whatever reason; perhaps your physical suffering; perhaps the gifts you were given when you were created; whatever the reason, you are now becoming one of those humans who is and has evolved."

I balked at the idea. It seemed ridiculous to look at me in such a way.

"I'm nothing." I answered. "I don't know anything apart from what you've taught me and I can't even do that properly."

He became stern. "That is not true. You, even now, possess more real knowledge than practically all the so called experts out there. What has befallen you over the last few weeks is an indication of that. Let me tell you this, and I don't want you to forget it: real evil in this world is not the gross acts of inhuman men and women against this world and its inhabitants—that's just down to their own depravity—but the very real and constant stifling of the human spirit on its upward path. When you get these little niggles, the disappointments, petty injustices and let downs of life, building one on top of the other, it's rather like a wounded animal being tracked by a predator: an oh so patient waiting for the pleasure of your fall; that's what maintains their interest in tracking you.

"Who are they?" I interrupted.

"Those who cannot bear your new and growing independence. To them, you are now alight; a bright flame that everyday begins to gather and build its strength. One more human light to dispel the darkness that they are intent on maintaining. One more human being who is no longer asleep. I know it sounds like science fiction or some B movie film script, but it's true. It is a common experience for those that are walking a true path. That's why integrity is all. Nothing can touch you if you retain your integrity; and, for the times when you know your integrity is awry, you must have some effective defence mechanisms in place. In the case of your mental body even simple defences which mean something to you, and have some power for you, are appropriate. Basing your consciousness in your physical body also helps. Not seeing everything as connected, but rather as individual incidents that need to be dealt with individually is also helpful. And do your best not to fall into victim consciousness—that makes stalking you so much easier. Obviously there's no problem at all in asking for help from those who help us on the path, it can be a powerful deterrent. But you must be clear that this type of obstacle is very real and it's something that you must attend to constantly."

I was stunned. I believed that such psychic defence was for the dabblers of this world; for those who lived enmeshed in an illusory world; however, I was wrong. When I returned home I attended to the matter in the ways he'd suggested, and my circumstances definitely improved. And, in the future, if I felt there was a pattern developing to certain incidents and disappointments in my life I paid attention to the defences of my mental body; uncluttered my thinking, and tried to integrate my bodies into one. It would work, and the rot come to a halt. It is also beneficial to cleanse and renew the defences of your home: often, in the unconscious, this represents oneself. It is obvious to me now that the malevolent forces out there are very real; whether they be the left-over mental bodies of evil people, thought forms that hold us in place as we try to move onwards, or actual beings, I don't know. There are other explanations I'm sure. However, whatever the true reason, these techniques work and that is all the proof I need.

He asked me to lie down on the cabin floor. I closed my eyes. This was the first of many times when he treated me with bodywork. It always induced a feeling of peace and calm in me, but also a peculiar in-between state of consciousness: not sleep, nor deep samadhi, but something that I'm still unable to name. He placed his hands in various positions on my body, sometimes gently moving them to facilitate the process. Bodywork from a knowledgeable human is one of the great 'carings' we can experience. I found that it took a number of sessions for me to surrender to the process: there was within a certain pride that wanted to deny any effects such treatment could have on my consciousness and my body. How could it possibly have any effect: surely I'd already learned and put into practice a long time ago any healing technique that had validity? But, you see, I hadn't experienced healing by consciousness before. In this process the healer themselves was of the utmost importance: their intent, their integrity, their light, their love and their knowledge would combine in that touch. The touch of one such human upon another is still the most powerful healing force available to us, but it absolutely depends on the integrity of the healer. That is why he only now began to teach me his healing techniques: it was necessary for me to begin to clear myself of everything that wasn't me, otherwise there is no integrated consciousness to bring to another. It is a powerful idea: that of the consciousness of the healer being integral to the act of healing, and yet it is so obvious.

After this initial session Nohona explained that he'd simply aimed to re-establish the communication between my bodies. The chakra centres that we all know of—the brow, neck, chest, solar plexus, pelvis and pubic centres—serve as gateways or doorways for the return of mental consciousness into the physical realm. From the body, consciousness should move through an area around the umbilicus into the soul body. From there it returned via certain

122

gateways back to the physical. There was one at the neck, one at each shoulder, one on either side of the chest and on either side of the upper abdomen—at the level of the liver and stomach—and one at the pubic area. Again, from the physical body, consciousness moves through an area around the base of the skull into the mental body.

Consciousness should flow easily between all these bodies, but often it could become disrupted for many and varied reasons. Work on these gateways caused a clearing of such blockages and the natural dynamics of our human anatomy would re-establish themselves.

I cannot say that after this initial bodywork I was stunned at the effects of it; rather, over the next few hours and days I felt again a familiar harmony re-establish itself. As with most humans, my soul could be likened to a vital and vibrant child trying to force the boulder of my mind to move. However, using many of the techniques Nohona had taught me, my mental self did, over time, change itself in invisible steps: hindrances simply evaporated, and character traits—which, using force, resisted any attempt at change—somehow transformed themselves without tears. Often it was difficult for me to realise that such and such a mental block had disappeared; to witness the actual disappearance itself. This particular characteristic of the way proved most rewarding when hate, anger, jealousy, or any other undesirable trait I had attached to a person, suddenly disappeared without work. Perhaps it is rather like being able to play a difficult passage of music after a few days rest from the instrument: secret facilitations are the birthright of all humans; and often how we think a solution can be found is not in fact the most effective way. It is the obvious in comparison to the subtle; the known against the secret; the night and the day. I had to remember that all were available to me: in the ocean of my being they were the secret depths to which I hadn't yet dived, containing hidden treasures I had no idea how to use effectively.

I began to feel more harmony within. This peculiar change of consciousness cannot be over emphasised: it is one of the keys to spiritual maturing. You could think of it in this way: there is an everyday irritating and superficial noise, which is so continuous and constant; so ever present during our lives, that it's only when we begin to concentrate on the much deeper and distant sound of our true nature, that this familiar and aggravating noise becomes differentiated from the deep musical rhythm emanating from the flame of our soul. Only with the knowledge of what you're paying attention to can your attention be directed in the right direction. The quiet between the breathing of the body; the suspense between the in and out of the tide; the space between day and night; that is the place when its sound is heard most clearly. All it takes is the encouraging and welcoming that the true seeker can offer; his or her dedication; the opportunity they provide for the quieting; the patience to hear its distant and faint calling sound; and finally the constant radiation of its song at the expense of the false and weak note of one who has not based their radiance on their intrinsic nature. The man-made is at best a representation; the Creator given is truth. Constant diligent encouragement is required to sing its song more and more frequently; until finally we sing its song continually during every breath of our life. I was a long way from this ideal and even now I sometimes hear something else which is not my song and the dissonance it creates alerts me to my error. However, after all this time, I find it easy to identify and easy to rectify. Nohona led me towards identifying and naming this sound. It sounded everyday of my life—I just hadn't listened hard enough—for it is a whisper at first; softly it said to me, "I am, I am, I am," until I caught a faint trace of its song. It took the rest of my life to hear its complex harmony. It took the rest of my life to sing that single note out loud. It is love.

Nohona was gentle with me over the next few days. He instructed me on some healing practices which would be of benefit to both myself and others. He completed this part of my training at a later date. Gradually I recovered my former strength and outlook.

One evening he said:

"I think it's time for us to walk in the night." We put warm clothes on as it had become a little chilly, and then set off into the dark. He took me to a place that had a clear path—reasonably straight, through the forest—which led, much further down, to the town. I was instructed to walk onwards—he would walk behind—and to give in to the trance state that such a silent walk in the dark would produce. I was to concentrate my sight about a foot in front of my face, looking ahead, and to try not to look at the ground. The night was still, the sky clear, and the moon shone out from the dark of space to light my path. I began. It soon became apparent that I had very little confidence—trust—in my body to regulate and decide its own pattern of walking; it took some time for me to allow my body to take care of itself whilst my consciousness sank into a state of one pointedness. As it happened for longer and longer periods I noticed that I walked faster; my feet were lifted higher off the ground and I felt light and unencumbered; I could have walked forever. This neatly fell in with the lesson I'd received about endurance: sometimes it really is our mental selves that inhibit and burden our bodies—all of them.

After what seemed like a few hours walking we stopped. The space I now experienced was utterly different from anything I had previously known. My eyes, having become accustomed to the dark, picked out shades and shadows I had never seen before. Here a small puddle of water, or a differently textured part of the ground, shone as if a bright light was within it. There, the arches, branches and trunks of trees became transformed into something I cannot name: living; moving just before or after my eyes had shifted; not ominous or frightening, but touching me in a way that I didn't recognise. I looked up at the sky. A huge skein of cloud, in the shape of a bird's wing, partly obscured a radiant silver moon. I'd never seen so many stars; glittering and sparkling lights scattered across the vast expanse of black space. They were uncountable and filled me with awe. I looked all around and was fascinated at the wonder of the night. Suddenly, in that instant, my fear of the dark vanished: somehow I felt enveloped and embraced by the depths and mystery of the night; as if the darkness had a life and consciousness all of its own. It felt benevolent and yet exciting, and was not simply the absence of light. Perhaps, because I was unencumbered by any man-made physical objects around me, my consciousness expanded and met something I hadn't experienced in my life before: what it was I do not know, and even now can only call 'the night,' but that phrase took on a whole new meaning to me as a consequence of this walk.

Ever since that time I have felt at peace in the dark. Is it because I am free from the gaze of other humans watching and criticising and judging in their own petty ways? There is only the presence of the natural and more fundamental forms of life; some may be malevolent, but most have their own lives and experiences; they have their own consciousness and life plans. If they saw me at all I would simply appear as just another of their life's encounters. Their indifference didn't bother me at all. In essence though, I experienced the night as a living being in itself; I'd separated what may happen to me during the night from the consciousness that is the opposite of day. There was a metaphor here as well, which related to my mental self: the covered, the mysterious, and the sometimes frightening are often not so when we look at them with a calm and rational mind. Illusions disappear; old traits and beliefs are nothing but ghostly clouds with no real substance; and the dark passages of the mind only need this walk of clarity and bravery in order for the mysterious power which they occlude to become part of our wholeness: for we cannot be whole without such a walk.

Again my consciousness had been expanded. My mind had to take in something more than I was originally aware of, or even suspected. It was almost as if an invisible travelling companion had suddenly appeared: I felt that all this information, all these experiences, were returning to me only because they were an intrinsic part of human experience; as if they'd been hidden at birth for some unjustifiable reason and only now revealed to the light. This aspect of the path's strangeness always impressed me: its ability to re-introduce me to my inheritance. Yet every one of those returns only made me more human. I began to expand into my birthright; the birthright we all have as human beings. If ever human society adopted such techniques in its education and social interactions what a magnificent way of life would ensue. But it does have to start somewhere; with any one person. Only when the weight of many individuals—with such an outlook—began to tip the balance of mass consciousness, was there any possibility of such a change. Until that time it was up to the individual to take care of and nurture their own spirituality. That is what I was doing.

The next day an unexpected guest arrived. As we were eating breakfast there was a knock on the door and a lady walked in. She was older than me, casually dressed, with a happy, carefree expression. They greeted each other like old friends. Nohona introduced me as David...Kawowo.

"Ah," she said, "so it's your name now."

They both laughed.

I didn't feel confident enough to interrupt their conversation so I just listened. She left us after a while to visit the temples.

Nohona didn't offer any comments until I asked him about her.

"Oh, she's one of my other apprentices." He had a look of satisfaction about him.

"So, do you have many you've taught; only I thought there weren't many?"

"No, you're right, there aren't: only a few. It's just good to see that she's doing fine."

After a few minutes I said:

"But you sound like it doesn't always turn out like that."

"It doesn't," he replied, "there are no guarantees. In the end there has to be the strength within to confront and endure the difficulties that arise—usually from the conflict between the society we live in, and the new centre that you radiate from. As you're finding out, it isn't easy. Sometimes there is very little reward other than to know that you are absolutely on the right path; and the only way you'll know this is by the continual process of clarifying your true nature. In the end I don't know the reason why so many dabble and so few endure. I'm just glad that one or two manage to make it."

She joined us later, towards midday, and we walked into the town. Again, I felt insecure: my questions and comments would seem stupid and idiotic to this well advanced soul. As we sat down at the little cafe I realised that she still had things to sort out, things she was still confused about; she offered her opinion about something and then asked Nohona's view on the matter. Then she would ask me. As the conversation proceeded I began to feel part of this group; that my opinions were as valid as theirs. They wanted my input. Then something peculiar happened. We were discussing something about which I had a strong opinion, and Nohona and the lady disagreed with me. However it became less of a discussion and more of an argument between us. It was something that I felt very strongly about and one which I had already justified to myself with internal debate and logic. I would not give in.

Soon the sun hung low in the sky and she had to go home. Our conversation had eased somewhat and I apologised for creating any ill feeling. My apology seemed to be accepted and we parted on good terms. Hardly a word was spoken between Nohona and myself as we walked back to the cabin.

"Listen," I said, "I'm really sorry about that argument. I'm sorry I spoiled her visit."

He didn't answer for a while. Then:

"Oh, it's OK, don't beat yourself up about it. It's good that you stuck to your guns. I could tell you felt very passionate about the point and you had some very good arguments. No, don't worry. Argument and debate is absolutely essential when we're creating and forming beliefs and opinions. You might call it spiritual combat; only in this case you never use techniques to embarrass, humiliate, or to put down your opponent, because you're trying to clarify your own mental outlook as well; refining and perfecting the edges of the jewel until they glint and fluoresce with light. No, I wouldn't have you any other way. It's just strange when an apprentice comes to the end of their apprenticeship; a bit like a child saying goodbye to its parents when he or she leaves home. There's this strange sense of relief and then again a sadness that things are changing. You've really grown during the last few months...its good...I'm glad for you."

We carried on walking. I wasn't sure that I'd heard him right and couldn't imagine that this was the end of my formal training.

"What do you mean, come to the end of my apprenticeship? I feel like I'm nowhere near ready. I'm really rubbish at this stuff: forgetting things, making an idiot of myself. I mean I was in a right state when I arrived this time."

"You see," he replied, "that probably means you are ready. You're fine now, that's the proof. Don't think that I can give you the answer to everything, because I can't. You don't have to worry, this doesn't mean you'll never see me again, and of course I can still teach you things that you want and need to know. But the truth is that it's my main duty to give you the true foundations on which you can build your own future knowledge and spirituality. They are unshakeable. They are unbending. And yet they are so simple. They are what you now know as truth. The three bodies. The fourth body. Living your life according to the soundless sound. Compassion and love for your fellows. Absolute respect for your environment and the world we live in. Realising that this is the one and only chance for you to physically live. And the knowledge that you, as a human being, are far more magnificent a creation than you possibly know. It's all really simple.

Everything else flows naturally as long as you keep the gateways clear. Once the rain falls, everything else is set in motion."

Nohona told me to go off on my own for the evening and to contemplate the meaning of my initiation. I was totally off guard and never expected to be initiated so unexpectedly. I felt unprepared; undeserving; and most of all had difficulty appreciating the fact that I had come to the end of my formal training. Surely there must be more to it than this. And yet, when I thought about it seriously, I had made huge leaps in my understanding. Confused teachings had been clarified; the sword of Nohona's perception had cleared a path back to the place from which the gold thread of true knowledge issued forth. I had sought clarity and truth and I had found them. Gone was much of my self indulgence—blameless or not, it had still obscured my light. Now I had rediscovered ears that hear and eyes that see. In reality, the eternal flame was lit.

I slept fitfully that night, my mind full of confused images: the jungle; that tiger again; of flying; walking amongst the bushes without a path; crying alone and lost in a place I didn't know; and then I would wake up and calm to my friend the night. I wanted to remember this special night; everything. It was a pivotal point in my life. I became acutely aware of the sound of the sea and the comfort of my warm bed. The distinctive smell of the cabin seemed intensified and I lay there with my heightened senses vibrating. I could feel waves of consciousness flowing up and down my body as I entered a trance like state: I was clear and strong; confident and wise; benevolent and loving. I'd felt a glimpse of what is available to us if our self imposed restraints are released, and we fully realise the light with which we are created.

When I awoke in the morning that exalted state had all but left me. I felt tired and depressed. If I acknowledged my initiation then I had to accept that this stage of my life was now over. I felt alone and lost again.

Nohona walked in the bedroom with a cup of tea. Chai jumped up and sat on my bed.

"When you're ready we'll need to get going. No rush, but we've a lot to do today."

Just as he was about to leave the room I had to say to him:

"I'm scared Nohona. I don't feel I'm ready. I don't want to stop coming here and having our conversations. It's not what I expected."

He sat down on the bed again.

"There, there. That's how it is for all of us. We all feel the same way. It's scary and unnerving to be given validation of your knowledge. Where else is there to go? Your life awaits you young man. The rest of your life awaits you."

He left.

We walked up to the temple complex before noon. After our customary greetings to the area—something that had become not only a natural and enjoyable act but absolutely essential now—Nohona asked me to go into the jungle and collect leaves, branches, flowers and any nice stones or pebbles I could find. Before I took anything I had to ask permission from those that were responsible for such things and was to treat the whole enterprise with a respectful and growing sense that we were preparing for an event. It was the culmination of the teaching process and marked my acceptance—by those who had trod the path beforehand—that I was a flamekeeper. As I walked off into the forest, my consciousness shifted to one of utter respect; utter thankfulness; and a growing sense of humbleness. The forest seemed so much brighter; the colours more vibrant. Everything seemed to come alive, as if to say 'they are here, they are here;' not in with any sense of reverence, but with a sense of anticipation for what was to occur. It was the beginning of my love for the plant life of this planet; love and respect for the utter magnificent and consciousness shifting ability which our green companions—on which our life depends— could induce in humans who were prepared to accept that dependence and learn from it.

When I came back to Nohona he was already placing the fern leaves and flowers he'd picked onto the walls of one of the temples. It was one we hadn't used before. I added my leaves, flowers and stones to the decoration and, as Nohona instructed me, did so with the express idea that we were preparing this place to be something that would be beautiful to look at; somewhere that, with each decoration, radiated the respect and reverence due to those who would watch. When we had finished the whole area shone with an invisible magnetism.

130

Nohona lit a fire, away from the temples, and we ate a small meal. The sun began to set and the sky fired its warm rays onto the sea. The temple complex glowed red and orange and was soon penetrated by the darkness.

"It is time," Nohona said.

We walked up to the temple, around which we placed three small fire torches which only served to add to the mystery of that place. In this light, and at this moment, that collection of great, ancient, stones was utterly transformed into a sacred place of great power. Everything became still and held its breath. There were others watching who were invisible to me; but I am sure they looked on with the collected memory of those who have passed through this stage themselves. They knew of the trials before and the trials after. They only looked upon me with love, although their eyes penetrated to the smallest atom of my being. I couldn't hide: there was nowhere to hide, for their eyes saw everywhere and everything. I didn't feel ashamed of my insignificance; the faults in my character; my pettiness; but I knew they were seen.

Soon the ceremony was over. It seemed rather quick after all that effort preparing the temple; but of course the preparation was also part of a ritual which gradually rose to its climax. We said thank you. I felt at peace; strangely full of expectation; wondering about what had really taken place in that short interval of time. I know now that it was much more than I had suspected.

I left that ancient space as a present day flamekeeper; for it is only in the present, and not the past, that we can find human fulfilment and wholeness. The spiritual has always been, and always will be, inherent in human nature. Without its acknowledgement a human is not complete; like snow without the cold; rain without the wet; sun without the warmth and light; love without the tenderness. I had become whole.

Nohona took me into the town and we had an expensive and beautiful meal in celebration. On that night the world was warm and fun. For a short time the trials and learning had stopped and there was just the happiness of being human: good company, lovely food, and the warmth of the earth.

I looked up at the starry sky. How many beings—how many worlds—were themselves enacting this stage of their evolution? Flamekeeping is universal. Now I had my own flame to protect and nurture.

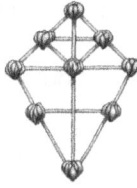

THE LIGHT

The shock of being born anew into the same old world hit me hard. Although I had realised there would come a time for me to be initiated I had put it aside as though it would happen in a dim and distant future, and I certainly hadn't wondered about what would naturally follow it. In some dreamy way I expected to find the world paved with beautiful stones; each painted with a clear arrow which led, inevitably, to a brighter and more enjoyable—more fulfilled— life. A life in which I was obviously and clearly supported—not only spiritually but, naively, financially as well.

I was mistaken on nearly all counts. My first reaction to being initiated was, naturally, elation. There was also a feeling of validation and approval. Again, I recognise how simple and perhaps childlike these reactions are; however, they are human, and I wasn't ashamed of them. I had worked hard; not only more recently during my apprenticeship, but also during the years and years of investigation and training I had sought and received during the whole of my adult life. However my life turned out in the future, I saw that the moment of my initiation was a direct connection between the past and the future. With that simple fact I knew that I was on the right path. I knew nothing of what would appear as its way twisted and scoured the future; and it took me years to realise that I did, in fact, know nothing at all of what was to happen to me.

Following my initial elation I became aware of a rather disturbing realisation. Until this point in time it was as if I had been goaded all my life to tread the path. Sometimes it had been with the temptation of new knowledge—gentle and soliciting—other times it had been nothing but cruelty beyond what I felt I could endure; and indeed, more than once, I doubted whether I would live to die a natural death. The strangeness I was experiencing resulted from the fact that, on reflection, both methods seemed ultimately to lead me forwards. Sometimes there had been a long hesitation as I began to once again re-establish an equilibrium between my experience, my philosophy and my spirituality; but still, inevitably, I walked forward. Always, again and again, I was standing on shifting sand that moved here and there; a wavering path which would buffet me gently and then prod me with the sharpest and most painful instrument I could imagine. Always, again and again, narrowing my path; selecting for me—or selected sometimes by my own hand—a direction to move towards. The path signs were, and still are, blacked out: that is the way it is. But, after my initiation—and quite unexpectedly—this invisible support and direction seemed to disappear. I was like a man left behind on a beach whilst everybody else had been rescued and was safe. In reality this was only half true: everyone else was not rescued and safe. Most of the time it seemed to me that they didn't even realise they were marooned in the first place. But, whatever the reason, I had been left utterly alone.

How do I describe a state that is so difficult to describe? It is not the dark night of the soul. I had, more than once, entered and emerged from that piercingly painful state. There was no desperateness, no melancholy, no intensely depressive and dark mind set. Instead I can only describe it as the disappearance of some invisible and vaguely suspected companion. Someone or something had aided me, even in great difficulty; lead and tempted me to carry on walking my path—even when this was the last thing I wanted to do. Suddenly though, the direction—or perhaps the director—of my life disappeared; as if I had qualified from university and was told that I could not study in this place anymore: with the most gentle and kind 'goodbye' I was pushed out into the world and the gate shut behind me. I walked on into an unknown land with neither map nor guide.

I was confused. Surely it couldn't be like this. I didn't know what to do with my life. I couldn't think of any way to proceed other than to follow the pattern I had previously trod. Perhaps, with the knowledge I now possessed, everything would be easier. A month or two after leaving Nohona I once again tried to set up my own business. Now, because of my natural desire for purity and clarity in the teaching, I was not prepared to compromise my healing methods: that would have struck at my hard won integrity. I should have known what the result. Only a few people were prepared to visit me; and I often found myself talking to them about far wider issues than they had expected from their treatment. No matter how many people talk about the idea of 'holism' it is still a disappointingly small minority who are prepared to enter a path of healing which requires something of them. I had found in the past how many erroneous expectations it is possible to hold and still be convinced that I absolutely understood what spiritual development was. Until recently I hadn't understood what it was at all; and, even at this stage, to define it was difficult if not impossible. The same is true of those who request healing. Very few are prepared for the journey that they may need to undergo; one that I suspect, in some cases, to be the real reason for the illness occurring in the first place. True healing amounts to far more than people suspect: it creates the space for expansion, evolution and freedom.

Over the next few months there came to me the realisation that this freedom was, in itself, part of my path. For some reason— and no one had ever told me or even suggested the fact—I always believed that my path led directly to that of being a healer, a teacher, or something similar. It seemed I was utterly wrong.

It took perhaps a year, or even more, for me to realise that the most important and ultimate aim of this teaching was to preserve the light of the eternal flame that had been lit. A flame of aliveness which had to be recognised and nurtured; a flame with that infinite core of light and love that is the given gift of life that everyone possessed: its manifestation being a natural consequence of the integration of the three bodies. I had felt it during the final weeks of my training, and since then had cultivated it as part of my consciousness. However, it was the initial integration of me as a human being which lit that everlasting flame. From my initiation onwards, no matter how dreadful life became, no matter what emotional or physical pain I suffered, no matter how much I wished and wanted that flame to be extinguished and for ordinary consciousness to reassert itself; it never happened. That is a consequence of becoming a flamekeeper—it cannot be otherwise. You can never go backwards where the evolution of your consciousness is concerned.

135

Thus it became evident to me that the first and foremost reason for spiritual development is to nurture and take care of one's own individual light; to clear the confusing image you may be presenting to the world; to base one's true self on the radiant perpetual explosion that is the soul. Even by accomplishing this you were manifesting one of the most important aims of growth. By holding this clarity, this consciousness, this vibration, it is grounded in our physical world. The light is made physical. Thus it becomes easier for others to awaken to their own growth and to achieve it: each person who becomes a flamekeeper clears the path in minute increments for others to follow, and contributes to an ever lightening world. I therefore felt that was beholden upon me to manifest, to the best of my ability, my ever growing integrity.

Only in retrospect did I realise that my life had actually become unified after my initiation. When I was younger I kept a diary for quite a few years. Written on those now yellowing pages were frustration and elation, the deep black moods, and the devastation of unrequited or broken love. It had the dual purpose of not only emptying my fevered mind, but also—and this effect I hadn't originally anticipated—of bringing everything into proportion. Perhaps there was a series of entries relating to a particularly painful episode, however, a few months later, I would be optimistic and happy: the effects from a devastating event had healed and life once again reasserted itself. To look back at these episodes of my life gave me a great perspective on the true strength of the human spirit, and also gave me the courage to cope with any new and unexpected events. However, sometime after my initiation, I realised that the diary writing had stopped: I no longer felt any need for it. The reason for this was really quite simple: my life had become unified and integrated; my awareness was bought to practically all my life situations and there was no longer a need to anchor each separate incident so that it would not be forgotten, because everything, every event, became part of my awareness. It was as if, before this point, my life had been surrounded by various threads, each one a different arena or concern; and I travelled to and from these separate concerns all the time. Sometime after my initiation these threads were woven together; they became one; this was the fabric of my being and of my life. I experienced all of it because those threads passed directly

136

through my body and my unified consciousness. At last I had captured the path.

In order that I maintain and refine my blossoming consciousness it was absolutely essential for me to perform a small ritual nearly every day. This would take the form of a few affirmations; moving between my different bodies; and maintaining connections with the consciousness of other forms of life. This was important for two reasons. Firstly, there is always a necessity to keep the gateways of communication between our bodies clear. Living in our society—the way it is formed—does not encourage the birth or maintenance of the whole man or woman, and in order for us to perpetuate and strengthen this birthing consciousness we have to give daily attention, even if for a short time, to the whole of our true selves. Secondly, we begin to develop the ability to bring the complete human into everyday activity, and ritual or habit can nourish this essential practice. This can have revealing consequences. No longer were all issues judged equally as important. Indeed, it becomes apparent when our immortality is known indisputably that, on first inspection, there is very little in everyday life that is of any real importance. What does this or that trouble really mean when held within the same view as the birth and death of stars? Yet, of course, to each human individual—created uniquely and with love—the minutiae of a life can have profound consequences on that life. However, by the maintenance of this dual consciousness—on the one hand an individual life and on the other the vast cosmos—a proper proportion can be given to the issues of that life. Whereas, beforehand, I might have obsessively worried about a particular problem, I realised now that when viewed against the backdrop of the vast history of the earth, or even the number and variety of terrible traumas afflicting sections of humanity at that very moment, I could easily put them where they belonged: categorise them as simple irritations to life that would, in time, disappear and be replaced by others. They are necessary companions once your body had breathed its first breath. Then again, other difficulties and issues stood out from these: they didn't diminish when compared to the whole of my life on earth, and therefore made themselves known as vital and important core issues that I should attend to.

137

Sometimes this consciousness caused problems between myself and those who were downhearted and depressed, or contemplating a total change in the course of what had been a good life because they had been treated abysmally by that life. Unless they too had some very real conception of all that—out there—then anything I could say to them would be useless: I appeared to be trivialising their pain, which was absolutely not the case. All I intended to do was help them to get a particular incident in proportion. Then again perhaps this is a symptom of having myself passed through similar traumas before, and realising—as much as I wouldn't want to—that, in time, I recovered. Therefore, I only really entered in to such discussions with those who had an inkling of such a perspective. Again though, it confirmed a subtle sense of separateness that befalls all on such a path.

And what of the aloneness to which Nohona had referred? About that, as in everything else, he had not lied. Ironically, because many of my own issues had been cleared up, I found it easy and rewarding to chat to many people during my daily life. However, when I considered how many real humans I could talk to with a sense of connection and mutual understanding, there were very few. I was intensely lonely at times, and learned to live a rewarding and fulfilling life when I had no real companionship whatsoever. But there were many times when loneliness swept over me as if cast into a chasm of utter bleakness and isolation. It was always difficult to endure. Of course there was Nohona and Kanaka Nui, but they were far away. I yearned for a partner to share my life with. It occurred to me that when the transience of this physical life is compared to one's own immortality, it seemed a tragedy that it took many years before I found someone to share my life with. It was well worth the wait though, for it was a true connection.

Because of the very real fact that my enjoying just one physical life had seated itself deeply into my consciousness, I became aware of an almost obsessive carefulness with my one life. When crossing the road I always took great care; when decorating or repairing my house I was very sure of my footing and used work tools carefully. For this reason I never took part in sports in which there was a real possibility of serious injury. For a person to risk their amazing—one time only—body for the chance to perform such and such a sport was something I couldn't understand. And it became apparent to me that often such people entered such dangerous arenas because it was the only time that they felt truly alive; stimulated and invigorated by life. For my own part—because I allowed the power of my soul to infuse my body—it took very little effort to 'feel alive.' And certainly I could be pleased and fulfilled with simple pleasures. I believe that this was, again, a great benefit of treading the path. To be a warrior of love and light didn't mean fighting battles with illusory enemies, or to throw ones life needlessly away in the pursuit of transiently bright awareness. It was to do with holding a consciousness that reinforced and radiated a perspective on being alive; on your creation; and on the potential that is innate within our very uniqueness. It was the bravery to embark on a journey into your own true self and to walk on defiantly when hardly any other human supported your endeavour; when negative forces might deliberately derail your journey, but where the absolute knowledge of one's intrinsic nature could be realised.

It also became clear to me that human beings are very special. I do not mean that we are given special dispensation; I mean that we are lucky enough to not only have the intrinsic gift of love within us, but the intelligence and self-awareness to bring its power into the physical world. We are capable of reflecting back to the universe our own, very human—but nonetheless absolutely valid—experiences of living in that very universe. The potential with which we are born is enormous. We are the only animals on this earth, as far as we know, that can actually nurture and protect other forms of life without obvious reward.

Of course we are the only animals that create so much destruction and cruelty. But we must not forget the huge potential that is available to us, as living, breathing, beings: love, kindness, compassion, care and gratitude; humour and laughter; music making; the written word; whole kaleidoscopes of art; and, of course, never forget fun, dance, sex and joy; community; self improvement and culture; training; healing; wonder and amazement. Peace. Great human beings, be they totally unknown or famous, are no more than the realised potential of ourselves. Praise is not necessary, nor is recognition—only manifestation.

As I have said, these realisations took a long time to flower. It is one thing to listen, to mentally absorb, and to fully acknowledge a teaching, but it is entirely another to bring that conglomeration of ideas and challenges into our world as a real and embodied knowledge. Even though my original interests were eastern in origin, it still surprised me how long it took to eradicate the all pervasive teaching that the physical body was simply a vehicle for the 'soul' or, mistakenly, 'the spirit.' Although there was an acknowledgement that the body should be healthy, it always took on a secondary role compared to the purification of the mind. It took persistence and determination in order for my consciousness to begin to settle into my body. Not just settle into, but also to enliven; to fill and to enjoy my physical body. It is very difficult to describe these feelings because, in reality, it is only the experience that illuminated my mind and my general consciousness. I can only say that it was as if I had descended into my body; rather than using my body, I became my body. After all, why else did we have a body; there is no good reason which stands up to challenge. It is within the physical dimension that ones individual light can truly live life; not as a thought or an idea; not in some illusory and dreamy trance state, but utterly physical. The senses allow us to revel and swim in this amazing physical world. Of course there are other forms of consciousness available to us here and also existing in the universe; however, the body we live in is our own. It is, once again, a gift. Because I had suffered from physical ill health during my life it was easy for me to curse my body and its physical form; so much easier to believe the tradition of treating the body as a vehicle which was cast off when 'earthly life' was over. I was wrong. Very wrong. For, with the acceptance and, furthermore, the full enjoyment and love of my body, came improved health. Indeed I could feel my skeleton, my organs, my circulation, my nervous system—all of it—expanding and relaxing with the invasion of my loving consciousness into it. It felt right. My body was not a 'tool' that I used; it was as fully an aspect of me as any of my other bodies. I had to work on this, as a daily short ritual in which I 'was' my body, for the idea to take hold. It was the full realisation that this really was the only physical body I would ever be; ever have; ever enjoy. It is shocking and yet obvious; the full acceptance of which only serves to preserve ourselves and others; to fully value the amazing sense and sense sensations that we can experience. I truly began to feel, to see, to smell, to taste, to touch, to hear. In fact, in reality, I began to live: for my body is the expression of my shining bright soul in the physical world.

Why do seekers spend so much time trying to escape this earthly life? It is as if they want to rid themselves of the unnecessary encumbrance of having a physical body. What sensations do they think are going to be available to them after this physical life? It is with these thoughts that I finally accepted and learned to value my physical self. I had friends who preached to me the value of hedonism because of this very fact, but that's not how I saw it at all. My valuable body was not to be thrown away on some questionable experiment— whether physical or mental—which, together with an almost suicidal drive, would become a 'peak experience.' The most delicate of sensations can fill me with pleasure. Using drugs to heighten this pleasure never interested me. I have never yet met a person who used drugs habitually and ever had anything of interest to say. And, even if some 'peak experience' had taken place, they never have the determination and endurance to really allow that experience to transform their selves or their life. Drugs as used today are an illusory path, and can often absorb the taker in a whirlpool of doubtful and dubious experiences. You just cannot afford to throw this once in a lifetime experience away so foolishly. To be fully grounded in physical reality it takes all of our consciousness and attention. The truth is that mortals live their life as if they are immortal; immortals live their lives as if they are mortal.

With these realisations, and especially the one that it was my own self that held and radiated consciousness, I was free to take up any work I wanted. I therefore found myself employment that didn't require much of me, did not conflict with my integrity, and paid me enough money to put food on the table. It is difficult to imagine now that I hadn't seen this more clearly before. My work was of little consequence as long as it didn't compromise my beliefs: again, my integrity is all. I understood completely that my identity was absolutely nothing to do with anything other than the feeling of being truly me. It was wrong for anyone to confuse their identity with their work, their possessions, even their beliefs, religion or philosophy. Everything I have just mentioned can change. One's identity is a

141

feeling: a feeling of not being anything else other than purely oneself; unsullied, uncontaminated and clear. It is a feeling of aliveness—of that which has existed ever since you were conscious. Suppose for a minute you took away your physical appearance; your history and name; even your nationality and race. What would be left? Still there would be a feeling. And that feeling is remarkably simple and open: it is loving, dynamic, passionate and radiating—but my words cannot adequately define it. To define it is to limit its potential and its identity. Therefore I simply had to feel what it was like to be me and it could not include, at all, any mental or intellectual evaluation of myself. My mind had to echo and resonate with that feeling, otherwise I had lost my integrity. So it was that whatever my work, wherever I found myself, and whatever I was doing, it was only required that I be absolutely myself.

Another error that is commonly held to be true also made itself apparent: that the ego should be snuffed out; pacified; denied its reign. I now understand that to be wrong, just as Nohona had told me. The mistake is in seeing the ego—the mental body—as an enemy or some kind of malevolent entity that voraciously and viscously seeks to deny any effort to find the truth: that is why it must be subdued. But that is not the case. What it needs is instruction, education, knowledge, wisdom and, above all, ownership and guidance. Remember that, just as is the case with the physical body, there needs to be an echoing; a mirroring with another dimension of the feeling of being oneself. Almost as if we are synaesthetic: we seek to translate sound into colour, or a taste into a feeling. That is how the ego should be treated: not eradicated or subdued, but moulded into a very real representation of your true self in the mental dimension.

Gradually and gently your ego becomes a reflection of your soul nature. It should be strong and powerful, but not overpowering. Your feeling—not your emotion—is the ultimate strength of your life. That is what reins in, and orders, the ego. And the only way you can do it is with love. The essence of the soul is love. Caress and tempt your ego with what it could feel like if it was an essential aspect of one whole integrated human, shot through with love and aliveness. It cannot resist that total feeling of integrity because even the ego wishes to belong; and as part of a fully integrated human being its well directed attention is invaluable. With such an integrity it complains only rarely because, once persuaded, it has the true model of your identity to guide and mould itself against. That true identity is an irresistible temptation.

One fact, above all, did become apparent to me. Much of my flamekeeping ability was supported by a gift: I could always leave behind me anything which I had outgrown. The fact that I was only interested in approaching closer and closer to the truth meant that, confronted by a good argument or personal experience—and free from dogma—I would, with little difficulty, move beyond that which I already knew. I had no restraints which could drag my freed self back into enslavement. I found that this leap was absolutely essential in order for me to move beyond that which can be taught to that which has to be known. My experience of meeting others who belonged to— or had for a long time been part of—organised religions, was that they found it incredibly difficult to throw their teachings into the crucible of light and only live by the few, true, purified remains. Even if the result freed them from false constraints and beliefs to fly with fundamental truth, it was simply far too frightening to contemplate a life without a manmade surface to stand on. Yet this is the leap that has to be made in order for us to find true freedom. It is essential to move beyond such received truths into the clear light. Without such a move you cannot hear the deep calling sound which sings without words, issuing forth from the magical flame which has to be nurtured and tended and is the essence of your creator-given identity. Its blinding clearness is the essence of life; of love.

And what of the Creator? Nohona never talked much of that elusive, ultimate, entity. It always seemed to me, and still does so, that whatever conclusions and explanations a human could come to about that which gave life to the universe, and to each and every particle in existence, couldn't possibly, even in the most detailed and philosophical explanation, approach the steps of that stupendous being. There always seemed to be explanations abounding: they ranged from the utterly banal, simplistic and insulting to those which wrapped themselves around convoluted and utterly futile expressions, yet only seemed to confuse and mystify those who honestly sought some clarification. Obviously simple explanations and platitudes are an insult to those who genuinely seek to know: they fly in the face of our experience of life on earth. They are like giving salt to a thirsty man: his desire to drink from that elusive glass of pure, crystal clear water can only increase. For myself I always preferred to keep the Creator a mystery: I believe that as soon as we name and qualify it, we limit whatever it is. Therefore it must be by reflection that we see a minute portion of its being. And that is why the inner journey can bring you some sense of the Creator: although you will never be able to name it, you are, of course, an individual result of its action in this universe. Yet another reason to discover your true self: manifesting anything else as self during your life is an insult to that which created you.

Because I had some faint sense of those who had not only already immortalised themselves, but had also decided to stay around the earth for a time to help those of us who wish to evolve, it was to these humans I decided to direct my prayers; who I performed ritual to; and who I thanked for occasional spontaneous insights that made themselves known consciously, in spite of my well defended mental self. These humans can, without doubt, pass on any request that it is not in their power to grant or deal with; or when it is not theirs to decide the outcome of a particular situation. However it was also clear to me that their intervention in the physical world did have limits and constraints; I know nothing of what they are. Therefore, I only tended to request their help with my own, and others', spiritual growth; trying my best to deal with problems that were obviously of the physical world for myself. In this way we seemed to come into some kind of harmony with each other and, with this in mind, I can say that inevitably, as long as my mind was open and flexible, I always obtained new insights and understandings as a result of any such request.

In spite of how these rather mundane and everyday thoughts might seem to mitigate against the normally expected visions and elevations of a spiritually directed life, I did, and do have, profound and mystical experiences which only serve to deepen that very mystery from which they were given birth. They appear quite unexpectedly, and descend without warning onto my everyday consciousness; perhaps a divine sense of peace and contentment, or an overwhelming sense of happiness and joy. Occasionally there was an expanded state of consciousness that somehow illuminated another life form's sphere of activity. It could be as simple as walking out of the house in the morning and smelling the unmistakable scent of spring in the air; or looking up at the depths of the blue-indigo-black sky of twilight; waking up in the middle of the night with a sleeping lover cuddled up to me, their abdomen rising and falling against my skin. Then again it may be the first few minutes of a new year's celebration or a still summer afternoon when the whole world seems to have fallen asleep. Each time there is something extra—something that cannot be spoken of. Sometimes they are sublime refreshments to my life—sometimes their effect is to strengthen and encourage my endeavours when otherwise they seem to have come to a halt. There are countless moments of epiphany during my simple life, and each one confirms and strengthens the flame within. As I have said before, this is yet another great benefit of the path: the experience of the mysterious and inexplicable only serves to deepen the mystery at the centre of life. It entices and motivates us as it calls from the depths of our being, waiting for our reply.

It was well over a year after my initiation that I next visited Nohona. I watched him from the edge of the forest as he pottered around the cabin. I realised that he was one of very few humans that I could communicate with properly. This secret man, in the middle of nowhere, held the whole world; a consciousness that tried its best to prevent the descent of the human race into a chaos of false and misinformed teachings; or else into the idea that humans were simply an accidental creation of no consequence; bags of chemicals and solutions that somehow, against all the odds, managed to survive. He was one of the hubs around which whirled the clear light of truth. There are very few such people on this whole, wide, magnificent Earth.

We greeted each other. He seemed genuinely pleased to see me. With the customary cup of tea we sat down on that bright and beautiful beach to talk of what had happened since we last met. The conversation was easy and light and I felt that our relationship had changed dramatically. No longer was it a teacher-apprentice relationship, but two real humans enjoying the challenge and entertainment of a conversation with each other: of course we could communicate, we stood on the same solid foundation.

At one point he looked at me:

145

"I'm so pleased to see you; it means a lot to me that you're here." He had tears in his eyes. "It's one thing to teach someone, but it's entirely another to see that they've grabbed the light; digested it; to see that it become part of their life. And I can tell. Look at you."

We laughed.

I responded, "Slow down there, I've a lot more to learn yet; in fact it seems like there's more to know now than ever before."

"Yes," he replied, "isn't it great."

Later on he said to me:

"If you want to, I'd like you to start to visit here as a caretaker for this place. I'm not going to spend so much time here. Think I need to spend more time with my partner."

He'd never really mentioned her, only in passing.

I asked, "Who is she actually. I've never met her?"

"Yes, you have." He said with a smile.

I thought for a few minutes.

"Oh, really." I'm so slow sometimes!

So it was that periodically I would spend one or two weeks at the cabin. Other caretakers visited as well. I didn't meet them often but we recognised each other instantly. We would chat and talk. It was a pleasure: the burden was not mine alone. Too much for one man or woman. The real interest in these meetings sprang from the differences and similarities between us. Each had a very identifiable nature; their character was well developed and shot through their whole being. Yet it was quite obvious that we were all very different from each other and proved, even if I needed it, that the truth of the teaching was absolutely directed towards the manifestation of the unique individual light of a human being: it enhanced humans and didn't restrain or oppress individuality. I consider the oppression of the human character a great crime: it is the darkening of that gift of love from whatever it is that creates us. It is the stifling of true life, true aliveness; and, of course, smothers the natural breath of immortality.

In time, of course, I grew older. But my age stated as a number of years always surprised me. I began to live according to the adage 'one minute and a thousand years old.' That really is how I feel. Indeed sometimes it is a shock now to realise how many years I have lived compared to someone who is only young, yet there is still the

146

enthusiasm, energy, enjoyment and inquisitiveness born of a soul-enlivened mind and body.

Looking back over my life, I can state absolutely that I found exactly what I was looking for: the truth. It didn't come to me via the obviously mysterious, in the shocking, or even the terribly frightening. There were no amazingly magical encounters or visions of terror. Yet everything I know now is more real than anything that would have resulted from such experiences. As Nohona had said, he simply re-introduced me to myself; the amazing creation that is called a human being. I find great pleasure in my body and its abilities; in my connection to the life of this planet and the planet itself. And there are those other elusive and sometimes sensed worlds and dimensions, and the mysterious questions they generate that I shall have to wait for an answer to.

And finally there is this: the full recognition of the act of your creation, when acknowledged, cannot fail to fill you with awe and wonder. Something went to the trouble of creating a unique and amazing individual and, when you really encapsulate the magnificence of that act, you will never again be an ordinary, average, human being; no one really is. Everything springs from that realisation, just as the universe manifested in one magnificent act.

I am an immortal, living my life as if I am mortal. I am undeniably grounded in this physical life and its beautiful experiences —the amazing birthright of natural experiences that human beings can encounter and appreciate. I am alive.

And there is love.

Gradually I begin to surface from my reverie. Somehow the rock has absorbed my attention and then replayed my life. I feel groggy, and my body aches from being in the same position for so long. I open my eyes; the sky is ablaze with the glorious streaming colours of the setting sun. As I begin to rise I notice Kawowo by the side of the rock. Sitting there so still; I hadn't heard or seen him until now. He jumps up to his feet and gives me a helping hand as I get down.

"Thank you," I say as I step onto the sand. "Now then young man, we'd better get something to eat."

As we walk along the beach he looks at me:

147

"Are you alright, I didn't know where you'd gone. All the cats are waiting for their food?"

I look at him. His eyes are more innocent than mine were, and he's wondering and worrying about the future: what it holds for him. Just like I did. I feel like crying.

"Yes, I'm fine. I've been looking back on my life. Now there's a scary thought for you. Frightening!" I laugh.

Nohona sent him to me. I'll bet it's because he saw that flame in his eyes—that eagerness—and didn't want it to be corrupted and confused by all the half-truths out there. How lucky to have encountered Nohona: I haven't seen him for years; not since we last met each other as I visiting the cabin a few years ago. We hugged with such love and care. Confident but sad that the next time we might meet could well be when we were both immortals; missing this physical earth and our amazing bodies. We chatted; and he became upset as he talked about Chai, who was getting older and wasn't very well.

"Just like Leonard, my first cat, I suppose we'll have to say goodbye soon. It'll be so painful." Unashamedly he sat there crying; his face streamed with tears. Still human. Absolutely human.

Kawowo and I walk in silence, over the hill and down into the bay.

As we sit down outside the cabin eating our food, with the cats—Shozan, Monkey and Rupert—all relaxing after their meal, I reflect on the day's reverie. Outwardly my life is very simple; not a life many would want. But my life's work has only enriched every day I have lived, as it will for little Kawowo here. And the richest investments of my life I can take with me, when my time comes to leave this body. But, for the moment, I sit here not only aware of this magical evening, which is utterly beautiful, delicate and transient; but also of my need to welcome Kawowo's very human nature into the light of self-knowledge and truth. He is becoming a flamekeeper.

The wind is warm. The sun has set and a beautiful dark blue fades to black in the sky above; the first stars begin to sparkle. Good company, food, the sound of the sea, and the smell of the forest behind me: I want to sit here forever. Why would I want my life to be any different from this? I am content. My older self was right: it didn't turn out how I'd imagined, but I am happy. I am very happy.

That is my story—make of it what you will. I hope that it begins to clarify what exactly you are seeking on your own particular path of spiritual growth and development.

You might like some clarification on the issues that are common to all true spiritual paths in order to begin your own path of discovery, or in order to check that the path you are walking at the moment is addressing the fundamental issues necessary for growth. The following section—On Being Human—will illuminate and clarify these fundamental issues.

After an interval of time it will definitely benefit you to re-read both the first and the second sections of this book. As we begin to evolve it is often the case that issues which were once thought irrelevant, or perhaps we hadn't even noticed, suddenly become important to us. For, just as in life, we see things we hadn't seen before as we begin to mature. The further you climb up the mountain, the more you can see. That's how you know you're growing.

The Handbook of a Flamekeeper

~

On Being Human

The truth about the way it is

You are one of the most magnificent creatures in this huge universe. Your wholeness, once manifested, can rival anything in any direction. You are distinctly and sparklingly unique.

So how do you manifest this? Answer the question now if you can.

If you can produce an answer to your own satisfaction then you need go no further; put this book down. You are lucky; blessed; congratulations, you truly are unique.

If, however, you cannot answer immediately, are not sure, or don't really understand the question, then read on. This book will help you to find the answer, and—only if you work on this yourself—help you to manifest everything that is uniquely you in this world.

So where do we begin?

You see it's like this: you first have to eliminate your ideas about what this unique you would be like. Some of you may have ideas about riches, comfort and power; saintliness or beauty; control; freedom from problems and difficulties: a fantasy existence. Adoration. Forget it. Forget all this rubbish. Dump it. Wave goodbye to the easy life.

Do you really think that trying to manifest your unique individuality in this world—and more specifically in a society that the human mind has manufactured for itself—will be easy? Surely not. It is the most difficult and challenging task humans can set for themselves. But, ultimately, it is also the most fulfilling way for you to live your one and only life on this Earth. It can be full of frustration, exasperation, desperation; trials and tribulations; set-backs and hopelessness. But, its rewards are joy; profound jumps in knowledge and insight; blissful moments, days or weeks; fulfilment more than you can imagine now; adventure; a never ending journey of discovery, and the satisfaction of knowing at the end of your life that you wouldn't have had it any other way.

Have I put you off yet?

No?

It's tempting isn't it, this rediscovery of oneself. You must admit to being just a little bit interested in finding out and manifesting the real you during this short life; because, of course, it can be the only truly rewarding way of living. Can you think of any better way of spending your time here? A journey that makes up a life, to a destination that—well, suffice to say that you cannot possibly be disappointed with the result, but more of that later. For the moment allow yourself to glow a little, to swim in the possibility of really owning yourself for the first time in your life.

Now, read the first paragraph again. Then stop and close your eyes. No thoughts; just imagine how it would feel if this were really true. True of you, my beautiful fellow human.

Death

Why begin with death? Isn't it obvious? It is the one and only thing that I can definitely predict about your life: you will die. So read on, because this absolutely applies to you.

It is said that in the past, to actually know the finality and certainty of death, many seekers after truth were sent to the burial places by their teachers. There they were forced to accept that we all must die. Your beautiful body; its marvellous organs trying their best to serve us through the whole of your life; your skeleton, muscles, and skin; your brain; your heart; a self regulating, self-healing, magnificence; together with all the history, profound thoughts, experiences; the love; the very beingness of us, all of us, can come to this. Death. An end. Sometimes it is utterly inconceivable that we will disintegrate into the earth. This wonderful functioning wholeness will be ended. It bloats and swells. It blisters and rots and smells and is eaten by creatures smaller than we can see. Or else it is burned to ashes and scattered to the four winds. Death will breathe down your neck, whether you like it or not. No one escapes its icy touch.

Have you understood this? Do you really know it? Feel it? What was the real purpose of this knowledge? The acknowledgement, recognition, and absorption of this fact—undiluted by petty dreams and fantasies—helps you to live; to live this one and only life. For it is not true that we are dying from the minute we are born.

We are only dying after our last breath.

Before that point we are still alive: still living. So, do not despair. Until that single and unique moment appears after your final breath, you are alive. Still capable of evolution and progress; integration; love; beingness; change. How wonderful.

It is one of the greatest teachings that you can ever embody. Try never to forget it.

Its most useful application is that it will help you to prioritise your life; to instil a sense of urgency to proceedings.

Death will always clarify complicated issues for you.

I shall refer to it constantly throughout this book. Realise that you haven't all the time in the world to put off that which has to be dealt with, or has to be experienced. You could die within a few minutes whilst reading this page, or tonight during your sleep; in a few days, weeks or months. Perhaps it will be next year. You may never reach forty or fifty, seventy or one hundred. Which time scale works for you? Which one scares the life out of you?

And don't comfort yourself by thinking that you will easily transfer into some paradise, into another body and another life.

Your continued existence after this life is by no means assured.

Truly, reality is wholly different than that. If you go no further with this book absorb this fact totally: you will die.

How do you feel about this? As you may have gathered, this book isn't full of fantasy. There is a saying that truth is stranger than fiction, and no where is this truer than in the real facts about life and death. So how do you feel about your death now?

You reply that you are not scared of death? It instils no fear in you. You welcome it? Do not be so foolish. Are you really saying that there is nothing, absolutely nothing, you enjoy and would miss about your life on Earth. So you have experienced everything have you? You have seen enough sunrises then; heard the pattering of rain or cracking of thunder enough; felt the sun's warmth on your skin; breathed the fresh air; heard the rustling of the leaves in the trees; felt the grass underfoot, all to excess? Are you bored with music of every kind; have you loved and made love enough? Have you heard enough laughter? You have been kissed by every kind of experience? Marvelled at and understood the countless other life forms on this

Earth to the point of boredom. Become insensitive to the true sensations of life coursing through your body? There are no secrets that you would like revealed?

Then you are already dead!

This brings us to a second point about the realisation that you will die: it can help you to enjoy more of this amazing life whilst you are here. Believe me when I tell you that even those highly evolved humans, who would appear as gods to us, sometimes miss this beautiful Earth and the basic and yet marvellous senses we possess to experience it by. So, do not throw this one and only chance at life on Earth away so discourteously. Everything I have listed above is free. Free to all. For every one of us here the sky is always above our head, the earth below our feet. Your heart still beats, and your soul shines its vigour into this world and other worlds. Your death will put an end to all this.

Understand this above all things: as you are now you will die. However, until the very point of death, until the time after your final breath, you are magnificently, marvellously and miraculously alive.

This is the absolute truth about the way it is.

Lies

As you will already have suspected, this book is not full of fantasy and imagination. In actuality the reality of real life is more fantastic than you can imagine. But, to realise this, you must address your attention to the lies that you live your life by.

When you were young, your parents or guardians told you the story of Santa Claus. This benevolent, cheery, laughing old man would give you what you wanted provided, of course, you were a good little child and followed the rules. That is always a stipulation, have you noticed? Can you remember the excitement and thrill of it all? If you cannot, watch the child you are telling the lie to now. And watch their face when they find out for the first time, as you did, that their parents lied to them. That young boy or girl knowing no better was lied to by everyone; nobody told them the truth. Until that is, as was probably the case with yourself, their intelligence got the better of the lies. There were flaws in the story; it couldn't possibly be true. Perhaps someone let the truth out accidentally or as a deliberate act. And, as a consequence, they grew a little. They were no longer the same little child; they had begun to mature.

So, why have many of you stopped growing in your understanding and knowledge of life?

Why are you content to sit back and perpetuate the comfortable myths that you have run your life by for so long; you know the ones, those only really suitable for children.

Oh, I'm sure you think that the Santa Claus lie is unimportant. Have you ever really distanced yourself from Christmas and watched it? It can be a very uncomfortable experience. But true, I'm using it as an example of a larger lie. A consensus lie. It really is time for you to grow up.

Some of you are taking comfort at this moment from the ideas, beliefs and excuses of larger or smaller scale religions. They are fed to you by people who should know better but don't. Do not misunderstand me. It's not the origin that is at fault. All religions, no matter how far they have come from the truth these days, had their origin in pure and crystal clear water. But it is extremely difficult to separate the sediment from the purity. Trying to look into the past through the lenses of bigotry, self-aggrandisement, ego fulfilment, wishes, politics, social control and plain misunderstandings that contaminate all that people take as verbatim these days is profoundly difficult. The easiest and most rewarding way to reveal the true knowledge at the core of these teachings is by viewing the examples and writings of others as parables; thought provokers; encouragement to seek out the truth for oneself. It doesn't deny that they may have happened, but here and now it is best to seek out the truth behind the words. Search out, for yourself, the knowledge and wisdom that are there; but do not view your results with the same attitude that you had to the Santa Claus myth: as a means of wish fulfilment. View it in the cold light of day; as an adult.

Use this as a guide:

Anything written or told to you which limits your expression as a self-actualised human being is not for human consumption. It is distorted and contaminated. And certainly when what you believe/believed no longer feeds your heart and soul then it is time to move on.

As an adult it is absurd to believe in Santa Claus. Why is it so long since you altered, changed, distilled and purified the philosophy and understanding of life that you have? It really is just a dead weight hanging around your neck, tethering you erroneously to a past which is just that: the past. But the fact is that you can only live now, here, at this moment. As you advance, so too must your philosophy of life; and vice versa.

Imagine that you were suddenly transported to a place and time where no one knew you. No history, no beliefs, no dogma; where

160

you could reinvent yourself without fear of retribution (that last point is important, read it again and again until it sinks in). You could express yourself as you really are without the constraints of a past; and the rules would be your own, not the society's you live in. How would you act and appear? How would you really want to manifest your true self?

If it is different than you are now, then you have some work to do.

Inside, you already know this. You have been putting it off; or you have just begun and that's why you are reading these words.

Do not be daunted, it is the same for everyone. Be enthused and a little apprehensive; but you must press on: it is the only way. Remember death breathing down your neck? Do you want to die an ignorant man or woman who no one really knew, because you never showed your true unique self to them? Let me point out again that you do not have all the time in the world; just this one short life. Discover and eradicate the lies. They are the equivalent of a too short string which tethers your kite close to the ground. Do you want to fly free and discover what the view is really like for yourself? There is no excuse that justifies your reluctance to change and grow and to discover the lies that have been told to you by other adults who should know better.

An adult who still believes in Santa Clause is an absurdity.

God

I am sure that you already knew I would have something to say on the subject of the Divine. But it isn't an easy subject to approach because people have such entrenched attitudes about God. Perhaps you have. I suggest that it will help if you first start to call whatever it is that created the universe by a different name. Oh, you will find many of them. This will enable some new feelings and thoughts to arise about the subject. Look at different faiths, beliefs and insights about the subject; learn what they have to say about the all that is. Ask questions, investigate.

Then:

THROW IT ALL AWAY!

Do you really think in your wildest dreams that that which created the whole universe, and because of that creation facilitated the growth of every creature, plant and animal, however small, however large, however intelligent; all that exists in this dimension and any others, could possibly be known and understood by you or any human being. I think that if you say yes then not only are you arrogant beyond all measure; not only deluded and egoistic; but most of all you are wrong.

It is impossible as a human on the Earth to understand and know the Creator.

Think about it, just for a minute, and you must realise it to be true.

We are but one aspect, as important as we may feel we are—and I'm sure we are—of the whole of creation.

I think that whatever the Creator is, it would appear so amazingly different to our expectations and understandings that we would probably disintegrate into confusion and shock; or else be reduced to a blubbering wreck at the staggering strangeness of its nature.

Here is another point that you might like to consider and may also surprise you: it is not at all necessary for your personal evolution or your life that you understand the Creator. That is not what you are here on Earth for. It will not enable your development during your life on this planet one iota. It really isn't important. I realise that this will not stop you from wondering and speculating. That is fine. That is in the nature of a human being. You can formulate ideas and practices of all kinds, but you will never know what it is; why it is; how it acts; while you are here on Earth. You don't need to.

Your task on Earth is to manifest your true nature to the best of your ability.

It is all about here, not there. Understandings about the Creator come later. But you will not get that chance if you do not try your utmost to manifest your Creator given uniqueness.

So many people try to run before they can walk. They spend endless years of their life seeking the unknowable, with their consciousness permanently in the clouds. And too late they realise that their one and only chance at life has passed them by; that they never really walked the Earth as they could have done. The majority of your time on this planet should be spent here in your body—not out of it: there is plenty of time to investigate these other planes later. What about the wonderful experiences and the very earthly pleasures available to you now? Please do not miss out on them; you will not be coming here again.

It is almost a necessity that we have this blockage in our understanding. It maintains the impetus for the adventure and is fuel and incentive for the journey. If everyone were able to know the Creator then all spiritual searching would cease. The driving force of many humans, a wish to know and understand this life and the universe we live in, would disappear. Maybe the purpose of being alive would cease. What would be the point of carrying on, for I'm sure that some or most of the true nature of God would be so very different to what we think it should be that there would certainly be some element of disappointment and disillusionment?

Suppose you did know, or suppose there was anyone on the Earth who really knew the force which shapes and creates out of the void—spirit, the very substance of the universe—all its countless forms. Yes suppose it was you who knew. How much incentive would there be for you to carry on this human life; to love; have sex; experience; to get angry and be passionate; to laugh and cry; to care and despise; to enjoy, challenge and flee; to actually love your life and aliveness?

None.

I feel that the single act of what we could call love, by the Creator, is to give us life. It gave you just one chance: a unique, never again to be repeated, amazing, challenging chance at life. The possibility of immortality. A one time offer.

Sure, it is fine and good to acknowledge thanks for your life, but don't be under any illusions that the praise and thanks you give is for anyone else's benefit but your own. Whatever it is, it really doesn't need the praise and thanks of its creations. You are thinking in human terms, and even a human can shrug off the praise of others, not allowing it to inflate the ego or sway a course of action.

You see, everyone makes assumptions that God is human. Why? There are far more insects on the Earth than humans, and we certainly can't eradicate them. Isn't God more likely to be an insect; or perhaps this entity is rock or plant like? Do not attribute human qualities to God. It is humans who have human qualities. And that in itself is beautiful enough. If you must have a concept of God, make it non-human and vague in form, something different to what you would expect. That must be much closer to the truth.

Today, as always, we have numerous people who claim to speak for, or are the embodiments of, some God or other; the Divine, the Creator, Brahmin, Dao, the All that is, the Great Spirit.

No one speaks for God. Certainly not me. It speaks for itself!

But, you will be pleased to learn, each one of you actually has a pure and clear aspect of yourself that resulted from the direct action of the Divine. It's as if a gift was made; a piece of the Divine was given in shape and impulse to each of us at birth. It is your soul body—your body of life energy—that is the essential, true, undistorted and uninhibited origin of your identity. It is connected to the Creator through a gateway which is above your head, through which the Creator maintains your life and livingness with its dispassionate input for as long as you are alive. Imagine we were each given our own personal lover, caretaker, wise person, guardian, adviser, coach and enthusiastic supporter when we were born.

**It is this which loves you more than anything
else in the whole universe.**

To some extent, if you are journeying or have attained some insight, it actually is you: your essence. It is impossible for another human to love you more. At your core you are it, it is you. It is that to which you should constantly refer. It is a measure of your integrity, your evolution, your congruency: it is you in a perfected form. It contains all your seed potentials, the paths through which you can best manifest your true nature.

**Remember that your soul loves you more than anything
else in the universe: its whole nature is love. All the
love you will ever need is already manifest in your
soul's love for you. Try never to forget this.**

When you listen to people who talk of having a revelation from, or an experience, of God; when they state emphatically that they speak for it; that they have been transformed by 'God's will,' then I think they are misinterpreting an experience of—and generated by—their own soul: that which loves them beyond anything they can imagine. The reason it seemed like a revelation or direct communication is because they were so cut off from their soul in the first place; perhaps because their gateways of transmission were obstructed. Many are. It is in the nature of a human life that we often have to leave before we can return, and it is very likely that some of

166

your gateways may not be functioning at their best. Unfortunately the vast majority of humans lose or forget the return address, some travel further away than others. Many cannot even remember the house in which they were born. But there are a few who unravel a string during their life and however taught or tangled it becomes are still connected to their soul. For others it is just a case of tracing their journey back to where they lost touch with the thread and making the required alterations to one's attitude and one's life. Sounds easy, doesn't it.

Your soul is the essence of you. It is your body of life energy. It communicates via feeling—not emotion! Each living thing has a soul. Each living thing is connected to, created by, and perpetuated during this life by something that we cannot know: yet. Concentrate, therefore, on your life.

And, for the moment, a final important point:

Your soul is not a saintly, devout, puritanical, sickeningly sweet natured creation. It is a vibrant, extravagant, enthusiastic, exciting, sexual, loving, scintillating, passionate force. It is you in essence.

Read this then close your eyes again:

Throw away the dogma. Throw away your preconceived ideas about God. Destroy all that doesn't encourage your self expression; anything that represses your true nature. Let in the words about your soul above; that is what you should be concentrating on; not discovering facts and thoughts about that which is undiscoverable to you here. Then feel how you feel. You cannot possible disagree with my description of your soul. Your essence. You.

Let in the light. Let in life!

Change

Change is frightening isn't it? I mention this now because it will be absolutely necessary for you to change certain thoughts about yourself and the world around you if you are to grow: for life itself is movement. Remember the example I gave you earlier: suppose there was no one else to care about; no retribution, no guilt; no history; imagine being in a different place of your choice, knowing only those people, if any, you wish to know. Would you be different than you are now? Of course you would, you know there would be differences, even if they were only small ones: no one is perfected.

Now, as something to aim for, begin to see how you would like that real you to be, not as a fantasy or a dream, but as something truly attainable.

You are not stuck with being who you are now. You can definitely and absolutely change.

Why is it that we all cling to that which is well past its sell by date? Do you know? Is it fear? Fear of change; fear of the unknown; fear of having made a decision that is irreversible? Let me tell you something: the only fact that is sure about change is that there will always be change as long as you are alive. Once a decision is made, you can be sure that it will be inevitable that you have to make others. So, if you really do not want to learn to deal with change then stay where you are now. Vegetate. Rot. Try desperately to cling to the past even though it is impermanent, ethereal, and no longer serves your growth.

However, there is an attitude that can ease the specific fear associated with change. Begin to look on your life as an adventure; as fun; wondering what is around the next corner at the same time as enjoying the challenge of the present. Go out bravely to meet your future. Yes I know it is frightening; I realise it is scary, but counteract those reactions with the more frightening and absolutely certain prospect of your death. Let it breathe down your neck and its icy touch shiver your spine.

You haven't all the time in the world to make the changes you wish to make. You need to begin to manifest the life, love, and happiness you really want now. The journey of a thousand miles really does begin with one foot in front of the other.

At the beginning, the changes do not have to be drastic. Start to toy with different ideas; allow some new information and thoughts to play around in that dusty room you call your mind. Pretend for an hour, a day, a week, that you have different beliefs than you do already. If your original beliefs were correct in all ways then they will be waiting for you, completely intact, after your sojourn into change.

All great truths can withstand the challenging onslaught of change.

Look for the habits in your life and deliberately change them. Look on it as a game. Get up earlier or later; skip a meal; throw out the studying for a few days. Change your habitual place at the dining table. Laze about if it's not usual for you or, if it is, design a rigid regime that you have to stick to. Go out for a walk; go to the library, or perhaps visit a few book shops. Investigate a new hobby, or something you've always wanted to do or know more about. Alter your daily habits around. Move the furniture into new positions. Use your body in a different way. Try being opposite handed for a day. Just begin to be a little more flexible. You will be pleasantly surprised at what an effect such simple actions can have. As you can see, change can be applied to the physical body and life as well as the mental. The two are interrelated. However, change in the mental world is often the most relevant to your purpose: growth.

Change is one of those peculiar subjects that nearly always arouses fear; yet in all honesty, if you look at your life so far, how many changes have there been which didn't at least result in new adventures, growth and maturity; insight; new lessons; new knowledge and even wisdom? I would be very surprised if there were many at all and, if there were, then you haven't used them as you should have: not as someone on a path of personal evolution would.

Begin to extract truth from the beliefs and notions you have at this time, and move on. As human beings we have an almost infinite capacity to learn throughout our existence. In fact life itself is learning.

There is always something more to learn about yourself and about the worlds in which we live.

So, although the thought of leaving a way of life or system of belief can prove to be traumatic, do not cling to it one second longer then it serves you, otherwise you become stunted. You are no better than an antique and, as such, will only be valued for your age. More to the point, you are wasting your time on this Earth. Yes I know we resent having to leave behind something that we have invested so much time and perhaps money in. But don't you see that it brought you to this exact point in your life. It was the surf board that carried you to the next beach. So thank it and wave goodbye because, although it was essential to your growth so far, it no longer serves you. We would look stupid as adults wearing the same clothes that we wore as children. They simply would not fit us!

The refreshment and revitalisation of yourself comes through bathing in clear, pure, water, not the stagnant pond at the bottom of the garden.

What are you bathing in at the moment? Does it activate, challenge, and enliven you; does it bring out more of the true you into the world? Or, does it weaken you; dull your light; deny your experience and the life you see around you? Are you a greater human being because of it; not in the eyes of any other human, or God—this is not about their approval or disapproval—but by the standards of your true nature. The real you.

171

Exactly how do you feel about yourself and your life?

You see, ultimately, it is only to your own self that you have to answer. No one else judges you, not in reality. How satisfied you are that you have lived and manifested your uniqueness? It is no good lying on your death bed—if you are lucky enough to have that luxury—and saying to yourself "at least I lived the life others wanted me to live; at least I didn't rock the boat." Does that sound satisfying to you? To me it sounds like a terrible waste of a "one time offer."

How much better to have the satisfaction of looking back and saying to yourself "Wow—what an adventure, I never could have planned that life. I lived my life; a life infused by my uniqueness. I shone into the world radiantly and brightly as myself and I am proud."

Each choice we make that is in accord with our true nature, no matter how small that choice is—cements our integrity, manifests in minute ways our original identity and its uniqueness. That's what it's all about. Life is about the manifestation of your own uniqueness in this world.

Of course, you have the choice not to do this; you don't have to take notice of anything you are told. That is how free you really are.

All life is movement on one scale or another. Do you really think that you are the one and only example in the universe of an unchanging being; the exception that proves the rule? Interestingly, it saps quite a lot of your vitality trying to maintain such a state of dormancy. That is why some of the old—and sometimes the not so old—are so tired and downtrodden. Energy and vitality can only flow where there is movement. So move!

Now, are you tempted to change just a little?

Indulgence

Indulgence pervades our lives. You would think it an unavoidable facet of the human condition for rarely do we see another animal indulging. So what do I mean by indulgence?

I am talking about a particular type of behaviour which saps your energy—your consciousness—your vitality; it uses up valuable life time, and discourages the manifestation of your soul nature.

This is a difficult lesson to absorb and put into practice because there is so much to let go of, and by its very nature we are reluctant to set it free. Indulgence will also present itself to you in many more subtle forms when you think you have left it way behind at the beginning of your evolution. Be on guard! It feeds off us and we feed off it. We are comforted by its familiarity; it is rather like an old friend that has been around for years: ever prepared to listen to our troubles, the tragic life we've led, the broken promises and expectations, but never suggests new modes of action and thinking because it doesn't want you to change. If you did, it could no longer exist. You keep it alive; you resuscitate it and, in return, it presents you with innumerable excuses not to change and manifest the beingness you want. In reality it is a dead thing and you are not: you are alive. Still, after this sometimes symbiotic—sometimes predatory – relationship, it hurts to say goodbye.

However, it isn't quite the same as a reluctant goodbye. In fact the best and most effective way to bid indulgences farewell is to get quite fed up with their presence. Become sick and tired—if you are not already—with their continued drain on you; the time they consume; the restrictions they impose; and their selfishness. After all, you are the most important part of the relationship, aren't you?

You, with a limited time on Earth, are being limited even more in your behaviour and your experience of life by this ugly monster which, ironically, you created yourself.

It always seemed so nice and comforting at the time: rather like a fictional animal that looked so cute when young but just consumed more and more food until it overshadowed your life. The sun no longer shines on you. How dare it restrict and limit your experience of life. How dare it surreptitiously lead you into a state of stagnation, hiding in the shadows, so that your growth has come to a grinding halt. How ever did you let that beautiful, bright sparkle that was you when you were born turn into this self-indulgent dullard who lets life pass by because:

'I can't get over him/her'
'I haven't got the strength'
'That's the way I am'
'You hurt me like that?'
'Poor me'
'My life has been so hard'
'No one has suffered like I have'
'I shall never get over it'
'I can't possibly forget'

Need I go on?

Yes, I absolutely acknowledge that we do need time to deal with certain shocks, situations, emotional crises and changes, but we must not hold on to them one minute more than we need to. Allow yourself to mourn fully; cry, get angry; stuff yourself with chocolate; get drunk (in private!); feel so sorry for yourself that you know you'll never recover. It is all quite natural and very human which is, remember, what you are. It is good to rail against fate sometimes. Assert your authority and uniqueness, the essence of you; remind the universe that you exist. Go into a private room and swear at fate, people, God and the universe; shout and hate it all. How dare they treat you like this. Repossess your power as a unique individual. Get rid of it all. Only in movement can there be cleansing.

174

Not until you have really expressed how you actually feel—not how you should feel, or are told to feel—how really upset you are, will you be able to let go of the crisis. And that is the only way to stop the crisis mutating into an indulgence. Some people would call the above techniques an indulgence. They are wrong, you are simply being human.

Why do you feel guilty about expressing how you actually feel?

Don't kill your passion. Allow yourself to be flesh and bones for a while instead of that oh so spiritual figure who is unmoved by anything in this world. You have no one else's ideals to live up to; or have you still not travelled to that paradise island where you can be your true self?

Usually, if you hold on to an incident, then there is something left unsaid, something left undone; some feeling of injustice; or perhaps restitution is required. Very often though, it is impossible to be recompensed for such incidents and you may well feel stuck and impotent. However, since this involves the mental world, there is a method for dealing with these situations. Relax deeply (there are many books that can instruct you if do not know how to do this) and re-create the incident, rather like a dream or fantasy, either by being there or watching it from a distance, but deliberately alter the end result in to as many new, different, funny, magical, self-affirming outcomes as possible. See yourself as powerful, and change the situation into one that is much more satisfying for you. Alter it; play with it until you feel good. Apologise; act kindly but firmly. Even wave goodbye with a tear in your eye. Now come back to reality. Surprisingly, something as simple as this can often have powerful results. Even if, in the physical world, things may not seem to have changed, how you remember them (the mental world) has. Do remember, however, that the physical world is far more awesome and mysterious than you can imagine and you may be in for some pleasant surprises. This is not wish fulfilment; nor is it done in an effort to bring an imagined set of circumstances about. It is simply done to review, alter and change a particular crisis in order to release you in the present from the grabbing claws extending from the past. Do you really think that your subconscious mind will worry about these new possibilities? The indulgence's parasitic tendencies will have been loosened. Later on, in the chapter on difficulties, you will find a few more techniques that will prove equally as useful.

One more important point must be mentioned:

Do not blame any one person for the way you behave.

It is fine in the privacy of your own room to criticise and berate anyone and everyone, but I am afraid you must start to take responsibility for the way you respond to events. Self-responsibility is almost the antithesis of indulgence: it disperses, nullifies and neutralises its power. Do not blame another for how you are feeling; acknowledge that it is you who are responsible. Own your power. Unless you are totally disabled physically and mentally, so much so that you could not read this, there is no excuse.

It has become fashionable for everyone to see the way they behave as an inescapable result of what happened to them in their early years. Parents, school friends, relations, society, are all at fault—of course they are, they are human! I absolutely acknowledge that some people have suffered lives which are terrible, painful, heart rending, dreadfully upsetting and not in any way deserved; to have survived at all shows real courage and the true strength of the human spirit; but when it comes down to it we are talking about the past, it is done; you have the rest of your life to live, with all its amazing possibilities.

The past only exists as a memory.

Your body cells replace themselves continually. Each minute you take in a new breath. You feed the past by constantly referring back to it. It devours your time and attention from the world; the mysterious, awesome Earth on which you live. So, use the resentments, hurts and resulting indulgences as fuel: burn them up in your fired determination to live the rest of your life as you want to, despite what happened to you, not because of it. For goodness sake deal with it then let it go.

To facilitate the letting go process, when you are truly ready to let loose the memory or events that inspired the indulgence, hold a ceremony just for yourself. Perform an event to signify in physical form the end of your indulgence and the severing of your connections to it. It may involve nothing more complex than writing the story of how you were hurt on a piece of paper and burning it, or burning a symbol that represents the event, indulgence or injustice. Then again you may put aside a day to celebrate the rebirth of yourself: a liberation from the past and the beginning of new growth. Rather as if you were pruning an old rose bush to encourage new and vigorous blossom. Breathe a sigh of relief and move forward. Remember from this point on that you really do have a choice about whether you indulge that incident or not.

You have a choice.

We are never too old to stop indulgence. Everyone does it, sometimes in many new and subtle ways. The most important skill is being able to recognise it as such. Again, do not stop this energy-sapping habit because there is retribution awaiting you if you don't; stop because you are heartily sick and tired of being the same old you: you are fed up of denying yourself that inspiring release of energy and, as a consequence, new experiences.

You have a finite number of years left on this Earth and you want to spend them enjoying and vigorously affirming your individuality in this world.

Life really is too short for you to wallow in the mud of self-indulgence. It will cling and weigh you down. It will dry and crack so that you cannot see your original features.

The major benefit you will receive from releasing indulgence is that you will always feel lighter, as if a burden has been lifted. A leak in your energy reserves has been mended. It is not hard or cruel to treat yourself so, but life saving, life enhancing; even a little frightening, because you can be sure that something new will be waiting to enter your life. It is time to burn the letters, sell the associations, or give them away. It is time to say yes, or no. Let go. Let the kite break away from the string tethering it to the ground. Spring clean at any time of the year. Decorate, move, go out, stay in;

177

create change. Change your indulgent behaviour into life enhancing freshness. Open the windows and let the wind blow away the cobwebs and the dust. Don't waste your life. The rest of life will move on whether you like it or not; are you content to hide away in a side stream? A place without movement; a place of stagnation.

Remember: all life is movement.

Movement to stillness, and back again. It is never just one or the other. If nature cannot manage it, then you certainly cannot.

So, from now on, begin to identify when you think "poor me." When "it's just my nature," when an excuse is just that. Do not let yourself be so easily swayed by others, or by the life around you. Don't wait for that telephone call forever. Turn the telephone off, or ring up yourself. Get a result either way, then you can get on with your life.

I cannot emphasise enough how important these realisations are for the present and future enjoyment of your life. More to the point, your spiritual development cannot move forward until this matter is dealt with.

With indulgence the lines on your face, the stoop of your gait, the tiredness in your voice, become more and more exaggerated each day. Rid yourself of your own indulgences to the best of your ability and you will immediately feel enlivened and vigorous, renewed and hopeful.

Of course, as is always the case with everything that I tell you, please be kind to yourself. Do this as an act of love and respect for, and to, yourself. And, as long as you know you're doing it, it is fine to indulge yourself a little. Time yourself for fifteen minutes during which you will not think of anything else but indulging in your habit of thought exclusively. I would be surprised if you can do it at all without thinking of at least one other thing in the process.

So, what is it to be; an ever increasing cloud of denial and self-mortification, or life? The choice is yours.

Read this chapter again and again until you recognise your own pitfalls. We all have indulgences; I know I have.

The first and most important fact is to recognise them as such.

Don't allow them to take the sparkle out of your life!

Responsibility

As you have probably gathered by now, many of the thoughts, ideas, and actions I put before you lead to personal responsibility for yourself; for your life, your thoughts, even, to a certain extent, your circumstances. Taking back unto yourself the responsibility for how your life is lived is a great boon to your immortalisation; it is indispensable. Your life was given over to you for your care. If you so choose, you can give it away; you can be thrown hither and thither by the currents and eddies of the raging river that is the water of life; or you can learn to navigate that river, to put in at a safe harbour occasionally and then to travel again, safe in the knowledge that you are acquiring skills to better and better ensure your passage.

It is only when we begin to recognise the pre-eminent part we play in our own lives that true change and our true manifestation can begin to express themselves in our world.

From what I have written in the previous chapter you can see how much indulgence has to do with responsibility. Blaming another for making you feel this way or that is indulgence: you give away your power to another. Self-responsibility on the other hand will lead you to ask "Why did I behave in the way I did?" or to say "If I want to, I don't have to act in such a way," likewise "I'm not going to let such an event/comment/action ruin my life." It is hard to break the habit of indulgence and learn self-responsibility, but, rather like an exercise regime, a little resistance at a time will enable you to ultimately manifest your true nature in the world—which, after all, is the whole point of your life.

Start to take responsibility for the way you live your life: realise that you have a choice whether to act in such and such a way;

and please try your best not to use the scapegoat excuse, "that's the way I am." Instead, try saying "that is the way I choose to be." See how different you feel when you start to use that phrase. The choice, as always, is yours.

It is important to notice and mentally, so much that self-responsibility does not mean self-blame; blame is not part of the equation.

It is highly likely that your behaviour up to this point has been defensive and self-protecting; you tried to the best of your ability to keep yourself intact, surviving and functioning. Something similar to the idea of "loving your disease because it's keeping you healthy." There is certainly a truth in this. It may be that you have been, by physical or mental means, protecting the delicate inside of yourself, because in reality you hadn't any true sense of what that delicate inside was really about; it's just that you knew it had to be defended and you didn't know any other way. Your error arose because you were identifying with the image in a mirror—your ego—and not with the true nature of yourself—your soul. Rather as if you had entered a hall of mirrors and believed that the image you saw was the real you, and defended it against what you actually looked like. No wonder you couldn't find clothes to fit you!

So, this approach is fine up to a point. But you have now reached that point. At a certain stage in your development—and I assume you are at that stage or you would not be reading a book like this—you have a choice. You can behave as an ordinary human being—full of the petty intrigues, indulgences and cynicism that are common to the majority—or you can choose not to act without a second thought: you will choose to look, no matter how reluctantly, at your own behaviour and wonder why it is that you act in a certain way. Why do you always do that? How come you are always riled by a certain person? Why do you accept their word for it when you feel that they are wrong? More importantly, why are you the way you are; why have you put up with behaving in a certain way for so long? I could go on and on with examples.

The importance of these words is in the fact that you have now read them! No longer can you plead ignorance.

Yes, you can carry on as you have always done, but you cannot deny that you now know a different way of acting.

Choose to stop indulging in behaviour that belittles the word 'human.' Grow up; be an adult amongst the children; not in the generally accepted way that 'adult behaviour' is classified—boring, staid; humourless, cold-hearted, couldn't care less, prejudiced, dogmatic, unmoving, know it all, fatalistic, rigid—but in a much more simple way: taking responsibility for the way you behave and for the beliefs and opinions you hold and express.

Nobody makes you feel the way you do; you are simply responding in a predictable way.

Now you have the choice to learn new responses, to break out of the mould that society has made for you. You can behave in a way that would not be usual for you if you want to. You have to take responsibility.

Do you know what the immediate benefit of taking responsibility is? Power. Power for yourself, not power over others. Now you are not the victim of the forces around you, but the navigator of your life. You have power over your behaviour; how you act, how you express. But I don't mean you need to censure your life. I mean that you begin to act in a conscious and aware state. No longer do you act in habitual and destructive ways. Indeed you may be in the surprising position of not knowing how to act in a given, often previously experienced, situation. There is a stoppage in the usual sequence of events; it is the no man's land at the middle of a crossroads where, for a short time, you are unsure. Let me assure you that this is one of the most important places for you to be in life, for only in this unsure place can the possibilities of new growth and new direction manifest themselves. You are beginning to own—to take back into your ownership—the life that you were given, where, of course, it should always have been. And the more responsibility you have for yourself, the more life itself will begin to show a new face to you.

So, have you expressed yourself today in a way that was below you; where you acted unconsciously?

Would you be shocked to be told how many actions of yours were not in accord with your true nature; indeed how many of them were self indulgent, childish and lacking personal responsibility. Have you blamed another for how you are feeling today?

Self-responsibility is a major key to the manifestation of your core nature: that which is truly you; something that is absolutely essential if you are to become immortal.

Beliefs

As a metaphor, let us imagine the idea that a child who is born into this world has little if any knowledge and personal beliefs, and is rather like an unprogrammed computer. As it grows—and for the vast majority of its early life—the child begins to programme its brain with numerous ideas, thoughts and experiences. But, if we choose to look closely, it is obvious that the vast majority of this child's ideas, thoughts, justifications and beliefs are programmed not by itself—as a result of its own experience—but by parents or guardians, siblings, peer groups, society, religions and the media. They are not the direct result of insight and reasoned and informed thought, but are given as a whole to be accepted rather than tested—a basic set of assumptions about which there is to be no debate. Yes, the child will learn much that is useful about how to function in our society, but its deepest thoughts and wonderings will go unanswered for the simple reason that most human beings have never sought any kind of justification, or clarification, for the very beliefs which they then pass on to others!

Now, think about how many of you reading this book still contain the programming given to you by everything out there, and how little there is about you that actually arose from within yourself; your own discoveries about the magnificent universe we inhabit.

It can be quite a shock to acknowledge how many of the basic assumptions and suppositions that our society runs on—commonly accepted 'wisdom'—are actually founded on nothing other than programming, prejudice and ignorance.

At a certain age, and it may well be different for different people, an important process needs to begin. Each one of those

185

programmed microchips has to be extracted and examined. It has to be minutely investigated to ascertain not only its true validity but also its relevance to the life you are living now. This introspection is a kind of meditation: taking a subject, looking at it from different angles—the objective and subjective examination of all you believe, all that you know—and the replacing of it back into your beingness. Sometimes it is simply polished, sometimes replaced and other times it is transformed into something totally new to you. And of course, there are some thoughts and beliefs that you will discard for ever. Without this process taking place, a man or woman will be unlikely to be able to manifest a good deal of happiness and excitement in this life, and may well endure the second half of their lives with that dull sense of 'coping,' or never really being happy; of looking back at 'all the good times' and not truly enjoying the present moment.

This re-examination of beliefs and attitudes is a constant and evolving process; a continuous refinement of yourself in the light of new knowledge and experience.

And, as a result, an interesting metamorphosis takes place. The constant testing of beliefs against the realities in which we live results in their transformation into knowledge. For, what are beliefs—nothing but subjects and opinions about something we do not yet have sufficient knowledge about. Beliefs are strongly held opinions or thought-acts of faith: that about which we have an opinion or want to believe is truth. They are not knowledge. Beliefs are an easy way out for those who are not prepared to test their opinions against the life we live and see, and the worlds which we inhabit.

It's as if a person viewed the realities around them through various filters which are attached to their senses saying "I believe everything is dark," or "I believe the world is pink," when what they should be asking is "is the world black; why do I see it this way; how do other people see it; it was such and such who told me it is so, are they right?"

All ancient systems of knowledge were directed towards the testing of what is experienced against what is believed—a true clash of the Titans.

Each and every day, people are expressing opinions and beliefs that clearly do not stand up to even the most cursory examination or challenge.

They resort to bigotry and "because I say so" opinions. I do not want to know what you believe, I want to know what you have found out about the world we live in; not second-hand experience, but real, first-hand knowledge. That is the only valid and useful guide to another's world and thence towards a truer understanding of the world we all live in.

You need to ask yourself this question about your beliefs: are they what you have knowledge and experience about, or are you simply reiterating the words of another? Are they a repeating sequence of words and sentences that have travelled through time and contaminated every individual that heard them, or have you found them to be true when applied to real life?

So, let the words you speak, the opinions you hold, and the life you lead be an expression of your own true knowledge, not the old decaying, rotting beliefs of others. Always, always, always test and investigate!

The Mental World

The last few chapters have been referring to your mental world.

The mental world, and the part of it you inhabit, is infinitely variable: it can accommodate practically every type of truth, every fiction, every delusion, no matter how outrageous or ridiculous it is. Just look at the humans around you for proof! It is fundamentally without form, and can therefore be shaped into no end of convoluted and distorted thinking patterns. It is deceptive without the deception being intentional. Because there are no right or wrongs there, deception, like everything else, is within its nature.

It is changed by our thinking; it is under our control. So what do we choose to do with it?

We shape it into a lie. A fiction. Because it's easier that way.

Instead of people's lives being based in the physical body and physical world, they live in a mental world of their own making. Yet it isn't one that is even constructed thoughtfully: it is a minefield of booby traps, false doors and phantasmagorical images, which in reality have no real substance; and still they choose to live there. The world becomes like some weird fair ground attraction, or a maze of mirrors which looks enticing from the outside but proves to be more and more nightmarish inside. And, like a fish caught in a net throwing itself around helplessly, there seems to be no way out of this confusing construction. Such people end up inhabiting a fictional, incongruous, deceptive, self-made mental world. They even see, hear, touch, smell, taste and think through the very filters of that false made world.

The difference between such a mental world and actual reality is similar to the difference between being told what an orgasm is and actually experiencing a full orgasm. The difference is really that dramatic.

The whole of western society is based on the mental world; it is a mental creation. That is why most people are so enamoured of it, and yet so unhappy. It appeals to the imagining mind, the desires and the ego; it is easy to imagine a picture of ourselves in rich and comfortable surroundings. We can imagine the emotions—mental world—that would be concurrent with such a scenario; however, in the mental world we cannot imagine the feelings—soul world—associated with such a vision: for those we have to inhabit the physical body. Are you now beginning to realise the difference between feelings and emotions?

It is usual for the emotions of the mental world to overshadow the feelings of your soul.

Part of the reason for this is that sometimes soul consciousness and its movement can be very subtle. But the main reason is that we do not inhabit the middle ground—the body—but are lop-sided; trying to view one side of a mountain from its opposite side. True perception can only arise when we stand on top of the mountain—the physical body—enabling us to see both sides clearly. The mountain and all you can see is the whole of you: both sides, together with the substance of the mountain, are you. Everything is taking place in one whole space—that which you occupy now—not far away, or left and right, up or down.

Where you now sit or stand is the exact place that your three bodies occupy. But you have to occupy the middle ground, the physical body, to become aware of this fact.

From what I have said you may think that I hate the mental world, but actually you would be totally wrong. It is a most incredible and fascinating realm which we need to master to the best of our ability.

190

The real purpose of the mental realm is to aid you in manifesting, in the physical world, the impulses from—and the radiation of—your soul.

Your three bodies need to act as one, but it is very rare for this to be the case. Instead, we find ourselves acting in ways which a few minutes, hours, days, weeks or even years later lead us to exclaim "whatever was I thinking of, how could I have done that?" It is altogether shocking and alarming to realise how out of control and easily manipulated we all are, and the very simple explanation for this is that we are living in the mental realm; in our own fictional universe. For, in our own mental world, we can justify any act, see ourselves in anything but the real light; we can easily alter and change not only our perception of events but the events themselves. In the mental realm, literally anything can be true. It really isn't surprising that the computer has taken such a hold on humanity at the moment. It swallows the attention of the mind—which is where most people live—instead of letting our consciousness wander around the physical and soul realms for a while.

Now do you understand how it is that so many different versions of 'the truth' are in existence? How easy it is to fit, distort, and stretch an experience into the existing mental world you already have, rather than deconstruct and build a new, more suitable, version of reality. This is why so many teachings are garbled and ultimately made useless. Their original purity is sullied by thought forms that we dare not let go of, because pulling down the scaffolding—or even digging out the foundations—around which we have woven countless thought forms to support our version of reality, necessarily means deconstructing or reconstructing those very thought forms at the same time. The skeleton of our mental body may need to be changed and, because we identify our true self with this supporting structure, it can feel as if we are being destroyed in the process. However, the fact is that what we identified with in the first place was incorrect, and this error can only be corrected by our own selves. It is what we have chosen to base our identity on that is ultimately at fault. In essence, this book is about where to place your identity in order to be true to your human life.

This is a heavy and involving task if you are prone to indulge in misgivings and lack courage. Yet the truth is that it is not that difficult. What usually troubles us is the life-time, perhaps money, and certainly effort, which we have invested in such systems: not their dismantling, but all the activities and emotion surrounding the beliefs that we now find to be erroneous. But you should approach this task in another way: thank those beliefs for bringing you this far safely, steps without which you would not have advanced; they were indispensable at the time, but now hold you back from your rightful future. Is it really so hard to say "that was how I understood it then, but now I have a clearer view and understand it in this way." If it is, then surely your pride is getting in the way of your evolution. And pride is, of course, a mental creation.

You can change your mind and still be very proud of yourself, unless the pride you have in being yourself depends on the approval of others.

The task of how you create your mental world is actually up to you. There is no particular and definite way it has to be constructed. Your mental body, on the other hand, should conform to your actual physical body in size, shape and appearance. How often we see those who haven't any real idea of their actual physical appearance, but have constructed a peculiar image of themselves to fit in with their distorted ideas and beliefs about how their body should appear. In order to construct a true reproduction of your physical self in the mental world it is beneficial to massage, touch, stroke and feel your own body without comment, but in full awareness: a strong awareness of your physical body impacts the mental body and alters it so that it is congruent with how your physical body really is. Rediscover your actual physical body. It may seem like a long lost friend.

Perhaps it will help you to better understand this mental body/world reconstruction if you think of it in the following way. Imagine your mind is like a hedge. In most people it is totally overgrown, out of control, and has no function or shape apart from the fact that it is alive. It is filled with dead wood and litter, old paper bags and rubbish; it is overgrown and dying from the centre for lack of light and care. It obscures the view of the green fields, the sky and sun above. Your task is to clip the hedge, tidy it up and feed it with nourishment; to bring its height down so that you can view your true nature—your soul nature—in all its radiant clearness. You can then mould and shape the hedge to exactly reproduce a mirror image of what you see in front of you. It will then become a resounding echo, a resonance of your soul nature; that which is uniquely and passionately you.

Retribution

Much of the way that humans behave is not driven by their true nature, but by the idea that unless they act in such and such a way they will be punished. Nowhere is this more applicable than in the various religious, quasi-religious and spiritual systems in use today. If you abide by these rules and no others then you are assured of an everlasting life in paradise; you deserve nothing less as a reward.

Wrong!

As an evolving human being you already have within you the perfect guide to how you should behave: it is your body of life energy, your soul. Man-made laws have been so variable during different periods of history and so variable within different religious systems, that they can provide no clear guidance as to how one should really act. And the truth is that they are inextricably linked to ideas about reward and justification: the words of another. Guaranteed life forever if only you stick to the rules that are laid out for you. These could be rules about wealth, or food, perhaps personal and sexual relationships; almost every facet of your life will be addressed. So many curtailments on being human—so much deadness. It's a wonder that any of us feel alive at all.

**The manipulation of the masses in the name of religion is
nothing but the abuse of power. They do not want you
to find out for yourself that you are your own
authority and do not need to refer to them.
It is so obvious, obnoxious and deceitful.
And it is a lie.**

This fact is the one that people find so hard to come to terms with: that they themselves are all powerful and there doesn't need to be an intermediary. To put it another way, you are your own saviour.

True growth and advancement can only come from within.
Only when your opinions or beliefs are tested against the
actual worlds in which you live can they truly be
known and embodied in your life. It is during
this process that you will watch your ideas
about retribution disappear.

What is important here is to begin to differentiate between the so often deceiving mental realm, and the never deceptive soul realm. That is most difficult and requires practice.

It is necessary, if you are going to test the ideas presented here, to rid yourself of the idea of retribution; of guilt. Because it is so ingrained in society that he or she will get their comeuppance—when clearly there are vast numbers of people getting away with murder, literally—this fictional idea that at some other place, at some other time, there will be justice, seems to warrant the insignia of truth. It is a comforter; indeed in some religions it is justification for cruelty, negligence and bigotry.

You must rid yourselves once and for all
of the concept of retribution.

No one is watching you as you steal a five pound note or a million pounds, bully another human being, are cruel to an animal, commit what you know to be a crime against your nature; and besides the victim the only person to suffer will be you—but that is not necessarily because someone else will punish you. By such acts you fundamentally delay your integration and, because you have a finite life, face the very real prospect of the dissolving of everything that is you at your death. Acts such as these can do nothing other than positively block the process of your immortalisation.

Clearly, unless there is something very wrong with us, we know inside when what we have done is against our true nature. I am not referring these comments to the millions of people who are so cut

196

off from their soul body that they couldn't possibly understand what I'm talking about. I am addressing them to you, the reader; the person who is interested in expressing your unique magnificence in this world. You know when it is that you go against your true nature; you know when you separate off the different parts of yourself in order to justify an action: there is a feeling, an uncomfortable feeling that often translates into guilt or self-justification. The excuses come thick and fast. In the quiet of the night you know that what you did or said was wrong, and instead of reinforcing your integrity, you reverse the process: you dis-integrate yourself.

Each time you go against your true nature you block the transmission of soul consciousness through to your physical and mental bodies; you actually delay your integration and the formation of your immortal spirit body.

I repeat again that you must separate off any ideas of what your soul nature is like from standard morality, social mores, religious and spiritual teachings.

Your soul body—the true origin of your identity—is absolutely human. It is a dynamic, vibrant form. It is sexual, it is passionate, it is exciting and enlivening. It is ripe for adventurous undertakings—whether they be physical, mental or spiritual—and it is interested. It is life.

How profitable it is for the religious and political life of a country to deny this truth; to be complicit in limiting your light. You are so easily controlled when the denying of a particular side of your nature results in spiritual retribution.

So, now the question is what do you do if you know you have committed a wrong. The real—true—'sin' as such is the deliberate hurting of another. So apologise! Make restitution. If that is impossible because of time or distance then make a committed statement to the fact that you genuinely apologise for the harm you have caused. Ask to be forgiven by the soul or spirit of the person.

197

Maybe you can give something away; money, or time, to another. Let your apology for causing deliberate or unintentional harm be distinctive and heartfelt. Clear your conscience.

**Understand that a genuine request for forgiveness,
when you are truly sorry, cannot be refused.
It is a fundamental law.**

So even if they are a million miles away it is still effective. But it is just as well to remember that you are making this apology in sight of the gods, and as such it is not a small or insignificant matter. Try your best never to do this again!

Unburdening yourself of guilt is an important step in the process of self-realisation. It is often true that the guilt we carry around with us is phantasmagorical: that in reality it has no substance, and elicits no action from the Creator—none of it does—it is simply time to let it go; let it fly away and dissolve in the sunlit dawn of your evolution.

**An important aspect of being human is to forgive
yourself and others for being human!**

If there are issues to be faced which, whilst being true to your nature, may hurt another, then kindness, consideration, and gentleness are required. Treat them as you would wish to be treated yourself. Take no great joy from disappointing or shocking them. Try your best to act in a way that, even many years later, you will not feel guilty about; realising that although an unpleasant situation had to be faced you did it in the best possible way for both of you.

**Act in a way that you can be proud of: proud of as an
integrated and compassionate very humane human.**

Remember death again. Would you wish to die carrying your guilt or sorrow for hurting another on your back; a combined weight which will only hinder your flight? Deal with it as soon as you feel genuinely able. You can then begin to expand and grow after all those years of inertia. Life is movement. Why would you expect it to be otherwise?

Identity

Who are you?

And don't dare give me your name. What's next: your occupation or employment; your hobbies; your hierarchical position in any of the familial, sexual, financial, religious institutions you are part of? Perhaps you identify with your nationality, your sex or sexuality, your body type or skin colour.

Primarily you are none of these. Your primary identity is obvious: you are human. A human being. You will be so forever. Forever and ever.

Does this come as a disappointment to you; are you downhearted? Please don't be. Your emotions around the issue may arise from the atrocities, the enormous harm, cruelty and thoughtlessness that can be perpetrated by man and woman kind. They are the converse side of the beauty and magnificence that is also human. Love, compassion, wisdom, understanding, bravery, excitement, inquisitiveness, joy, and sexualness are all parts of the human experience. The former are the penalty clause of the, sometimes named, shadow self, which can do nothing but exist. As it is said: the brighter the light, the darker the shadow. In order to progress you must own your shadow self. It is part of you, and only by ignoring it can you do harm to yourself and others. So, own up to what you really are. Own all the parts of yourself that exist. Remember, there is no retribution for admitting that you have certain thoughts or you acted in a certain way; that you imagined or did something that was embarrassing or shaming.

You are human. Forgive yourself.

Your shadow self will always be with you; all you can do is shine the light of knowledge and insight onto it. Never let it get up to anything of its own accord without you being fully aware of what it's trying to hide behind your back. To look bravely into these aspects of yourself is bravery indeed. Truly, bravery is facing your own self and being able to keep your eyes open at the same time: the act of a courageous man or woman. It is the bravery of a real human who wishes to evolve. Accept your beingness. It is part of the human condition that these challenges and confrontations with one's counter nature come about. To be truly human, and to integrate effectively and completely, you have to own all of yourself.

The truth is that even if we are progressing we are capable of great harm. That is why the most fruitful and ultimately the most magnificent evolution is done in steps; not in one shattering, mind blowing realisation. In time the explosion is but a memory, and such an explosion can lead to an oversight, a temporary ignorance of the darker side of such knowledge. Sooner or later it will show itself to be uncontrollable, untameable, because you have not eaten and digested it in palatable portions. It may overwhelm you. What is desirable is the gradual, one step up at a time approach: times of enlightenment, amalgamation, steadiness and integration. It is as if you are in a subterranean network of passages, a quick flash of light will quickly be forgotten, but if you lit, ventilated and then came to know the part that you occupy, a safer and surer knowledge is accrued. Enlightenment is like this; like the waves on the sea; like the weather and seasons; like the growth of an organism. Look at how the world around you evolves.

There is no once and forever enlightenment.

You can only be enlightened about that which you presently search for, in a manner you can take in and understand. Otherwise it is simply experience.

I am only reminding you of the natural way for us humans. And, since we are all human, let us think about what the universe would lose if humans ceased to exist. Certainly the bad things would leave, although I am sure there is quite enough—unintentional as it may be—cruelty and savageness on this Earth, let alone in the universe, to keep it going without us. No, let us for a moment concentrate on the great and beautiful qualities of being human. What is it that actually makes you human; that which makes you different as an animal and a being, something which has caused some spiritual teachings to place us at the pinnacle of creation? Whether this is true or not, there are some matters about which we are undoubted leaders. Think for a moment about human passion; the passion that you can live your life by, and when combined with inquisitiveness and adventure leads us to discover that which is hidden; spurs us on when the case seems hopeless to new heights of adventure and discovery. What other animal appreciates the world as we do, trying sometimes in desperation to recreate the beauty and awesomeness of the physical world in all manner of artistic and creative endeavour, sometimes losing that life at the expense of its creation. What animal is filled with awe and wonder at the sights of nature, the sunset and sunrise, the weather, the starry sky and the heavens above our head .

Think about the sharing of joy and harmony with others. Laughter, truly one of the great gifts, lifting us from the mundane to fun and light-heartedness. The sharing of an experience with another human, whether it be serious or simply enjoyable. Companionship, camaraderie and friendship enabling us to endure. Think about the fun and excitement of sex and sexuality, the sensuous and sexual pleasure that having a human body allows us, and the heights of ecstasy that can be reached. Dwell on the risks that humans take not only for each other but also for other animals and plants that are in no way close relations and cannot of themselves reward us.

Now think about the kind eyes of a friend who is trying to help us, sharing in our sadness and distress and offering us a hand when we are down. What about those who offer us care and protection when we are ill and unable to help ourselves. There are others who will try to ease our loneliness and seek to illuminate and make whole again that which has been fragmented.

And the voice that asks you not to end your life.

What about the distinctly human qualities of honesty, integrity, joy; and perhaps behind and greater than all these, must be the quality of human love: that magnificent, indescribable feeling of the love we have for another human being or fellow traveller on this planet. The concern, care and time—that most precious asset—dedicated from this finite life for another. Love. Feel it.

Truly, if humans ceased to exist then a huge beacon in this enormous universe would no longer shine its light out. The whole universe would know that something unique had been lost.

I am describing you, fellow humans. You all have these qualities; they are denied to none. They are essential ingredients to your nature—without them you could not truly call yourself human. So, hunt them out, dust them off, spark them with life and own all the parts of your human nature; not just the dark places, but also the unique glittering jewels that make up the totality that other beings envy. Feel proud to be human—a fully realised human being exhibiting your true identity.

Uniqueness

This "proud to be human" attitude extends one step further into "proud to be me."

Another fundamental understanding to take away from this book is the fact that in essence you are absolutely, unequivocally, and undeniably unique.

- **You are a once in a universe creation and will never be created again**
- **No one has experienced or experiences anything in exactly the way that you do and you are a valuable being because of those unique experiences.**
- **You have as much right as anyone who has ever existed to express your true nature in the world.**
- **No one should deny you life.**
- **No one is actually any more valuable than you are.**

How do these statements hit you? Are they difficult to swallow? Difficult to digest? How about actually living as if they were really true of you? Of course, if you accept them as true of yourself then they must necessarily be true of others. They are unique as well. They will never be re-created. That's a kind of tough one isn't it; until you realise that I'm talking about their soul nature, their essence. That is unique. Of course their bodies and minds are also unique, but their true essence—that which is Creator given—is their soul. That is the blueprint: it is the template to which you can, and should, refer. That is what you must accept. You do not have to respect their opinions, or their actions, if they do not originate from their soul;

and you will know when that is the case because they will be life denying, not life enhancing. You'll know them by the kind of feeling—not emotion—they arouse in you. So I do not mean that you should tolerate all behaviour, not at all.

Anything that denies you the right to manifest your true nature on the Earth does not originate in the soul.

Providing you pay attention to the caveat 'without deliberately hurting another' it is fine to oppose such opinions or instructions if you feel that is necessary, for they can be nothing but a mental creation. Look at the issue as I have already said: that which is life enhancing will expand you, whilst the life denying contracts and deadens us. It's really not that difficult is it?

It is the tradition in many religions and spiritual sects to view the universe as ultimately one, or even to view it as "not two." It is not a difficult position to arrive at, as we are all created out of the void—spirit, the background of the universes—then it could be said that we are indeed reducible to one. Even logically we can take this position. What I would like to ask you is why would you want to do this in the first place? Why dismember and dissolve something that is unique? Admittedly they are opposite poles of the same unity: oneness and diversity. It is even possible to live within the unity, though this cannot be done with linear thought and language as they can only get in the way. But I ask you again why you would want to do this? Perhaps there will come a time in your future evolution when your individuality necessarily dissolves permanently, I doubt it, but I do not know. On Earth, however, you must value your uniqueness. Do not get too bound up in reducing diversity into oneness. You were born separately, you think separately, your physical body and its genes are unique, as is your soul body; you are full to the brim with uniqueness. Perhaps such an act is a way of not confronting the difficult situations that necessarily make up a life lived exhibiting ones individuality; or maybe it is an escape from the past or a possible future, but it is not a satisfactory answer. To value your uniqueness does not mean a lack of respect for others, it means value for yourself. I am sure that you were not uniquely created in order to dissolve that very uniqueness into anonymity.

It is the uniqueness of the soul which you are seeking to reproduce exactly in both the physical and mental realms. As this process takes place and you become an integrated being, you impress the fundamental nature of the universe—which we could call spirit—with your manifested individuality.

By this process you can truly create a spirit body which survives the death of the physical, mental, and soul bodies—all of which will definitely die.

That is what being and becoming immortal means.

That is why your uniqueness is so very very important.

Congruency

**It is impossible to immortalise yourself unless
you are a congruent being.**

There's the rub! You knew there would be a draw back. It is absolutely necessary to be true to oneself: you must have integrity. In fact, as silly as it sounds, you cannot have integrity unless you have integrity.

This is a vital point. More and more your actions have to spring from an integrated beingness. Only when the soul-body-mind realms are practically inseparable can you hope to imprint the nature of the universe with your beingness. Think about it. If your mental world is different from the physical world, and the soul is different from them both, who are you exactly—a body, an ego or a soul? How can you possibly hope to develop enough force of beingness to imprint spirit, there are at least three different possibilities!

Imagine if your three bodies all met each other on a street, would they recognise each other? Perhaps they would pass each other by with only the faintest glimmer of recognition thinking, "I'm sure I know him/her from somewhere; where have I seen them before?" Would they even want to go up to each other and introduce themselves; go out on a date in order to further increase their knowledge of each other; how would your three bodies act together? Rather like the proverbial three legged race, if they're not in rhythm and unison you will fall down or, put more simply, be unable to advance.

The vast majority of people on the Earth are like this. Are you one of them? You can often identify this lack of integrity when they behave in a totally different, unusual or extraordinary way: the "I've never seen them act like that before" situation. You can be sure that they still need to work on their integration. Often it is in the contrast between work and leisure where we see such incongruencies: the "wow, I never realised they were so serious," or "she's got a great sense of humour," perhaps "he's so romantic, thoughtful, philosophical, physical." Why haven't you seen this aspect of their beingness before? Perhaps because it would be frowned upon at work? So your work denies an important part of your beingness does it? Do you see what structures we have created; how they deny intrinsic aspects of the whole of us? If your work does this to you then you need to begin to change how you are at work, or get out; create a change that enables you to manifest yourself more fully. Begin to work towards how you really want to be.

No one has the right to deny you your right to manifest your true nature.

Watch someone you know, when they are unaware of it, and see from where they are expressing themselves. Is there indeed any behaviour that exhibits their true nature? Now, look at yourself, and I warn you it is a difficult process to go through. What aspects of your self are not expressed fully, or are suppressed and hidden from the world out there. This suppression actually feels like pain sometimes; like a deadening of life; a dulling of sensation; a boredom with and a denial of life itself. It is like a flower withering on the stem for lack of water or sun: its potential may never be realised. This is particularly relevant when there is a newly discovered aspect of yourself and it is being denied by those around you as "not you." That is when it hurts most. The map showed you where the treasure was hidden and you discovered the treasure chest, but there are those who will try to tell you that it isn't real gold; inside there is only plastic; you couldn't possibly have found anything of value; you are misguided. Listen to them, yes. Then carry on. Know for yourself whether it is true or not; do not take their word for it. Often it is the case that those who are closest to you are not able to adapt to your changes, and they will try their best to disable your congruent actions. Nevertheless you must try, at least, not to lie about what you know, although you may need to adapt yourself to the level on which they function if you are to communicate at all!

Is the world so full of laughter, love and excitement; passion; discovery; fun; philosophical debate; communication; adventure; satisfying, loving and sexual relationships; individualness; anticipation; success; that it couldn't possibly take any more. Of course not. The world is crying out for the manifestation of unique and magnificent individual lives.

It is often the case that this congruency and integrity can be found through particular paths that are personally suited to you. That may be to do with a talent or interests; feelings of difference, be they sexual or racial; to do with disablement or health problems: many paths which act like a conduit, a channel to recognise your own uniqueness. The important point is not to make these differences and gifts into causes in themselves, unless injustice is rife, but to let them lead you along a path of self-discovery—out into a wider world. Rather as if you had discovered a tunnel from a particular vantage point and, after a while—where you adapt to the dark or the stress of the journey—you are led out to a new and higher—more complete— view. One that is new to you, or perhaps the same scene becomes visible again but is viewed from a higher lookout. Although the tunnel was essential for your journey it is not the point of the journey. The travelling is, but not the tunnel itself. However, the destination confirms the journey's necessity. Bear in mind that in this example it would be very wrong for you to go back to the original starting point and laugh at others if they try to use the same or a different tunnel, just so that you don't stand out from the crowd, or because you are embarrassed. In such circumstances you can be sure that your mental body is causing you problems. The soul will be shaking its metaphorical head, wondering how you could deny such an essential aspect of your true self. You are lying. You are denying the truth as you have discovered and experienced it.

You will never be immortalised if the majority of your actions are incongruous. They must be integrated into your beingness. They must appear in your everyday life on this Earth.

I do not mean that in every encounter all aspects of your being have to be expressed; simply that the core of you, the true impulse, should be visible, as a motivating force behind your actions and words. This core, especially at the beginning, may well feel like a very tender part of you; the part not often exposed to others for fear it will be taken advantage of or misunderstood. You will remember it from times when you have been at your most vulnerable: at the death of a loved one; the break up of an intense love relationship; in the middle of the night when everything seems dark and unfriendly and old hurts that haven't been dealt with resurface to trouble you yet again. When you know you are alone or lonely. Remember during difficult times like these that it cannot be destroyed, this delicate core, but it can become distracted or detached from your consciousness if you do not attend to it on a regular basis. It is this core self which keeps you going through adversity in spite of all other circumstances.

Your true nature—that feeling of being you—is the most beautiful, significant and magnificent aspect of your consciousness.

Don't hide it away. It is the light in the eyes of human beings. But, in spite of this—like a muscle that must be exercised to become strong—that core of you has to be manifested in the physical and mental worlds, albeit gradually. It has to be exercised, nurtured, and tested, to strengthen it until that time when you are a congruent being. Only in this way can you hope to manifest your true nature. Only in this way can you hope to become immortalised.

A fully congruent being is truly a force to be reckoned with.

How often have we have seen or read of individuals who preached one type of behaviour and yet, in secret, practised another. You will be pleased to know that hypocrisy is certainly one way to ensure that you do not become immortalised. Quite a gratifying thought. Such people have not accessed their own experience of life, and the mental world has somehow fractured or hived off into separate sections: work, private life, sex life, religious, social and political lives. Do you see how untenable this situation is? Not only does one harm oneself, but also there is the possibility of hurting a large number of others, both human and non-human. It is directly opposed to the life you were made to live. How could such a fractured individual imprint spirit, the fundamental nature of the universe? There has to be a powerful expression of you in all three realms before you shine out like a beacon in this universe.

Hypocrisy is an important area for you to work on. Are you being hypocritical about anything at the moment? Are you not facing up to something, a situation perhaps, which you know deep down must be dealt with, but about which you are not telling the truth? Is it easier to go along with the crowd? Not wanting to hurt another is admirable, but only as long as it is not an excuse for your lack of courage. Using false words or expressions is also part of that duplicity. You say one thing and believe another, and the truth is that you not only hurt others by your actions but you seriously damage yourself. After all the excuses, you are simply being a hypocrite, plain and simple.

As an exercise, look back at decisions you have already made concerning love and relationships, work, belief systems, actions you took which have surfaced into your consciousness again, and see if you could have acted any differently and still been congruent, if you were at all. Sometimes it is the case that we would act in exactly the same way, because it was something very important to us. Never mind the heartache, the pain and discouragement that resulted, there really was no other way to act and still be true to ourselves; true to our core. In other matters we may now be able to see that we acted foolishly and in accord with the desires of other people. Was this done out of fear; love for another; an inability to assert yourself; lack of self worth; lack of clarity; plain dishonesty or simply not caring less? Each one of these is different and the difference is important. But, at the foundation, is a lack of congruency in oneself—hopefully something which you are now beginning to address.

Acting from a congruent source will not necessarily make your life any easier.

213

However, I can assure you that it is the only way to live properly as a human being; the only honest way. It is one of the measures of your worth.

I would like to talk for just a little while more on a related topic to this one of congruence. If we wanted to simplify it even further we could call it honesty, or perhaps honest responsibility. Here I am referring to the idea that as a developing, or developed, self-actualised and manifested individual, you have responsibilities. You need to own them and recognise them as such.

As such an individual you have enormous choice. No longer can you act as an ordinary person: there will be many other possibilities available to you and you may have to think before you make even the simplest of decisions. Recognising this fact often presents you with something of a dilemma. One of the more subtle and surprising instances where this kind of dilemma may arise is when you are wondering whether to intercede in a given situation or not. You suddenly recognise that it is your choice whether to interfere. Do you see what I mean? As an evolving human being you need to be crystal clear about your motives for acting in either direction. That is where to start from. Again this comes back to the issue of owning all the implications of honesty and integrity.

You are part of the whole, you are part of the universe; a unique and valuable asset because of that. You are part of the life on this Earth, not separate from it.

If you stand aside, do so knowing your true motives; do not use untenable arguments to justify your lack of commitment or care or concern. Please realise you always have a choice to be honest or not in a given situation. Some modes of behaviour, which until now have been your constant companions, will be forever lost to you if you decide to evolve—you can no longer be an ignorant human being. Remember—no retribution.

It is up to you, your conscience; it is your decision whether to act or not.

Do you see what owning yourself and manifesting your true nature requires of you? Your integrity and congruency is such an important issue that it can make or break your greater evolution. The mirror of your being must be polished continually, or a true rendition of your self can never manifest. You could imagine it as if our incongruities show up as dust on the mirror of our true self, and we then have the opportunity to identify them and wipe them off. Yet again, though this issue may require real determination from you, please be gentle and kind to yourself; use the overflowing love that was given to you at your birth as your guide.

You have decided to walk the path. Now you have to be honest with yourself and the world you live in; you have to take onto yourself the full implications of living a wholly congruent life, from a fully integrated beingness.

You will become an adult in a world of children.

Relating and Relationships

I hope you now realise how important congruency and integrity are. The establishment and refinement of your own congruency is a lifelong task. Each new situation—and there are uncountable numbers in a life—offers you an opportunity to test your integrity, shine light into a dark area of your life you would rather not face, and to act from your core self: your soul body. However, it is rare that this can be more powerfully made obvious than in your relating to society in general, and to individuals in particular.

Many spiritual traditions, and their followers, carry with them an ideal picture of how they would like to live. Perhaps it is alone on a mountaintop with a convenient stream of fresh running water close by, friendly animals, and the radiant sun shining down on them; a quiet contemplative existence. For others it may be in a monastery, ashram or community where all is peace and light.

Yet, in some spiritual systems, the most respected of all adherents are those who choose to live in the everyday world.

The life that you and I lead. The struggle, competition and challenge of living in a society directly opposed to you finding your true self and, perhaps, a different way to live, is highly respected. Truly it requires courage, dogged determination, strength and, perhaps, an ability not to take oneself too seriously!

As if living in the world was not enough, we then have human relationships to deal with. Human relationships can be a nightmare. And if you do not agree, then you probably haven't had any! It is in the field of human interrelating that we all find out how many Achilles' heels we have; how inadequately prepared we are; how much more work we have to do on ourselves; and ultimately, how human we are. That is their joy and their drawback.

Do you find it easy or difficult to create new relationships, to perpetuate them, to enliven them or to finish them? It may take much inquiry before you can honestly and congruently answer all these questions. But I can assure you that it is important not to be afraid of entering into relationships for fear of hurt or embarrassment. Much better that you courageously go forth and not isolate yourself from life; for how can your advice be of any possible use to another if you are not speaking from a congruent, confirmed core.

In the field of relationships there is much to correct in the mental world. Remember how I stated that all the love you will ever need is within your self already. The implication of this is that you should not go looking for a relationship to validate you as an individual—that is not its prime function. It is, in essence, the bringing together of two human beings; it is the effects, implications and ramifications of the interactions between them. They are a measure of how well you can adapt and change; how firm you can be about your congruency; how honest and straight forward or manipulative you are; whether you really want or need this relationship at all. They can help to clarify who you actually are by the mirroring of yourself in another's eyes. And there is, of course, a special type of consciousness which echoes and resonates between two people who love each other deeply; one which supports and emphasises the individuality of each, whilst creating a safe but challenging arena for new growth and evolution.

Deep love and affection between two humans is a powerful force for positive change within and without.

It is certainly worth working on, for it is a unique and valuable experience of your human life, and as such is irreplaceable.

Never ignore human love. It is the core expression of your humanity.

If an important relationship has just broken down or is faltering, re-run the events and see if, even initially, there were hints

218

of incompatibility. Did you disintegrate in order to facilitate the relationship? It is important to realise that the fact that it has gone wrong is irrelevant; what is important, however, is how you reacted and behaved during the relationship: did you become incongruous; have you compromised too much; did you allow yourself to be trampled on; were you too aggressive; afraid of commitment and deeper feelings; the reasons can be many and varied. Find out, and use what has occurred positively. Ultimately, if nothing in you has changed, and there has been no questioning, then I am sure you have wasted a valuable opportunity for growth and evolution; for your refinement. Remember, not only do you have to be congruent, as discussed in the previous chapter, but the consciousness passing between your three selves must be clear and uncorrupted.

Do you see the point of relating now? It is possible for you to do all your work in the mental world, changing yourself, your behaviour, opinions and beliefs; the very way that you are; but unless it is tested against the wider physical world then you will never really know how well, or otherwise, you are doing. It is not that you are looking for approval or disapproval; you are simply testing your changes. You may well receive all manner of negative feedback from those who are important to you. Listen to it and then analyse where their words have originated from: did they spring from their mind or their soul? The difference is important. What is more important is to ask yourself how their reaction affects you emotionally—mental—or feeling wise—soul. Again it is important to separate the two. Often we can find ourselves in the most desperate circumstances, yet if we detach from our mental consciousness and concentrate on our feelings we can, surprisingly, feel good about life. In such a case you can be sure that you are exactly where you need to be, even if it is not where you want to be!

We all need times of withdrawal opposing those of advancement in order to absorb the events and occurrences of our life: to take stock and to judge honestly what has happened to us. These times can feel very lonely and be difficult to endure. Again, it is important to separate from each other your ideas about this 'living alone' and what society may have to say on the matter. The truth is that there will actually be a sizeable minority who envy your aloneness and the freedom which it can facilitate, both physically and mentally, and there will be others whose opinions cannot be separated from their fear of having to experience the very aloneness that you are experiencing. It is possible, during these times, to make remarkable advances in your evolution, ones that may have been very difficult within your previous relationships. But this does presuppose that the reason you separated from your previous relationship/s is that your evolution was not welcomed by your friends/lovers. Only you can really know this. But, ultimately, we must all re-launch ourselves into the melee again for the very reason I have stated before: in the mental realms all things are possible. It is an easy matter to fool ourselves that we are advanced and mature and all the rest of the oh so seductive dream—as it is equally possible to convince ourselves that we are useless, unlovable and unloved—but we must gather more information in the physical world before we can truly know what is actually the case; only then can we convert it into knowledge and truth about ourselves.

Your soul will provide you with plenty of opportunities for growth once you are on the path, some of which may seem hard to endure. Many times, because the gateways connecting the soul-physical-mental bodies are blocked, your soul will organise events in the physical world which hopefully will alter your mental perception of reality and cause you to seek an answer within yourself, or to search in new directions to facilitate your growth. Do you see what a marvellous strategy this is? All is not lost if the connections to your soul are blocked or not functioning correctly. Events are sometimes organised to make a strong mental impression on you; to change your mental world and literally change your mind, allowing it to become more amenable to the messages from your soul body. Life changing incidents can arise from such a cause. That is how to use them positively.

Remember that it's often only in the no man's land of indecision and confusion that new roads can be found, new paths followed, and new growth ensue.

When you are on the path of self-development and congruency you can be sure that many of the incidents that assail you during your life are directly related to your path and your growth.

That does not mean that your life is pre-destined, but it does mean that through these incidents your true nature can be uncovered; it can be recognised and refined almost like the refining or purification of metal from the ore in which it is embedded. Think of the incidents of your life as an aid to untangling your confused and chaotic mental webs, enabling the resulting reflections to be differentiated into relevance and irrelevance. By comparing them to the light which shines through the template of your soul, only that which fits the template need remain. The incidents of your life should help to determine and differentiate between what is confusion and misinterpretation and what has resonance with your original uniqueness; so that, one by one, all that has become embedded in the mental realm that actually has no meaning to you in reality can be disregarded and rejected. Rather like the deprogramming of the computer chips in our earlier metaphor, you are using the happenings of a life lived in the world of the everyday to determine and define the truth at the centre of your being: something truly extraordinary. Relationships will often be the stimulus for such an investigation.

However, there is no need to question and investigate everything in minute detail; rather you should view happenings as unique rhythms, or wave patterns, which have behind them a similarity, a common purpose or direction. As an exercise, try compacting the whole of your life so far—and include the future if you have an intimation of it—into the now; as if everything happened at this moment. You will find there is a common thread, a pattern, an impulse that drove each seemingly unconnected incident and meeting; all those love affairs and friendships; all the happenings of your life. Recognise this impulse. It may point to smaller rather than larger changes; in other words you are not that far from the target; or it could help you to realise that for much of the time you have resisted a change that you have already recognised as necessary, and explains the reason for it coming up time and time again in what you thought were different guises. In a case like this, rather large transformations and change might be necessary. Whatever, do try compacting time; look behind the challenges and relationships of your life—both those surmounted and those not faced—and see the impulse behind them. Then you will have found a key to your personal evolution and growth.

As you may well have gathered, this particular chapter answers one of the major criticisms of this kind of path: that of selfishness. Often the idea of spending attention and time on your own development is seen as a somewhat immoral act, as if you had only been born as a sacrifice to the greater good. That is not true.

The reason why you are alive is so that you can manifest to your greatest ability who you are, your uniqueness. It is that uniqueness that should relate to the whole world.

What good is a man or woman who does not question their thoughts and actions? They are like the proverbial bull in a china shop: crashing and breaking humans without a care in the world because they have no purpose, no control, no insight; and really no care about the consequences of their actions. Rather the bull had learned to balance; lost a few pounds; referred to a map in order to plan the route and had a "controlled folly" of a journey.

By inter-relating with the world out there we are offered enormous opportunities for our personal growth and evolution.

So much of this life is stimulation and challenge that simply to survive relatively intact is a credit to any human being. But wouldn't you rather pass with flying colours, with a certificate that says "dealt with and mastered the vigorous testing of the world." Sounds good doesn't it? Relating and relationships may well be one of the more relevant paths through which you can discern your true nature.

Remember: as you grow, so another beacon lights up in the universe, and everywhere there is an almost audible sigh of relief.

The Physical World

I cannot over stress the importance of your physical body. It is the medium through which the clarification and purification of your mental body can take place. It is the vital middle connection between your body of life energy—your soul body—and your mental body. Without it there could be no possible connection between those two dimensions, and therefore not the remotest possibility of immortality.

It is impossible to have direct mental knowledge of the soul; what is more, it is impossible to mentally perceive the Creator in any way. The mental world helps you to formulate, clarify and understand what it is you have experienced. Because all manner of manifestations and distortions are possible in the mental world, it is only with and through a physical body that you can validate your beliefs and opinions and transform them into knowledge. Furthermore, the passage of consciousness through the translating medium of the physical body will facilitate a never-ending cyclic exchange of information between all three bodies. The soul needs to know the present moment, and the mental body needs information from the soul to perfect its rendition of your true nature. Both need to manifest in the physical world.

Without a good deal of your time being spent in your physical body you will not become immortal.

So, contrary to what others have told you about how the physical world is nothing but illusion, a diversion, a vehicle, in actual fact it is essential to your growth and development.

The physical world itself is definitely not an illusion, how you perceive it however, may well be!

There must be a time during the day when you become fully aware of your physical body and your physical existence. The tissues out of which you are formed must be informed and infused with consciousness. All of the crude and subtle sensations that are available to you should be observed: the awareness of the gross and refined movements of your body is a boon to your development.

Begin to see the physical body rather like a telephone exchange, where the feelings of the soul and the emotions of the mental body are translated and made understandable to the opposite world. Also, of course, the infusion of your physical body with soul consciousness—which, remember, contains the blueprint for your DNA—has enormous physical benefits; and a clear connection to the mental body will accomplish congruency between your body language and your true emotions and thoughts.

Some time—some conscious time—should be spent in your physical body each day.

This need not be a vigorous pursuit such as ordinary exercise, for during vigorous exercise it is often the case that everything but the physical body is thought about; however, with full awareness, it can be done. What is more appropriate is some form of awareness connected to movement. Dancing, and the more gentle or soft martial pursuits come to mind, as does yoga, or walking with a full awareness of your body; but even picking up a cup of tea with full physical awareness is beneficial.

Remember that awareness is not thought.

Read that last statement again and again as you pick this book up and put it down until you know the difference. If awareness allows thought then it becomes a reflection of the act and, unless you have both of them well differentiated, you will find yourself enmeshed in thought processes and the mental world again. This indeed takes practice. One added benefit to this kind of awareness is that it brings you into the present moment, and that is the only way to actually know anything!

Often, once this difference is understood, many previously romanticised observations can be placed into proper perspective, such as sensations and feelings associated with connections and workings in the natural world. Instead of rationalising and making an incident understandable, you can look back or recreate the situation simply by becoming aware of what happened in your physical body. Remember that in the physical body you can have an awareness of the movement of mental, physical and soul consciousness: it is truly the place to really know an experience. Afterwards, if you choose, you can postulate and propose various explanations, but you are unlikely to benefit from a true transformational experience if it is a purely mental process. Many ancient peoples, who lived much closer to the physical world than we do, valued in their traditions—beyond all others—the experience of physical awareness, physical sensation and the physical world.

It is also true to say that many beliefs and religions frown upon the physical body and its sensations. This, in light of the above explanations, can be seen as a method to disempower the individual; to convince him or her that the answer could not possibly be within—which of course it is—but without, in the form of a powerful human who could dispense wisdom and advice in return for the perpetuation of that power. Hence the reason why some of the strictest taboos seemed to surround the physical body and its everyday functions.

The fact is that your body is you in the physical realm.

It can certainly take effort and determination to break down the mental thought forms associated with the physical body and its processes. From your very early life there have been admonitions and even punishments associated with your body. The one thing that you actually own outright, that which was given to you free of charge, is somehow put into the hands of others; or else is actively possessed by various factions such as parents, peer groups, the medical profession, lovers. But it is yours and yours alone, you can do what you want with it. You own it, you are it, it is part of the whole of you; you should be its keeper, its preserver and its guardian. It allows you your one and

225

only chance to become immortal. It is always annoying to watch how easily a physical body, an aspect of your totality, is almost freely given away to others for them to do their bidding with.

Never, ever, let another human being do anything to your physical body which you are not happy with.

Your physical body is so very important. You need to not only enjoy having a body, but to do your best to respect and nourish it. This concentration on—and awareness of—your body, keeps clear the gateways through which consciousness can flow to and from it. It is important that that consciousness is full of respect, thanks and love.

What better nourishment could there be for the physical body than knowing that it is adored and loved by its owner.

Your body usually owns six senses. None of these should be ignored if you are lucky enough to have all six—the kinaesthetic sense is here included. There is not a time during the day when you are not using at least one or two of your senses because they are always, at least unconsciously, feeding information about your surroundings into your brain. You could even think of your body as one vast sense organ. What uncountable pleasures their mixing and matching can bring us; what variations of sensation. Here again we can see how thankless we are to our physical body for such unrecognised, unrecreatable and singularly individual sensations as those that flow from the senses. How different our lives would be if we had no senses at all, floating in emotion and feeling—assuming we had a body of some kind—unable to identify what is us and what is not. Is it not peculiar then, after my previous comments, that there are so many taboos against the utilising and enjoying of the marvellous physical body you have? Do you now begin to appreciate your physical body more?

There is nothing sinful about your body and its functions.

Every one of them is vital for the tissues which make up your body to remain healthy. Start to contemplate the incredible importance of your digestive processes, urination and defecation. It would be impossible to live without them. Value all of your body's functions. Contemplate the stunning sensations of sexuality, your sexual organs and sexualness. Think about and enjoy your sensuality.

You have a wonderful, unbelievably complex, sensible, sensual, sexual body; so enjoy it. Value it. Love it.

Ah, now that last one can be a real problem for a lot of people. Loving your body is difficult if, at the moment, it seems to be letting you down. Have you considered, however, that it may simply be drawing your attention to the fact that it actually exists; that it needs some consciousness sending to it. Otherwise it may be making visible in the physical world issues which you have to address. One possible reason for many long term chronic conditions can be a desperate effort from the soul to bring awareness back into the physical body—and thus in closer proximity to the body of life energy—after perhaps years of neglect, or what has become a natural tendency to ignore it. Even though you are not prepared to fully descend into—and be aware of—the whole of your physical body, illnesses, both chronic and acute, can force you to spend some time being aware of at least a part of it, keeping communication and contact at least partially alive. Instead of thinking of your body as if it were a necessary evil, think of it as if it is an essential intermediary between your soul and your mental realm. Illness may even be an important part of your evolution, asking you to search for new information and thoughts that would not otherwise occur to you. This is yet another way in which your physical body proves indispensable to your growth, maturity and evolution. If you are not sure about this and suffer from a chronic illness, think of how you would be if you had never suffered as you do: you may be surprised when you see what you could have turned out like.

Perhaps your physical problems may begin to ease if you simply start sending awareness, respect and love to your body. With this in mind you can mentally vacate the relevant part of your body—eliminating the negative thoughts associated with it—and simply allow the ever present love of your soul for your body to fill and refresh that space. To accommodate this, if it is difficult for you, simply contemplate the amount of possible pleasure that can be derived from having a body—literally mind blowing! Begin to take pleasure in movement; becoming fascinated in gross and fine movements and how they can be performed without a thought. Explore the sensations that exist within your body. Sensations from the very obvious to the incredibly subtle exist there, believe me. Touch your body; it is a sensual pleasure. To touch and be touched with awareness is one of the great pleasures of our lives. Start to challenge and re-evaluate the taboos you have about your body, realising now how important and unique it is. Above all, remember that your relationship to your body is pivotal to the process of your immortalisation.

There should be freedom of movement in all parts of your body, but most important is a freedom of movement in your pelvic and abdominal area. This is a crucial area for the transmission of sensation from your physical body—which may have translated impulses from the mental body—to your soul body. This area needs to be clear and not constricted, otherwise you will be acting blindly: for your essential reference guide, your uniqueness, the template to which you need to refer, will be as if non-existent. How can you know, without this transmission, that your development is not a mental construct; divorced from the reality of your body of life energy? You would be like a tree which is still immature, rejecting the help that a firm wooden stake could provide. Every storm would pose a very real threat to its existence. Much better to use the support that was already in place from the moment of your birth in this world.

Remember that—besides the purely informative consciousness that it transmits to your body—your soul communicates with other soul bodies and can organise enormous and relevant developments in your life.

Now you may understand why in most so called primitive dancing, pelvic mobility is very obvious. The people may have forgotten why this is so, but they still know the value of such movement. Your pelvic area is the "heart" of the physical body; the centre from which movement should take place. A young child always initiates movement from its hips and pelvis, only later does the head become dominant.

Obviously, now you can see one of the benefits of sex: it is no accident that there is a gateway of consciousness near your sex organs. Although a complete orgasm should be felt in all of your body, it is centred in the genitals and pelvis. It clears the gateways for the passage of consciousness in your body as well as performing important functions in your physical body. So, even if you do not have a partner, remember the value of orgasm and please rid yourself of the taboos about masturbation. It is your body and it is pleasurable. Enjoy it while you can.

This is the only time you will ever have senses in this form.

How could it be possible that you were created with the ability to perceive such fascinating sensations and be constantly denied the pleasure of using them? Stop martyring yourself; stop feeling guilty for enjoying what is a free gift! This attitude is far too common amongst the supposedly spiritually advanced: the denial, the sin and guilt of something that is one of the great glories of a life on Earth. The whole of your body is valuable; all of its functions are necessary. Do not accept some of them and not others.

Again, as I always state, there is no need to be brutal or uncaring about these new insights and thoughts. Proceed with respect and love to challenge some of your deeply entrenched beliefs about your physical body. Loosen the roots a little at first; play with possibilities; enjoy a new found sense of adventure; revel in new freedoms which have constrained you for far too long.

You may be surprised to find yourself coming up against jealousy and bigotry in this new adventure, often from people who should know better; however, you are to carry on regardless. They envy your expansion into the wider world of who you actually are, for all men and women seek liberation from constraining morals; morals which are often only symptomatic of this time period and not at all common throughout history. If this is a problem for you, begin to remember your death; remember that you have only one life on this Earth; only one chance to enjoy and revel in a physical body. Close your eyes and think about that for a few minutes. However, this is not an instruction to indulge yourself—you will have your own internal feeling about how you need to proceed; about that which is false and not true to your true self, and that which is rightly an embodiment of your own true values. Now begin, slowly, to change your attitude about the sensuality and physicality of owning your body. It is pleasure and excitement; it can be blissful and challenging at the same time. As long as you do not deliberately hurt another against their will, use your power over them, or put your physical body at risk for a transient pleasure, then your body and your life are yours and yours alone. Tune into the soul and allow the soul's vibrancy, enthusiasm and passion to invigorate your body. You will be transformed.

If it wasn't for your body you would not be alive today.

Health

You may be reading this book because you are facing a crisis concerning your health.

It is often the case that not until we are faced with serious or life threatening illnesses do we even consider pressing questions about our life and our death.

Perhaps you have a long term chronic condition which responds little to orthodox medicine, yet doesn't actually threaten your life as such, but deadens the experience of it. Perhaps you suffer from a condition which can occasionally become very serious and threatens your life directly or indirectly through the suffering it causes you personally.

There can be many causes for ill health. Certainly the environment and our modern lifestyle present a very real threat to the effective physical functioning of our bodies. It may surprise you to learn that many illnesses in the human body are actually the result of dosings received from allopathic medicine. Yet, of course, in desperate circumstances we would be foolish to ignore the help that is available: it can literally mean the difference between life and death.

However you look at it, no one who is on the path of self investigation and growth can fail to acknowledge that we are more than flesh and bone. Most humans have no problem in identifying that they, as a whole, are the result of more than just chemical reactions. It is a point that is hardly worth disputing. Even medical science has direct knowledge of the effects of psychosomatic, stress and anxiety states on physical health. Let us look therefore at disease from the viewpoint of a complete man or woman.

Health in itself is not the state of never being ill. That is a mistaken belief. Health is the ability to respond to illness with effective counter measures that return us back to health. The natural state for human beings is overall health with occasional illnesses, after which we return to health again.

The soul pattern in your body of life energy contains the blueprint for your physical DNA.

It is absolutely necessary that you allow its message to penetrate into your physical body; the tissues of which should be pliable and flexible enough to absorb and translate the consciousness transmitted. In this way you invigorate and remind the cells of your body how they should be. However, the situation that we normally see is fundamentally different. Not only is this invigorating and healing effect of the soul denied to the physical body, but the mental body is all powerful and its distorted patterns and behaviours influence physical health to an inordinate extent. From this diagnosis it is possible to see how effective healing can take place. The life energy pattern must invigorate the physical body, whilst the mental body and its patterns are changed to reinforce the soul pattern; rather than usurping and denying it its power, the mental body will reinforce and resonate with your soul. However, it must be said that this is much easier said than done.

If we acknowledge that life in this universe is governed by movement, then we can also see that movement itself can aid health. Movement of your physical body on no matter how small a scale—and of course awareness of it—can facilitate your healing. A means of physical therapy, combined with flexibility and movement, is necessary to aid the translation and transmission of this consciousness from your other two bodies. And it is for this reason that all true healing will result in certain subtle or great changes in the character of a person. They should be more open, less restrained, grow and evolve, and in some way become more 'free flowing' than before. Fundamentally they will express more of their real self than they have in the recent past: they will actually be more alive—which is a desirable state for any of us.

It is obviously possible for us to recover from illness without any of the above taking place—a measure of the miracle that is the physical body—but, as a human being who wishes to express more of your individuality in the world, wouldn't it be more profitable for you to use illness as a teacher rather than to view it as a nuisance?

The truth is that most of the time your body goes about its business of healing and repair without your conscious intervention. A cut heals without you thinking about it. We should have more confidence in the body's ability to heal. But in order to aid these processes we need to allow the body what it needs. Perhaps it needs more rest, better food, or more or less activity; whatever it needs we must start to listen to its messages. Here, again, it is easily possible for the mind to override these requirements. Is it really important for us to reach such and such a goal; to overwork so that we can afford our lifestyle; to snack because there isn't enough time for a cooked meal; to forget sex and physical affection because we are stressed? These are all excuses made in the mind.

You may simply need to take better care of yourself; something which could entail paying more attention to the food you put inside your body. After all, how can you expect it to run efficiently if you do not feed it correctly? Deeper than this is the impulse behind such negligence: that of not valuing oneself enough to take care of such matters. How often do you hear people say that "it isn't worth it just for myself." With this attitude is it any wonder that the physical body rebels.

It should go without saying that you must value yourself or, if you don't at the moment, learn to. Read the chapters on death and uniqueness again.

More usually, illness can be the result of thought patterns and behaviours that are life denying rather than enhancing. This does not entail an instruction to live an entirely hedonistic lifestyle however; it may surprise you to learn that often such behaviour stems from an insufficient respect for oneself and a lack of value for ones life. It is a needless and pointless act to throw your life away in a whirl of experience, the whole point of which is often simply to regain the sense of adventure and vitality that should be a part of your life.

Realising that you have one life and one life only should sober up your attitudes to risk and risk taking; whether that be with drugs or in physical activity.

Originally, drug taking was not only a means to loosen up social and moral constraints in order to allow some freedom for the denied aspects of a human being, but also a means to shatter and dislodge the strict belief that this is the one and only reality. In actual fact there are countless dimensions interpenetrating the space you occupy now; the experience of which gives one the definite knowledge that the universe is more mysterious and awesome than can be ordinarily imagined. However, many of these realities can be intrinsically dangerous to human beings because they have nothing to do with us or our evolution. They can therefore damage us, resulting in mental instability, insanity or death. You will observe that people behave differently after taking drugs, often exhibiting their true colours; of course I am also including alcohol in this discussion as it is the major drug of our time. If you wish to learn from the experience of disorientation and new perception that taking a drug can give you it is necessary to ask yourself the following question "what is it in my normal everyday life that stops me from expressing myself in such a way," or "why do I need to drink etc. to do so?" These are the secrets that are available to you if you choose to look at your life in such a way.

I do not advocate the habitual taking of any drug. It is the easiest way to put off tackling a problem or disturbance in your life. And simply on the physical level its deleterious effects on your body could have life long implications. Ultimately, you always suffer the risk of becoming a slave to its effects, the surest way of never manifesting the life you would like and the way you would like to be. Often it is the case that drugs will cover up a real lack of physical pleasure in existence: an obvious way to prove that your body itself is so blocked and armoured that the only way pleasing and pleasant sensations can be experienced is with the use of a drug. You could liken this type of use as akin to putting a sticking plaster on a huge sore: the underlying necessity for using it in the first place must be addressed.

Sometimes drugs are resorted to when life is too hard to face or too painful to endure on an emotional level. Again it is necessary to realise that life is not a bed of roses, there will often be times when we will be depressed and unhappy, just as there will also be times of happiness and love. Drugs will not change these facts; they will only help you to ignore them!

Many of these thoughts are directed towards freeing up the mental attitudes that can cause illness.

Unless you care for yourself, you are of no use to either yourself or the world at large.

Loosening the constraints that you limit your life by can radically alter your state of health. If you try to remember that life in general should be fun, adventurous, enjoyable and satisfying then you may learn to take life more easily and to begin to seek out enjoyment rather than be content or resigned to suffer.

One more important point about health needs to be remembered. As I have already mentioned, it may well be that your ill health is a part of your life for a certain time to enable a process of evolution to take place. Without it you would not have been spurred on to find the solution to complex mental and spiritual questions. It is a positive aid to your evolution and growth. It could even be that it precipitates in the physical body a problem or obstruction in your mental body that would otherwise prove an impossible obstacle to the furtherance of your personal growth. It is also the case that there is a certain sensitising process that takes place, in that the suffering and limitation you have experienced in your life enables you to understand and comprehend that of others.

At the heart of being human is this understanding of the dilemmas of another; of the human experience.

We have this unique ability to identify with other humans and other life forms. That ability can be heightened through illness: you will be more whole and have a more expanded awareness than you would otherwise have had. It may not be recompense for the suffering you have undergone, but it may well be the only way you would have reached this level of understanding in the first place. I put it to you that if you had never experienced your illness it would have been impossible for you to have evolved as you have done. If you have used your insight to fuel your journey you have indeed acted with wisdom and courage.

Try listening to your body and not your mind: in this way you can hope to recover from illness with the positive side benefits of new insights and growth. Often this is why those seeking more from healing will visit alternative practitioners, because at least there should be some new insights into life, the universe and everything. If there isn't, then they have no right to call themselves alternative!

In essence it is important to find out what you can learn from your illnesses, not necessarily why they happened in the first place. You will find countless lessons to aid you in your growth.

Difficulties

There is nothing more sure than the fact that you will encounter many difficulties on this path of growth and development.

It would be so easy for me to tell you that this path will be a bed of roses; that it will seem natural and free from problems, but that is not the case. The truth is that all this should be really simple and straight forward—however, there may be many obstacles to your growth appearing from the most unlikely sources.

Part of the problem lies in the fact that we have created for ourselves a society that is fundamentally mental in its orientation—in both senses of the word—not soul or feeling based, but a rather hard and unforgiving culture that really is of our own making. How different this is from a life lived as advocated in this book will become painfully apparent as you try to bring into operation the principles I am suggesting.

One of the major confrontations you will face—apart from the one which involves the confrontation between your ego and your soul nature—will actually be with those people in your immediate environment. Friends, family and partners may all actively discourage your evolution: partly because of the very real fact that with the act of you changing they must choose whether to follow you into a place that is new or uncharted or to stay put, and partly because many people simply haven't the courage to move into a space involving the unknown. I use the word courage deliberately.

It takes bravery and determination to listen to guidance from a new voice in your life: the change from the mental—calculating—impulse to the soul—feeling and growth—impulse.

Although it will involve many trials of strength to subdue the mental self and its fears and anxieties—some of which may actually be legitimate—still it must be done. Rather like bringing under control an unruly pet which has hitherto been allowed free reign, the mind needs and enjoys a certain amount of firm but compassionate discipline. This tussle can result in difficult times, but perseverance and determination will ultimately win out. We all have these difficulties—they are an aspect of your complete life—but do remember what I said about the soul sometimes organising events in the physical world to directly alter your mental world.

There may well be times when it will seem that nothing is working. You feel lost and alone, lonely, given up by the universe around you; forgotten and rejected. Yes, I do speak from experience! Dealing with these periods can be a turning point for you. With dogged determination the path is to be walked. Just like the scaling of a mountain, you can expect there to be periods of extremely comfortable walking, times of rest and recuperation, challenges that you thought insurmountable, days when the weather is fine and sunny, and periods when the clouds loom large and it is cold and unfriendly. There may be risky ventures; paths that seem to lead nowhere, and unexpected events that alter the plans you had. What I am describing is nothing other than the journey of life itself. A human life. And only in retrospect can we see how far we have come. The journey, the adventure, is a goal in itself, not the final destination. That is the making of you as a man or woman.

Often it takes time for the physical world to "catch up" with advances you have made in your understandings and knowledge, and these periods of stasis can seem unbearable; but you must hold tight to the impulse that you are on the journey of life itself—hold firm to the knowledge which you have discovered so far. Know that it is truly darkest before the dawn. It is often the case that after periods of stillness that seem positively retrograde, there appears, within perhaps a few minutes, hours or days, a breakthrough; new insights and understandings abound, almost too many to take in and remember. It is as if some consciousness had to build up, some power needed to accumulate—like water building up enough force to break through an obstruction—before the next step could be reached.

Each new insight and understanding, each new experience resonates through your whole being. It needs to be integrated into your wholeness to enable it to change and transform—sometimes by gradual steps, sometimes in rather large leaps—the whole of you.

They must be expressed in the mental and physical realms to the best of your ability in order for them to resonate through into your immortal spirit body.

It seems that there is often a long delay between the arising of knowledge and insight and the significance of it being manifested in the physical world; as if the physical world took time to catch up with your knowledge. Perhaps, each time these radical insights flood your consciousness, new possible futures need to be formed, and manifesting them in this mysterious, mystical, and awesome physical reality takes time.

Whatever the reasons, it is still important that when confronted by difficulties you are fully aware of their effects on you. What part of you is being prodded that wants to remain comfortably asleep? How are you being challenged to think or act differently? Are long neglected talents you didn't even know you had being dragged kicking and screaming into the light of day? This can all be very disturbing to the mental body, and can sometimes feel like a dismantling of the ego you have come to both love and loath. At such times you must remain anchored to the feeling of who you are at the core of your being: these difficulties must be faced in order for you to get the full picture of yourself and the whole picture of your journey. Difficulties can indeed be teachers. They are absolutely, unfortunately, part of the whole. They may require you to dig deep into your reserves and adapt, however reluctantly, to something new; invoking fear and anxiety, and frightening us into immobility in the process. Such is life!

Let me share with you a few ideas that may help you to endure:

* Firstly, get things in perspective. Try to look at your life as another—enlightened—being would see it. Look upon your life as a whole. Or see yourself as very old and very wise, and

ask this older and wiser you about your situation and what you should do. Indeed, would it even be of any importance to that older and wiser you?

* If you hit a blockage in your development and don't seem to be able to make any progress, do not keep pressing against it. For a while concentrate on something totally different, another aspect of your life: from the mundane activities of the everyday to artistic, musical or creative pursuits. Return hours, days or even weeks later. You will find that you have probably moved beyond that particular obstruction without even noticing.

* Move! Very often we find ourselves sitting sullen and static. As much as it may seem like the last thing you want to do, try to force yourself up; put on a favourite dance record, something directly opposing your emotions of the moment and move. Lose yourself in your body and its feelings. Depending on your nature, even gentle or vigorous exercise can have the same effect.

* Try writing your thoughts down. Keep a spiritual diary that details the varying periods of growth, insight and difficulties you go through. One of the prime benefits of this is to give you a correct perspective on events. If you can look back and see that you once wrote how you would never love again, or feel again, how life would never get better, and can then look a few pages further on and see that things changed, it will hearten and strengthen you in times of difficulty.

* Try allowing nature into your perception again. Walk in pleasant scenery, feed some animals, reflect on the staggeringly difficult lives that many animals have. Try empathising with their tragedy and suffering; realise that such incidents are part of every life. Remember the courage of animals, especially the small ones that struggle to survive against all odds, sacrificing their lives for the future of their offspring and species.

240

* Remember the environment around you; the elements of air, fire, water and earth. Lie on the earth in a place that seems special to you. Ask the earth for help in releasing the present health/emotional/life problem. Now sink the consciousness of your body into the earth, as if you were being cradled by the ground, as if it were hollowing out to adapt to the shape of your body. Allow its consciousness to infuse your body. Relax and, if possible, fall asleep. During this time thank the Earth, the animal and plant kingdoms for supporting you this far: the air you breath, the warmth of the sun, the water you drink, and the earth you walk upon are gifted freely at your birth. Now, after such a time, indeed at any time, give a token of thanks to them. It doesn't have to be substantial, although it can be; perhaps some seed for the birds, some herbs returned to the earth, even some hair from your head or some saliva from your mouth placed on a tree; in fact anything you can think of as long as it is done with purpose and awareness. You really are part of the whole, as insignificant as you feel at such times.

* Write down your suffering, or make an object, drawing, or picture that personifies or symbolises it. Now, with full awareness, burn it; ask that any beings or forces that are benevolent to humans help you to transform the situation. Watch it burn to death. Concentrate the situation into the flames and the process of transformation that is going on in front of your eyes. When the flames have died, take a few of the ashes into your hand to signify that you are willing to help yourself as part of the process.

* Pamper yourself. Look after yourself. Treat yourself to something you have wanted—if you can afford it—or simply prepare a tasty meal just for yourself. Perhaps take a leisurely bath with some candles to light the room; but most of all take your time. Give yourself a massage. Take a day off work and give yourself a chance to breathe.

* At such times it is no coincidence that we often fail to breathe fully. Our breathing is shallow and only just feeds us. Remember to breath deeply and completely, knowing that you are willing to take new life in to the full and expel that which no longer serves you.

* Take care of other humans, animals or plants realising that this minute will never re-occur again and will be lost forever if not used. Animals, plants, and humans have limited life spans. Can you afford not to miss an opportunity to appreciate their beauty? Express love, admiration and care for them; touch and physically please them. Remember, if you are lucky enough to have a partner who you love and who loves you, not to take them for granted. Don't put off what you really want to say to them. Tomorrow they may not be here.

* Realise the impermanence of things. Imagine yourself in ten or twenty year's time. Try really hard. How does the time span affect the problem and its significance? Will this particular trouble matter then? No? Then it isn't half as important as it seems to be.

* Remember death and how it is your life's constant companion. Let death fill you with an urgency to explore and experience the world in a new way this very day. Why waste your life in reflecting on the misfortunes of your life when that finite time could be better spent.

* Expand your awareness into the physical universe. See this beautiful, stunning, blue, green and white globe spinning in the vastness of space. Think about the sun; our solar system; the galaxy; expand even further into history and time. Now compare that with your problem if you can still remember it! Perhaps you had forgotten the true significance of life; how valuable and unique it is. Value even the bad experiences because they prove that you are alive!

* If the worst comes to the worst, mope! Feel one hundred percent truly sorry for yourself. That is fine as well. Again it is part of life. Know that you are indulging but indulge nonetheless. You have every right to feel sorry for yourself. After a while, when you have done it to excess, you will get heartily sick and bored with it and will want to move on.

* Cleanse and cry and shout out all your emotions and thoughts; clear them out. Bang the couch or bed. Get drunk— in private—be bitter and twisted—again in private—rail against fate. Shake your fists at the gods—they can take it. Remind them that you are really unhappy at the moment. Have your say. Complete the cyclic nature of consciousness by putting in your—considered—two peneth. If it involves a particular person, can you write a letter with all that you really want to say in it? Be honest even if it may seem to diminish you; in reality honesty never diminishes you. Then send it to them, or burn it so that its message floats on the air to their ears. Finish it and move on.

* Discover your own particular successful strategy to approaching and surmounting difficulties. Refer to your diary and try to recognise what you did to help yourself to recover from a previous setback.

* Forgive. We are all human, all capable of error and wrong judgement. You wanted and expected them to behave in a certain way but they didn't. The universe did not respond in the way you wanted. That may or may not be an error; whatever, you still have a life to live and so do they. When you are heartily sick of allowing their actions to have an effect in your life then cut the memory loose. A small ritual or ceremonial burning will do. This time throw the ashes into the dustbin, flush them down the toilet, let them fall into a river or stream and ask the elements for help with healing and forgiveness. In order to forgive you must have recognised the lessons. Honestly evaluate events, how they unfolded, and thoroughly mull over them. Take away whatever you can that

243

is positive from the incident. Grow and evolve. Now forget. Please try to remember that however your life has been lived, you too have committed acts that need to be forgiven; no one has led an entirely blame free life; that would be ridiculous. You have transgressed also: I am not talking about any kind of divine law, but you have certainly acted against your better nature. Perhaps you too need to ask to be forgiven.

* Understand that not every day of your life has been misery. There have been times, no matter how few, when you were happy and content, and there is no reason why they cannot return in a new and surprising way. Whilst you are alive there is always the hope and very real possibility that things will change; if you kill yourself that can never happen.

* A technique which is quite advanced consists of simply standing side by side with your difficulty, neither fleeing nor challenging it. Rather as if an angry dog was bearing its teeth at you but instead of running away, or fighting the dog, you actually just spend time in that space. It is a difficult thing to do, but is well worth the effort. In fact it takes no effort at all. What it does take is courage; simply stand there in that space and be with your difficulty. Sometimes you will find that if you stop fighting, all the energy goes out of the situation and you can breathe again. Breathe again and learn. There is always something to learn! Try it, you may well be surprised.

* Realise that, as an evolving human being, you really do have a choice whether to deal with a difficulty in a habitual manner, or in a new and different way.

You have a choice whether to sit there and indulge or to stand up and do any of the above.

They do work I can assure you. As stated above though, it is fine to enjoy being miserable as long as you realise it is a choice. Now you have read the above I have given you choice. Try as you might you cannot deny that you now know alternatives to your usual behaviour when difficulties arise.

You will find many other methods for dealing with difficulties in other books. Sometimes though, it is actually necessary to have some faith that life is working out exactly as it should be for you. That is difficult, but not impossible; yet looking back we can often see that a new plateau of understanding and insight was reached after a period of darkness and stasis. When you know absolutely that you have behaved as well as any human could, with the highest and purest of motives—even if these only occurred to you after the event, as you rectified and completed the situation—then you can do nothing other than you have: your conscience is clear. It is only when the river reaches the shining sea that it can understand what the real purpose of the journey was.

Life is a rhythm. There is nothing in nature that doesn't have rhythm.

Even the mountains were once under the sea. Then, after they have risen, they are broken down and return, as sand, once more to the sea. Why do we humans expect life to be constantly wonderful? If it was then we would never know what happiness is. Do not yearn for mundaneness. Each moment can never be repeated again.

If you are experiencing difficulties do not think it a sign that you are on the wrong path, or an indication of failure: it may well be the opposite. All seekers after truth face difficulties; if it were easy then everyone would be doing it! Clearly that is not the case; only a few are drawn to investigate. Do not envy those that appear forever happy and joyful, clearly for even an advanced soul there is sadness and upset during a real life on Earth.

You are one of the not so many throughout history who have sought understanding and enlightenment on the human condition. Join hands with them during a meditation; hug and greet them; look into their eyes and see the self same burning desire to know. Speak to them. You will shed tears together: they are your fellow travellers. They will inform you that there is no ultimate enlightenment but many enlightenments and illuminations on the path. After all, you can only be enlightened about what you are concerned with at the moment, for other knowledge may seem to be totally irrelevant or unintelligible to you.

The path of self-discovery lasts for ever, that is its beauty; and you, as an individual unique expression of your true nature, illuminate the whole universe with your sparkling never-to-be-repeatedness. Do not be downhearted, press on!

Destiny, Fate, Karma, and Time

Following on from the thoughts in the previous chapter, there is another point worth making: it is often the case that we blame fate and destiny for our difficulties. I am afraid that the normal usage of those terms offers neither an excuse nor an explanation.

The only sure fact about your life is that at some point—and even that seems not to be pre-determined—you will die. However, if you are on a path of self discovery, and in contact with your soul nature, this is unlikely to be at any early point in life. I am excluding, of course, those who die young through illness or injury.

To understand destiny or fate it is necessary to resort to a metaphor. Imagine that the whole of your life can be represented by the space within an elasticated boundary. Within that boundary are a number of coloured marbles, each of which represents certain probable opportunities for growth and self-manifestation. Notice that they are not necessarily incidents as such, more like potential routes through which your individual manifestation can best be realised; rather like conduits which can boost your evolution, or tools which help you to uncover more of your potential. They are the subtle impulses behind situations. These marbles are not laid out in a pattern; they are totally mobile; the elasticated boundary, likewise, is flexible. Thus the shape of your life expands and contracts to accommodate the fulfilment of your potential. It is possible for you to do practically anything with your life, however there will only be certain routes that have the potential to bring out the best of you; they act as the sun does when it encourages a flower to unfold. Although the rain and soil are essential, sometimes the flower dies on the stem for lack of sun. That is how choices can make a difference in your life. There are paths that you are intrinsically more adapted to—that may seem to be destined in retrospect—and not only will they allow you to flower, but will also draw out specific qualities that may otherwise have remained dormant; qualities that are ingredients of your uniqueness. Many gems do not look beautiful in a natural state but, having been polished and cut by a skilled craftsman, glitter and shine so as to take the breath away. That is like your life. Do you see the subtle but important difference here between what is normally considered destiny and fate and these thoughts? It is not necessarily the case that you could only shine in one particular light, there may be other paths via which you could show your true nature; but yes, it may be that only a few paths—or even one alone—are rigorous enough to bring out the best of you. But this is different from what is commonly called destiny. In actual fact you are not destined to be anything at all, apart from human.

Everyone, however, does have the potential to become immortal

But it must be said, however, that there are good and bad decisions made during a life. Often it is the case that you actually learn from the bad ones, but it's quite possible to gain just as much information from the good decisions, it depends on your level of maturity. If you are in doubt about a decision, try compacting your future life: see yourself in ten, twenty or thirty year's time having made this particular decision. Does your soul have any comments to make? Sleep on it. Do not fear that if, in retrospect, you realise you made the wrong decision then the opportunity will be gone forever. Only the chance may well have gone for good but, and this is important to remember, if it was one of the important marbles in your life shape, then a similar situation will reoccur again, but perhaps in a different guise. Because of the flexibility of your life shape it will adapt to circumstances as they are now. Do not let this make you complacent and uncaring however. Learn from all the incidents of your life. Better that you ascend in spirals rather than go round in circles.

With these concerns in mind let us now consider a particular programme which needs to be retrieved from your mental world. It is the one which tells you that all accidents, deaths, misfortunes, diseases, even ordinary meetings, are purposeful, are predetermined and fated or meant to be. These are practically always excuses and explanations which are trying their best to rationalise the wanderings of this chaotic and freewill universe we live in.

Events can definitely be random and totally meaningless in themselves; without rhyme or reason they can descend onto the person lucky or unlucky enough to be in that particular place at that particular time.

You can be a genius and go unrewarded; you can be a shameful example of a human being and be wealthy and loved. Clearly, even a cursory look at the world around you will confirm this. You will have a much clearer view of reality—and be happier and more content into the bargain—if you can accept, or at least allow for the fact, that random events happen randomly. Not just to others but to you also. Pure chance. Do you see how this immediately releases you from your guilt and worry? No more "why me, I didn't deserve this," or "what was the meaning of that," more "OK, if that's how it is, I'll deal with it," or "what can I learn from this situation?"

Sometimes, with the best intentions in the world, your plans and hopes will fail. I cannot tell you why. The making of you as a human being is how you deal with these adversities.

Accepting the possibility that they may well be random is important. You can choose to deal with them in the present as challenges to be faced and conquered; enticements to help you draw on resources you never knew you had. To be sure we are all more powerful and resourceful than we acknowledge. In order for you to remember the ever present and ever emerging true nature you are uncovering, it will be helpful if you approach such situations with these thoughts in mind, instead of blaming fate and destiny. Sometimes you are simply unlucky; it is as plain as that.

Notice that I do not mention that very popular explanation: karma. The truth is that for the vast majority of people on the Earth karma does not exist. Karma is not carried over to a new life because there is no entity called you that existed before this life, and you are born and live on the Earth only once. Karma only has any relevance for those who have at least a vestigial immortal spirit body. How can consciousness return to an individual if that individual has no integrity: it would be returning to something so separate and fragmented that the source of the original act would be unidentifiable. In the case of a reasonably integrated human being karma, the result of actions, returns, if not immediately then within a few days or weeks. But then, as an integrated being, you would know when you had acted wrongly; not in accord with your true nature; your conscience would inform you strongly and you would "feel bad"—soul nature—about an act. It is not a sophisticated act to know when you have done wrong, just one that many people simply choose to ignore; they have become so used to the rude selfishness of their lives that the way they treat other humans and the life on this planet has little impact on their stubborn and closed consciousness. However, as an integrated being, your response would involve a "setting to rights." An act of contrition would need to be performed in whatever practical or symbolic way you felt appropriate. Karma, in its true form, would really indicate a pricking of your "spiritual conscience," or guilt about an act. As such it would be self-induced in the developed individual; almost as if a barometer or circuit would be bought into operation indicating that you had acted against your true nature. Karma exists only when people have a conscience about their acts. Karma, as understood by numerous people in the world, is a political and religious tool to control human behaviour. Ultimately, of course, because a "bad human" would not be acting in accord with his or her soul then death, annihilation, would definitely be the end result of their lives. Perhaps not as satisfying as it could be, but at least there would seem to be some form of crude justice!

Besides fate and destiny, we also have another factor to consider: time. Time is flexible and contracts and expands. Sometimes it disappears altogether. Remember I informed you, as I myself was informed, that the soul itself lives in a timeless realm. There is no concept of time passing in that realm at all. Your soul forms, exists, and at a certain point no longer exists. This means that information passing to the soul is doing so concurrently with information from your past and future, assuming that at such times there is communication between your body and soul, something that is by no means certain. This is a difficult concept to elucidate on further, or even to think about logically, but you will find it easier to understand if you do not think linearly. Just hold the idea and its ramifications in a kind of limbo for a while, do not dissect too much; allowing an understanding to fruit in its own time. Actually there are many spiritual ideas that should be treated in such a way.

What this means in practical terms is that you can contact and consult the soul for its feelings on matters; you can also decide whether a particular occupation, opportunity, love relationship etc. is relevant to you at that time as an individual. By referencing the appendix on the subtle anatomy of humans you will find out where the connection is between the body and the soul. You can imagine the sensations from both your body and present emotions to be in the form of running water which gathers around, and forms a whirlpool disappearing through, the umbilicus. Send your emotions and thoughts through into the soul realm, into the eye of the whirlpool, and feel them dissolving into the depths. Three basic responses are possible: a feeling of expansion, or/and warmth and relaxation; a feeling of deadness, contraction or tension; or no response at all. The only one which needs to be explained, as the others are self explanatory, is the last. In this case the lack of feeling response means that it is fine to go ahead, but it is unlikely to have meaningful ramifications in either direction. So enjoy if you wish to!

Time can be seen as the relating of events into a linear framework. But actually there is another way to see such events. Living in the moment—in the now—enables you to eliminate, if even for a short time, the passage of time. What is more it somehow compacts the past-present-future into the present, and as such also eliminates judgements about incidents or yourself: things simply are as they are. It is not only a way of dealing with difficulties but is also one of the true ways to be happy, to be happiness. It is never sufficient for you to reflect afterwards that at a particular time you were happy, you need to be in happiness at the time to know it. That means no reflection or thinking. Pure awareness is the key. Within that pure awareness something happens, yet it is something that cannot really be spoken of. It would seem to be true aliveness. After all, how much of our time is spent reflecting on the past, whether it be recent or distant, about possibilities for the future, from simply getting up and going to work to planning fifty years ahead. It may be reflections on intellectual questions and problems, or else a comment somebody has made. All these thoughts rob us of being totally present; and, since the present is all that we can actually know, your life is actually being impoverished by no one else's hand but your own. You are the only person who can stop time and experience life.

Living as such, you simply are. It is an immediate way to contact the body of life energy. Pure awareness—or consciousness—of being. And, as you would expect, it is by no means easy; but it is well worth pursuing in practice. Again, not too rigorous or serious, experiment with it for short periods or you will eliminate the fun of the adventure from your life. Truly, all work and no play make Jack a dull boy; however all play and no work makes Jack a lout! Resorting to my metaphor again, the desired result is that the elasticated boundary of your life shape is of a desirable tension; not so tight that each decision becomes critical and not so slack that you are hardly aware of being alive.

Remember the jewel that comes free with your life: the gift of immortality. Remember death? Immortality is not one of the marbles in your lifeshape, it is a pearl. Are you going to grab it, or sit there looking at it in a day dream. Begin today.

The Soul

The word soul has so many connotations and connections with different forms of thinking that first of all I need to separate the word into an isolated definition: for the purposes of this teaching it could equally be called your body of life energy, a body of energy formed from the medium of that realm—the soul realm. That is what I mean by soul body. Try to separate this definition away from the moral and judgmental attachments the word has in our society. I am not using it in a religious sense, simply as a practical and factual word to describe that particular body. As you already know, we each possess three bodies: a physical body formed from the physical world, a mental body formed from the substance of that realm, and a soul body formed in the soul realm. All exist in the same space that you now occupy.

You are a multi-dimensional being.

In truth, getting in touch with the soul body is sometimes difficult to perceive correctly. If you feel the movement within of waves and vibrations, the more gross manifestations of the movements of consciousness, it will almost certainly be the case that you are perceiving movement associated with your mental body, which in itself it is beneficial to be aware of. But the movement of soul consciousness—also known as the power of love—can vary between being enormously impressive and unmistakable or, more usually, incredibly subtle; almost a perception of movement once removed. It is a feeling, but sometimes a sensation. It is an awareness but not a thought; akin to something happening but not having the words to speak about it.

253

It may be better to think of it as a template or reference. It is the core of your uniqueness; it is life itself. It is a connection with something outside our usual perception, and at the same time it is the heartland of your true self. However, do not make the mistake of thinking that it is above your head or up in the stratosphere somewhere: it is here, now, surrounding you and within you.

If you want to recreate a clear perception of your soul, imagine with intense vividness the time when you felt the happiest in your life; when you felt vitally alive. Now simply concentrate on that subtle feeling of expansion and vibrancy—aliveness— that is the movement and perception of the soul body.

If you were boiled down into a concentrate, so that all that is extraneous and not really you was burned off, it is what would be left. If you are on the path in the correct way then it actually is you, and you are beginning to be it.

As stated before, it is passionate and adventurous. It is joyful and exciting. It is sexual. Through contacting your soul you will be both more enlivened and yet, ironically, more at peace with yourself. As if you had come home after a long journey. Its timelessness is comforting and calming, but when its energy is aroused and invigorating it will spur you on to new heights and endeavours.

Each person will perceive it in a slightly different way. But you can be sure that when you feel expanded, excited, blissful and happy then you are in good contact with soul consciousness.

Think about when it is in your own life that such feelings invigorate you. Is it a hobby you have—dancing; speaking and communicating with friends; when you are doing a certain type of work; when you are alone; perhaps an artistic pursuit or making; music; making love; a special celebration; viewing a sunrise or sunset? I could go on and on. Do you see how your soul loves life itself?

You can be sure that if you rarely have these feelings then you need to orientate your life towards a more fulfilling and soulful existence; one that simply makes you feel more alive. Interestingly enough, the only healing a soul ever needs is to allow its manifestation in the physical realm; the only way you can hurt a soul is by closing off its manifestation and ignoring it, which is a strange thing to do really, to ignore your self! In such a case the soul body actually shrinks and the person concerned will feel cut off from life.

Sometimes your soul consciousness will be perceived by your mental body as disturbing, oppressing, driving, and passionate; perhaps even too much for your ego to deal with.

These are the urgent needs of a soul—one desperate to be expressed in the physical world.

In order for you to get a better perspective on what is really taking place in your life, you may need to begin to differentiate between the desires and opinions of your mind and the desires and concerns of your soul. It is quite possible to be worried, fearful, and emotional about a situation, but by eliminating the mental symptoms and concentrating on the physical body and soul feelings—which will actually be felt in the physical body—you will find that you actually feel quite good. You see, sometimes your mental body—in the form of your ego—may well have a different agenda than your soul body; sometimes it certainly does not want to change and move. Believe it or not it may simply be scared about what will happen as a result—that it may have to alter itself to accommodate a new truth. Your soul body may desperately need you to change in order for you to live a more fulfilling and self-realised life. If you can differentiate between the impulses arising from your soul and those from your mental realm, it will give you a better perspective on events and help you to feel more secure about changes that may need to take place.

Now you truly understand the meaning behind the phrase "in spite of everything I actually feel good about this."

Have you used that phrase without knowing its true significance? Now you do.

Your soul certainly has a lust for life. That is why it can sometimes be perceived as an incredibly disturbing force within you. It can even cause a kind of abstract pain. You feel you are being torn apart, driven to distraction by something which you cannot identify. It feels as if your soul is trying its best to undermine the structures you

255

have built around yourself in the mental world which, in actual fact, may shore up a fictional and inappropriate self-image. At such times it is important to move, dance, exercise, or otherwise be in your body. Concentrate on your body feelings and sensations. It could well be that in a few minutes, hours or days you will understand what has to be done. It takes time for the mental body to translate the body feelings you have experienced into something logical and understandable; perhaps it might well be unable to convert them exactly into linear thought at all; but in some mysterious way you will know what has to be done.

Understand that the soul does not communicate to you in words or pictures but the mind may well translate the feelings it receives as such. The pictures it may produce as a result are not the message. Decipher them and understand the true significance behind what you have experienced.

With that last idea in mind I want to talk a little about something that may not be clear to you, something that even well advanced people seem not to understand. Often when workings are done in nature there is this perceived element of vision and clairvoyant perception. Peculiar journeys and visualisations may ensue. More often than not these are the rationalisations of the feelings you experienced within your soul and body of whatever it was you contacted. The movement of consciousness within your body was entirely genuine; the rest may be entirely symbolic. Search behind these pictures and words for the true, occasionally abstract, spiritual messages. Usually this type of investigation will result in a certain knowingness that can never be doubted. The knowingness is more than belief or opinion. It is the certainty of a knowledge perceived through the physical body; that which is pivotal in the relationship that exists between your soul and your mind.

According to some philosophical models of thought, all that we perceive is illusion: but this is not the case. It is true that much is ill understood and misinterpreted, but there really is knowledge available to those who truly wish to know. That knowledge flows from your soul body and the soul bodies of others, into the physical realm. The physical world is so very important to the life of humans, indeed it is highly likely to be important to our universe as a whole and exceptionally important to all things that live. It is entirely possible to misinterpret the physical world before us, but that is down to our own mental structures which although allowing us a social reference, also limit us as seekers. Allow more possibilities into your life, even what may seem to be outlandish. Your mind will get the idea eventually and your true knowledge of this universe will grow as a result.

Our three bodies communicate using different aspects of consciousness. It is as if three humans were born of the same mother but bought up in different countries. On meeting each other they speak different languages and have to begin to interpret what each other is saying. The human born in the country of the soul, however, is the least sullied and the most pure expression of all of them. It is the teacher and leader. The body is the translator: the mind the interpreter, and so on back and forth. If this process of communication is encouraged and facilitated you will, in time, be hardly able to differentiate them from each other, so similar are they. Does that help you to understand?

Without the physical body to translate and transmute,
without the mind to interpret and discern,
the soul would be impotent.

As stated above, the only way you can actually injure your soul is to deny it its manifestation. No soul needs retrieving. No soul fragments. It simply loses heart. It is defeated in its primary urge to manifest itself.

If, for a minute, you imagine this core uniqueness which is called your soul, do you see it as happy or sad; as jumping around and active for at least sometime during your day, or is it morose and defeated? Is it overshadowed and its messages drowned out by an enormous ego shouting down and bullying your sparkling soul, throwing a cloak over its light? Think about this. The answers will aid you on your path of development, evolution and manifestation. Your one and only human life.

The Modern World

How strange it is to try to pursue this journey in the modern world, where the spiritual search seems so easily undermined and rebuffed. In times past the closeness of human life to the natural world enabled, and often encouraged, a connection between a human body and its soul. Indeed all the thoughts laid down herein shouldn't really be necessary.

This process of immortalisation should be a natural consequence of your life on Earth, simply part of your evolution as a human being.

When our lives were spent in natural surroundings, when we had to concentrate so much on physical well being, food and shelter, and when the natural processes of life such as eating, defecation, physical contact and sexual activity, were not taboo, then the evolution of humans was often natural. The expression of one's uniqueness was all part of the whole; indeed, unusual and what we might call eccentric people were often given specific roles to which they would be adapted and well suited in some enlightened societies. There was a place for almost anyone. Thus all felt part of the community in which they lived; all were valued. However, it has to be admitted that this has only actually happened a few times on the Earth. Often there were societies that were not far away from this ideal, but they fell short simply because of power struggles between religious ideals and the politics of the community. Even in large communities it only takes one human to undermine what could have been a marvellous life for all.

What seems to be missing in the modern world, and has been for hundreds of years, is the valuing of our eccentricity: for in essence we are all eccentric. Certain individual behaviours and expressions should be a natural expression and component of each life; the particular mode through which individuality is expressed. Yes, there may well be other, more common, expressions but the urge to demonstrate uniqueness and individuality and, what is more, for it to be valued, is one of the strongest urges in human kind. Intrinsically we all recognise our uniqueness.

But, living in the modern world, our task is made enormously difficult. Yet, in some strange way, it also presents us with enormous possibilities for growth. The challenge of our personal evolution is actually facilitated by the huge number of fellow humans we have to deal with. Ironically, the plethora of individuals on Earth at this time has not of itself produced diversity, rather people seem to attach themselves to particular groups, cults or tribes, within which they feel part of the whole. How strange to realise therefore that we all already belong to the tribe called human, and within that we should express our individuality. In this way, uniqueness is not lost within the mass. Whether you belong to a tribe of a few individuals or to one which encompasses millions, it is so important not to lose yourself in the rules, regulations, and admonitions of that group. The group is not in itself an end, your expression of yourself is. It is so often the case that people will join such groups because they identify a commonality of interest between them, yet they then lie down and accept everything that is required of them in order to remain a part of that group. It is not good enough, for the sake of peace, to agree to something which denies individuality and uniqueness. Do not be afraid to leave such groups if they no longer serve your growth: doing so will polish a vital facet of the jewel at the centre of your being and it will sparkle a little brighter.

Without a doubt, deep personal evolution is not happening at present. The reasons have all been laid down in this book. So many humans think that they occupy the real world when in effect all they do is live within their own mental creations. Many of the values of present day society are completely alien to the soul. Indeed, if it thought as the mind does, it may well be perplexed as to why it would seem that our society never truly values the soul's uniqueness. Imagine the situation as rather like a child who is always spoken for by a parent, "But mum I would like to..." "Yes dear, I know what you want to do." But they rarely do, and the child's growth is stunted. Now reverse the situation and see how idiotic it all seems: an out of control child telling its parent what to do. Do you understand?

It seems that we have to learn again how to express ourselves; not from the mind, but from the soul. To do this will involve all that I have mentioned.

It is time to repossess the whole of you and learn not to constantly subdue your true passion; passion that is from the soul, not the distorted meanderings of an out of control ego. We are surrounded by constant admonitions to behave in such and such a way; to toe the line; to be dressed and presented in a certain way, and told that we have no value if particular material possessions are not part of our life.

All this is rubbish. It is simply a case of you giving away your power. It is also the case that you are not valuing your own lessons and experiences of life on this Earth; in effect, your own uniqueness.

You know inside that the way a person dresses, the way they talk, the colour of their skin, their sexuality, does not in any way reflect their value as a human being.

It suits the lives of the majority to think otherwise though; they belong to a particular tribe because their strength as an individual is lacking. Likewise, it suits the majority if you do not work on yourself and your evolution. Your progress illuminates their doubts. Their prejudiced and uninformed opinions will be challenged by much that you say and do. That is why difference is not valued today, and yet is indispensable for your continued evolution.

This seems an appropriate opportunity to cover another related topic, one very distinctly of the modern world. There are great moves afoot today to have us all believe that what we actually are is simply the result of genes, chromosomes and chemical reactions. Everything is seen as ultimately explainable and elementary. What these people have in common with others who share their beliefs is that they deny their own personal experience in an effort to explain and contain their lives. The possibility of other dimensions to their beingness cannot be allowed to exist, because that would mean that they had to allow for the mysterious and unknown to play its part in their lives. And that would be far too frightening. It is not enough, as

I have stated before, to discover such and such, or to believe that is the way things are, your personal experience must be entered into the equation. You are your own apparatus and signifier; you do not have to build machines in order to perceive what you, as a human being, know to be true.

When you look at the stars at night; when you fall in love; when you grieve at the loss of a friend, you know you are more than chromosomes and chemicals. The exultation at the birth of a child; joy, laughter and ecstasy, are all very human and all innate. Not only do we experience them, but we experience them with our own sensory apparatus: our consciousness.

I do not need anyone else to tell me when I am happy or sad, to prove by dials and readouts that I am in love. I know this.

Scientific machines are tremendous applications of human discovery and ingenuity, but they are not the whole story. They never will be. Do not think for one minute that the trend that is inherent at the moment is all truth and innocent investigation. At its core is the basic and inevitable desire for power. Pure and simple. Who will be the genius who leads us to physical immortality, freedom from all disease, the discoverer of a pill which induces true happiness? NO-ONE WILL. YOU ARE HUMAN. Once you recognise this fact—and own it—you will realise that the whole of you can never be discovered or denied by others, only by yourself. In your own world you are all powerful. Isn't it about time that you owned that power? Never let them tell you what you are; how you are nothing other than explainable phenomena. Of course some of the actions and reactions of your physical body can be explored and explained, but that is only part of you, not the whole of you. I give you the right to allow yourself to be more magical, mysterious, knowledgeable and awesome than you can possibly imagine.

You are a mystery. An awesome mystery. Never forget that.

Surely, the modern era is one of the most difficult times for a true seeker to pursue the goal of completing their personal and spiritual evolution. On the surface it may seem like there is enormous opportunity, but scratch that thin layer of freedom and you will discover that there is only encouragement, at every turn, to discontinue your pathwalking and submit to the group consciousness of the present moment.

The truth is that society cannot really change until individuals work on themselves; that is the way of real progress.

And that is what you are doing now, isn't it?

The Natural World

Humans originated as part of the natural world; we were not planted here as fully formed beings.

From our earliest beginnings we were an innate part of the life of this planet. Each of the billions of cells that we are made from is derived from those that originally swam as single celled organisms in the sea of life. Think about that for a moment; trace your natural history back through time and think of your lineage. We have so much in common with all of the natural world.

The antidote to the modern world is the natural world which, despite all the attempts of man, still holds sway on the Earth. It is the healer of your injuries both physical and mental; it is the regenerator of vitality. It is and always will be more powerful than the mind of humans. You only have to look at any number of natural disasters that happen each year to see how powerful the elemental forces of this Earth are. Human beings will never overpower nature, nor will they control it.

There seems to be much sentimentality, particularly at the moment, about nature. Only one side of the enormous equation is viewed, just as, often, only one side of human nature is seen. It is as important to see the seeming cruelty, heartlessness, and tragedy that are an intrinsic part of the natural world at the same time as the beauty, diversity, and stunning allure that it undoubtedly possesses. The Earth can crush you without a thought, the wind destroy you, the water drown you, and the sun burn you to death. The evolution of the spirits which control such forces may have absolutely nothing to do with human life. Often they have their own agenda and course of development to follow, and may not occupy similar realms to humans. They will, however, have a soul. All that lives has a soul body. But trying to control such forces for our own ends is not to interact with them intelligently.

Once you realise that these natural forces are more powerful than any of us, your urgings to control them vanish and are replaced by a proper sense of respect, investigation and inquisitiveness. Notice that I said we cannot overpower them, but that does not mean we cannot learn from them. There is always help out there for our dilemmas. Much original and inspired thought and philosophy can be traced back to the observation of nature and its ways. How could it be otherwise? We are nature. We are part of the universe—an important and valuable part.

Without the support of the environment we could not live. Where does the water you drink, the food you eat, the shelter you take, and the air you breathe come from originally? What is it that warms us; how come this planet supports any life at all? Our existence here is balanced on a knife edge and yet, although the forces were not in themselves meant to be our teachers, some are more than willing to help us on our spiritual and evolutionary path. However, you have to ask and value. You must give thanks to them as I directed earlier.

Answers will come in many abstract forms and will need to be deciphered by your mind. Sometimes such knowledge will never be understood linearly and always remain a feeling, a knowingness; an intuition. This type of knowledge is especially valuable as it opens up whole new ways of observing and interacting with the world we live in. How could the wind literally talk to you; how can a tree see as you do; a stone has no ears; the earth cannot taste the herbs you scatter on it. It is the consciousness behind such impressions that has significance: and it is the quality and motivation behind your initial contact which will have a significant bearing on the type of interaction that is possible. It is as if you were setting up a telephone wire along which communication can flow.

**Always approach nature with respect and reverence
and a genuine desire to know and learn.**

As I stated earlier, you may simply have intuitions and impressions; fleeting thoughts and feelings. These are simply to be experienced. Analysis comes later; understanding, perhaps never.

Still, the act of communication with nature expands us, breaks down boundaries and long held mental blockages; it nourishes our human nature. Nature will humble you. Then watch, observe and learn.

Imagine yourself as one of the cells of this planet. Are you helpful; does it have pride that you are here, or are you a cancer or disease that the Earth would love to eradicate?

Human values must be separated from those of nature. The sun will shine on you irrespective of your creed, colour or morality. The Earth will nurture you without a care for your history or your positive and negative qualities. Really try to understand this. See that what the forces have to give you is available to all, and that includes you. Knowledge is there for the asking and investigation. However, as I have stated, the correct method of approach is all important.

How very easy it is these days to feel alienated from everything. When we feel cut off from the world around us and the society in which we live, the panacea for your problem is actually all around you: nature. Primarily you are first a part of the nature of this planet rather than a citizen of a town or country. That is where to begin if you are feeling alienated and alone. Try reflecting on some of the following:

* the oxygen your body breaths is produced by the plant kingdom—the carbon dioxide you breath out is used by the plant kingdom.

* tons of cosmic dust fall onto the Earth each year and is then integrated into the soil. The food you eat, whether vegetable or not, grows in and is made from this dust. You are made of the stardust of this universe.

* when you switch on the electricity or gas, eat food or drink water; wear clothes, live in a house or shelter, you are partaking in a network of production and distribution whose origin can be nothing other than the natural world.

* without the Earth to nurture you, without the sun to warm you, without the atmosphere to protect you, you would be dead. You would never have the chance to live and experience, nor the possibility of becoming immortal.

* however you have lived, whatever life you lead, it affects others, even if in the most minuscule ways. And, believe it or not, your consciousness affects the whole universe in some way or other.

Like it or not, you are part of the sum total of this universe. If your light goes out, so does something which is unique and never to be repeated again. Even if you feel that absolutely no one else values or cares about you, you must learn to value yourself.

The acceptance or rejection of you by other human beings means absolutely nothing in the great scheme of things. It does not affect your chances of immortality one iota.

One of the major results of contact with the natural world is a stimulation and invigoration of your powers of awe and respect. Read books, watch films, and analyse for yourself the incomprehensible diversity and magic of life. When you are feeling disheartened and disillusioned, watch the natural history of practically any animal or plant. They struggle against unbelievable odds, even in the face of huge disasters and disadvantages; in spite of frailty and injury, they persevere. You cannot fail to be moved. For all our knowledge we cannot even recreate a single cell from its component parts. Yet there are billions of cells in your body, and they work without a single request from you. How is it that plants and trees shed their leaves in autumn and re-clothe themselves in spring? How do animals migrate, raise young, battle against practically insurmountable obstacles to survive until the next year? From whence did the impulse for the creation of this universe arise? How big is this universe? How did this planet and the solar system really come to be? What is the true age of man?

What is the true potential of a fully realised, self actualised you?

The physical universe is far more magical, awesome, and mysterious, than any of us can comprehend. This is also true of you. So, when you advance into nature as a counterbalance to modern life, do so with these thoughts in mind. There is so much that we do not know, so much to learn, so much to simply admire, and so much of it will forever remain mysterious. There will always be something in the natural world to investigate further and understand better.

But that is part of the fun of being here!

Summing up and beyond

The whole emphasis of this book is on the revealing of that inner jewel that glitters and sparkles like no other. In each person it has a unique colour and lustre; an individual number of facets; it may be rough hewn or cut; big or small; opaque or clear. None of these qualities is more important than any other; it is only important to reveal that jewel in the first place. Rather as if a man or woman carried a gem around with them and kept it secret, but gradually and experimentally began to show it to his or her friends, work colleagues, people they met in the street; parents, relations, lovers. That is how the true nature of you begins to shine in each "transaction" you have with the world out there. It should also shine when you are alone. These instructions are a way of describing the stages of development, and the information necessary, to enable the process of immortalisation to take place. It is rather like the clearing of a bank of fog to view that which was previously hidden. Deconstruct the ego and reconstruct it on the pattern of the soul or self-nature. This fluid, flexible and integrated consciousness imprints the very substance of the universe—what you could call spirit or the void—and your immortal spirit body begins to form. Beingness could be further defined as the consciousness emanating from the centre point of that spirit body. You could liken your ego development in ordinary life as to that of a child; the development stage of your self-nature as akin to adolescence; and your spirit body formation as that of a true adult: fully formed and acting from this imprinted beingness. It has to be activated from a fully realised self-nature, which itself acts as a catalyst to enable your spirit body development. Beingness is both the infusing, or infusion, of spirit with the consciousness of your true self-nature, and the conscious occupation and manifestation of that state.

I am talking about an ideal, a target to aim for; in reality it is a hard won prize.

In spite of this difficulty, I am informing you of the way things actually are; I am not giving you a metaphor or model through which to view reality.

However, do not expect it to reveal itself quickly; even if it did it will take a monumental effort to bring its influence to bear in everyday situations. We can forget it for hours, days or months, even whilst we think that we are trying our hardest to manifest it, which can be a rather strange realisation. At other times, when we are least aware, our true self can be revealed easily and without intention, only afterwards do we appreciate what happened.

In reality it should take no effort at all to reveal your true nature. After all, it is you! But, after a lifetime of building an ego structure brick by brick which—due to the false plans that you had in front of you at the time—bears little resemblance to who you really are, it cannot do other than take time, effort and determination to complete your task. That is part of the fun though: the journey, the investigation, the introspection, the testing against reality out there. It's just that it takes time and, as humans, we seem to be naturally impatient. Now perhaps you understand why in some systems of learning the acolyte will be asked to cut off all connections with his or her previous life, with all the relations and friends and work they once had. In one fell swoop they are reborn without a history, the ego that has been built up over countless trials is cast aside and they walk out into the world like a blank canvas. That is one way, but there are others. Very often you are never as bad as you think you are, everything in your ego is not wrong; indeed for a lucky few there may only need to be a gentle repositioning and refinement of ideas, beliefs and attitudes. Moreover, what are usually amiss are the patterns that we have created for dealing with the world at large. These patterns in themselves have served us through our lives until this point but, if they are designed to defend an ego structure that in itself is distorted, the situation becomes untenable; we had better dismantle them and begin again.

The result of this restructuring is that if your ego is a pure reflection of your true nature, then nothing can assail it: it cannot be disturbed by any incident because it is based on a true picture of your original uniqueness, of what and who you really are. That imprint is indestructible.

Unfortunately it is practically impossible to create this true likeness of you in the mental world immediately. Even if it were, we all have structures in the outer world which reinforced that older-style you. They, and this includes all the people you know, will seek to strengthen the older structures and to destroy the new. It gives rise to the classic comment "but that was then and this is now," "I'm not like that anymore...I've changed." Why do we find it so difficult to accept these statements from others? The image we have in our minds of who and what they are is a static form, one that doesn't allow for change. Better that we have a somewhat nebulous "abstract" thought-form associated with their name; rather as if we were interested in finding out more about them each time we meet, than to compartmentalise them at all.

If you allow for change in yourself then you must also allow others to change.

Likewise, the structures you have built up around you in the physical world may also need to be changed and bought up to date. This can take much time and effort. Yet again though, this helps to clarify more and more the "who you really are." The processes of conflict and change, difference and self-examination, will all help by reaffirming and renegotiating—both with yourself and the world— that real you. A challenging but worthy task.

When you have a good sense of that real you, then you will more easily identify when you go against it. Again, this helps to crystallise the soul-nature throughout your whole self. As this process takes place you will begin to imprint the very nature of the universe, that undifferentiated background—spirit—with your true nature. As a congruent individual it cannot be otherwise: you begin to form your immortal spirit body.

**This is how you can live on after the death of your three selves;
for you must make no excuses to yourself about the fact
that they will all die at the end of your life on Earth.**

Perhaps the mental body, if it is strongly held in a rigid pattern, will survive for some years afterwards; a phenomenon which gives rise to the present day fascination with channelling and the spirit world. However, this is not a permanent state because the mental body will eventually disintegrate. Then you will die forever. It is perhaps right that only with a supreme effort to clarify your true nature will you be able to manifest an immortal body. In this way, all the beings that have immortalised themselves justly reflect how they were originally created. Can you imagine how awful the real realms after death would be if everyone, no matter how distorted their mirrors, was immortalised. The universe would be nothing but a rubbish tip, rather like the ever increasing number of satellites and junk circling this beautiful Earth.

Even this immortalisation is not the whole point of the process. It is a bi-product.

**The whole point of your life on Earth is to
manifest who you really are.**

In the end it doesn't matter what you do for work, what religion you are, what colour your skin, which sex you make love to, how you spend your leisure time; nothing else matters to the universe other than manifesting your true nature during your life without deliberately hurting another. There is no more reward for dedicating your life to millions of people instead of being a mechanic, a street sweeper or a housewife. The universe does not work like that. After having read this book you should already realise this fact.

**You are not a child being chastised by a parent; you are an
adult manifesting your uniquely created life.**

I see this emerging true nature as concomitant with the word 'spirituality.' At the present time spirituality is another of those words that has both thoughtful and unpleasant associations. In this

274

understanding you can have a better idea of its truer and more relevant meaning. It is the interest in, the working on, the effort towards, and the manifestation of your soul nature and the creation of your immortal spirit as a consequence. It is not a holy or religious endeavour, one which tries to deny the true nature of humans. If you are in any doubt read the chapters which describe how adventurous, sexual, passionate and life enhancing the soul actually is. There is nothing there that you wouldn't want to take with you; nothing that you would regret leaving behind. It is not even concerned with spirits and gods in any religious sense, even though they are, of course, a reality. It is about you.

So, how will you change as a result of walking on this path? Who can say? For some reasons beyond understanding some who have suffered greatly manage to retain a contact with the real heart of themselves, others fall by the wayside. Perhaps your life has been relatively easy and yet you have lost touch with who you really are. This is the working out of individuality and free will in the world. We do not need to understand why. Whatever your present state, there is always work to be done on defining your true nature. Try not to use, as guides, external or internal images of how you will be. Prepare to be surprised. Use your sense of beingness. I cannot describe this to you in language. I can only say that you will recognise it when you begin to make progress. It is not a thought or an emotion. It can begin as a feeling about what and who you are, but as you become more and more congruent with your true self you will simply understand and acknowledge this sense of beingness. You do not reflect on this beingness, you simply are. Yet what you are is a different aspect of the whole of creation. Whatever it is that maintains the state of being alive is common to all, but this is not what you need to manifest. Perhaps a metaphor will serve our purpose. Electricity causes a light bulb to shine. Electricity is common to all light bulbs, yet light bulbs in themselves are different: different wattages, shapes and colours. It is the nature of the light after it is transmuted through the medium of the glass that we are interested in. As I have already mentioned, do not believe others who tell you that in essence we have no individuality. That is like saying that all books using the same language are the same. Clearly that is not the case. It is interesting to reach that state of non-differentiation, but not an end in itself. For some it can even be an escape route from the trials of living an individual, self-actualised life. What you are trying to do is to find out who you are. Do you want to live as part of an undifferentiated amorphous mass, or shine as an individual unique creation: yes part of the whole, but as a truly differentiated aspect of that whole? Recognise your connection to—yet your difference from—everything that exists. Yes I know these are two poles of the same continuity, and much mystical thought can be attached to its realisation—that of being one and of being one of many at the same instant. I leave that discussion up to you. That is for you to explore and will be your knowledge. My stipulation is that you discover yourself first. It is impossible to see your attachment to the whole whilst still being undifferentiated from it. A two dimensional being cannot know its position in space without pulling out of it into the third dimension. Two people who are passionately in love lose themselves in each other, but that stage should ultimately be left behind and be replaced by an admiration and love of the other as an individual, something which gives birth to respect, love and understanding. Your manifested individuality is the best thanks you can give for the gift of your life.

I do not think that, as individual human beings, we are specifically supported by that which creates us after it has done so: its love does maintain your life for as long as you live, but you do not receive more or less because you understand this fact. It is up to each one of us to take care of ourselves and each other—and of course the environment which supports us. That is a measure of our independence, freedom, and responsibility. Is that not the greatest gift you can be given? As a human being on the Earth we are one of many. As a planet part of the solar system we are one of many. As a solar system part of a galaxy we are one of many, and as galaxies part of the cosmos we are still only one of many. We cannot know the workings out of the universe, its purpose, if any at all. Even in the very small incidents of our lives we cannot take in all the possible ramifications of our actions; the consequences of failure and success. We can try, but we will never know the end result whilst we are here. The meandering stream that trickles from a spring into others, making a river which has rapids and waterfalls, pools and tributaries and an estuary, never knows what the journey was all about until it reaches the shining sea. Only then can it appreciate and understand the trials it has been put through.

Your uniqueness is that spring. Your life its journey, and the sea into which it flows? That is for you to discover, many years hence: but you will never be able to find out unless you make the journey to discover the uniqueness of that gushing clear spring in the first place.

Read the first paragraph of this handbook again. Do you begin to feel its truth now, or is it still far away? I can tell you that I absolutely know this to be true, not only of myself, but of each and every one of you.

Imagine an Earth full of glittering, sparkling, multicoloured and multifaceted jewels; imagine them all shining into space. Imagine that you are one of those jewels, adding your individual sparkle to that which is known throughout all dimensions as human.

Begin to feel pride in being yourself.

Be!

Amama ua noa!

Appendix

Whilst reading this book you may have become a little confused about the position of the different gateways, and the spatial relationship of the three bodies as I have referred to them. This section will help to make things clearer.

Strangely enough, after all you have read, you may well find this the most contentious and challenging of all the ideas in this book. As I have said more than once, at present there is much information available which is distorted and very far from its original source—no where more so than with information and instructions concerning your three bodies. However, no matter how disturbed you are by it, please read this section carefully; I am not presenting a model of human subtle anatomy—this is how it actually is. So, at least let the ideas rest lightly on top of your thoughts for a short time and, perhaps in that way, they may become saturated and gently sink into your nature. After all, why would I lie to you?

First of all it is necessary for you to be clear about the fact that you are a multi-dimensional being. Out of all the dimensions that interpenetrate the very space that you occupy here and now, a human being partakes of only three which, for the sake of clarity, we call the mental, physical and soul realms. These three realms communicate with each other through what we can call gateways; these are like passages through which information in the form of consciousness can pass to a connected body in another realm. These gateways are specific and in particular positions within the space of your physical body. There is no gateway that connects all three bodies—that is why I have constantly stressed the importance of your physical body: its position in the scheme of things is unique. The gateways, as I have stated, transmit the consciousness from one body to another, thus enabling the three to communicate with each other. Without clear connections between these gateways it would be as if you were not just one, but three different people trying to lead each other forwards—none of whom can talk, touch or see each other.

As explained earlier, your physical and mental bodies should be identical in shape, and occupy the same area spatially. Your soul, although it exists in the same place as your mental and physical

279

bodies, is not the same shape. It is oval, larger, wider and longer than either of your other two bodies. At its highest point above your head, it contacts, through a gateway, that which created you and maintains your aliveness. At its lowest point below your feet, it contacts the Earth. Within it is a pattern, a spiral from above the head to below the feet—known as the soul pattern—which is the absolute pure essence of you. Around it is gathered the oval body of energy or substance of that realm. These two function together as a unit until you die. This is your soul body.

Your physical body—being pivotal—has two connecting gateways, one to your mental body and one to your soul body. Thus the incoming messages from your mental and soul bodies are translated and transmitted by your physical body and its consciousness. For once and for all time remember that your mental body does not communicate directly with your soul, it can only do so via your physical body.

The gateway from your body to your soul is at the position of your umbilicus, in depth it is at a midpoint in your body. It is not a physical structure but an energetic one.

For consciousness to pass from your physical body to your mental body there is a gateway at the base of your brain, approximately at the position of the medulla oblongata.

Many people know about the chakras these days. However, what you may not know is that they connect your mental body to your physical body; mental consciousness passes from your mental realm into your physical body through the chakras. These are each located near your spine, facing forwards at the level of your pubic bone, the base of your sacrum, your solar plexus area, the area of your mid-chest, your neck and your third eye. There is also a spiral pattern, sometimes known as the caduceus, which extends from your top to your bottom chakra at a similar position to the spine.

Now onto your soul's connections to your body. There are eight to be concerned with; one at your throat, one each near your shoulders, one on either side of your chest, one each at the level of your stomach and liver, again level with each other, and one at the level of your pubic bone. They too, like the umbilical gateway from your body, are at a position mid-depth in your physical body. There

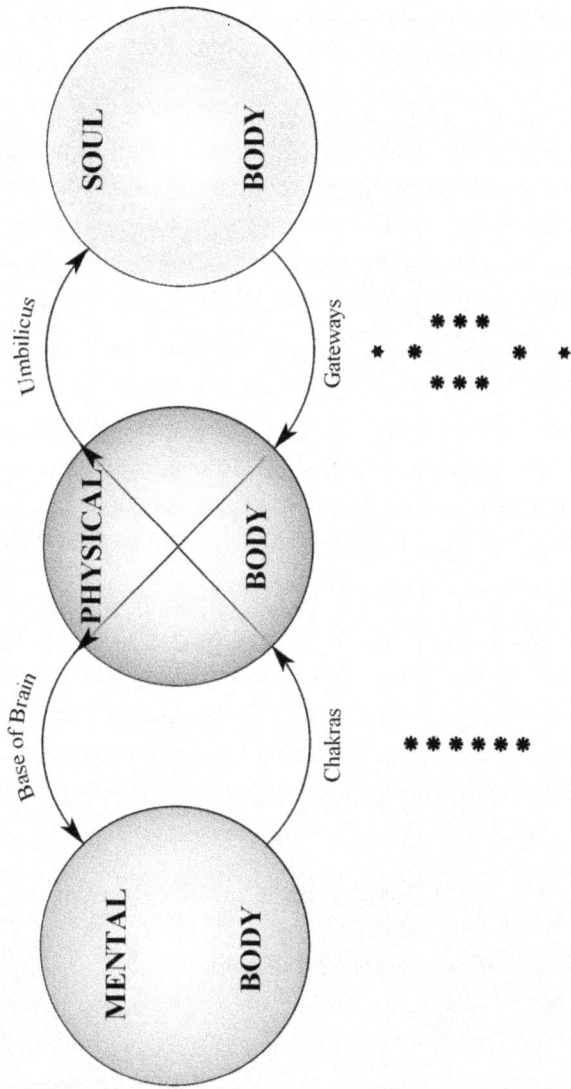

The movement of consciousness between the three bodies

are actually two more gateways, one above your head, the other below your feet.

The immortalisation process that I have mentioned takes place when your three bodies are so congruent that they impress the very nature of the universe, the original nature from which your bodies—and everything else—was formed. Interestingly you do not have to try to occupy any of the other realms that exist to allow this process to take place, indeed as I stated, many of them may have nothing to do with humans and could be very dangerous to you. Think about that.

The diagram on the previous page may help you to understand the communicating links better. Please bear in mind that they are not in reality side by side but all here, wherever you are sitting or standing, at this moment. You see I am right, you are an amazing being!

In fact the whole of this book and the processes it concentrates on are simply concerned with the free flow of consciousness between the three realms. It sounds easy doesn't it? But as we all know it is only mastership which makes things appear easy.

I give you this knowledge. Do not waste it, for it could literally save your life.

You may contact David Kala Ka Lā by email at talktokala@hotmail.com

Other titles from MasterWorks International

Available from all good bookstores or direct form MasterWorks International.

Quinta-Essentia by Morag Campbell

A study of the Five Elements of Ether, Air, Fire Water and Earth.

A Promise Kept by Morag Campbell

Autobiographical account of a profound spiritual adventure set in England and ancient Hawaii.

The Art of Mental Wellbeing - The Polarity Of Mental Wellbeing and Mental Disorder beyond the Medical Approach by Tony Caves

An exploration of sacred geometry and energy in relation to mental health.

The Power of Love - A Guide to Consciousness and Change by Phil Young and Morag Campbell

The ancient Polynesian viewpoint on spiritual development retold for the modern world.

www.ingramcontent.com/pod-product-compliance
Lightning Source LLC
Chambersburg PA
CBHW031945090426
42739CB00006B/95